GANDHIAN PROTEST

GANDHIAN PROTEST

B. ARUN KUMAR

RAWAT PUBLICATIONS

Jaipur • New Delhi • Bangalore • Mumbai • Hyderabad • Guwahati

ISBN 81-316-0130-7

Published by
Prem Rawat for **Rawat Publications**
Satyam Apts., Sector 3, Jawahar Nagar, Jaipur 302 004 (India)
Phone: 0141 265 1748 / 7006 Fax: 0141 265 1748
E-mail: info@rawatbooks.com
Website: www.rawatbooks.com

New Delhi Office
4858/24, Ansari Road, Daryaganj, New Delhi 110 002
Phone: 011-23263290

Also at Bangalore, Mumbai, Hyderabad and Guwahati

Typeset by Rawat Computers, Jaipur
Printed at Chaman Enterprises, New Delhi

Contents

Preface

This book focuses on Gandhi as thinker who has advocated the theory of protest that is well known by the name of *satyagraha*. Not inclined towards a theoretical enterprise like conventional academician, Gandhi was more interested in *praxis*. Imbued with a scientific spirit he desired to experiment and to change according to the conclusions he derived from these experiments. Yet he struck to a steadfast adherence to certain inviolable essentials which he acknowledged in the form of truth and its various manifestations like *ahimsa, aparigraha, astheya,* etc. Like his entire philosophy, Gandhi's theory of protest also reflects these essential aspects of his conviction.

Originally a thesis submitted for Ph.D. this text has now been expanded and also revised to incorporate more details and updated knowledge in the field and thereby contribute to the Gandhian theory of *satyagraha*, which has been one of the aspects of the growing interest shown by people world over in Gandhian philosophy. Thus, the book tries to examine the various concepts and theories of protest and Gandhi's understanding and contribution in this regard.

The *'Introduction'* throws light on the significance of protest, Gandhi's theory of protest and a brief description of the studies undertaken so far in this regard.

In the second chapter *'Protest: A Conceptual Analysis'* the meaning of the term 'protest', the essential elements that lend to it a distinct form and a brief description of its historical evolution have been dealt with to make understand the concept of protest.

In the third chapter *'Protest Theories of the West'* an attempt has been made to highlight the nuances of protest theories of some of the noted contributors in this field in the West like William Godwin, Henry David Thoreau, Albert Camus and Georges Sorel.

In the fourth chapter *'Theories of Protest in Gandhi's Contemporary India'* the contribution of Gokhale and Tilak, who respectively represent the moderate and extremist view of protest during the independence struggle of India, has been analysed.

In the fifth chapter *'Satyagraha: Conceptual Concern'* Gandhi's theory of *satyagraha* has been examined to delineate its philosophical foundation or elements, various forms and techniques of implementation.

In the sixth chapter *'Practice of Satyagraha'* the various *satyagrahas* launched by Gandhi have been critically examined to throw light on the *praxis* of *satyagraha* and the relevant significance of each *satyagraha* in individual as well as collective respect in the form of contribution to the entire philosophy of *satyagraha*.

In *'Conclusion' satyagraha*'s place in the galaxy of protest theories and its contextual and perennial relevance has been highlighted.

This effort to bring out the book in the present form would not have been possible without the support and encouragement of many people. I wish to thank them all from the core of my heart. I would also like to avail this opportunity to express my gratitude to my parents and elders as well as, wife and children for their encouragement and cooperation. One special person to whom I shall always remain indebted for his continuous inspiration, guidance and support in my academic pursuit has been Prof. Naresh Dadhich, who is now the Vice-Chancellor of Vardhaman Mahaveer Open University, Kota. I shall be failing in my duty if I do not record my gratitude to him and his very generous family members.

In the end I would like to thank Shri Kailash Rawat and his team at Rawat Publications, Jaipur for bring out this book in its present form.

1

Introduction

Gandhi is undoubtedly one of the most charismatic personalities of the 20th century who has left a great impact on the socio-economic and political forces of this century. As a political leader having mass appeal, he successfully mobilized the poor, despondent and dormant mass of India and effected its liberation from the domination of one of the mightiest empire known to history. In the process, he propounded a new theory and innovative method of protest and became responsible for a new epoch of saintly politics in the Indian political arena. Besides the loftiness of his personal character, wherein action was in perfect harmony with his idealistic thoughts and advocacies, he was a ceaseless activist and a great humanist who expressed his deep concern and love for the suffering people and worked for mitigating their sorrows. His whole life and activism was characterized by an effort to analyze and seek solutions to the perennial problems of human existence. Thus, his concern not only transcended all aspects of man's individual and social life, but also that of the territorial boundaries drawn by nation-states. Gandhi's emphasis and exhaustive exposition on morality assigns him one of the top positions amongst the class of moralists that the world has known so far. Thus, Thomas Weber rightly remarks, "It has often been remarked that Gandhi provided a signpost for moral living, leaving us with some valuable insights about the way life should be oriented so as not to become dysfunctional to the self, society or planet. For many of those who knew him he was influential as a father figure or charismatic leader, and for those who did not come under his personal sway there was the great world-renowned moral authority he wielded and example and teachings he left behind."[1]

The inadequacies of the existing institutions and practices in his contemporary societies, both of the East and the West, profoundly disturbed him and instilled in him an urge to seek solutions to the problems posed by these. In his analysis he concluded that unless these were not reconstituted on certain moral or ethical principles there is little scope for achieving any real progress and happiness of humanity in general. This, thus, became for him the *yugadharma*, indispensable for the contemporary societies to transcend their moribund state and regain vigour and resplendence.[2] In the process Gandhi proffered a vision, underlying which were a few principles or values which were not completely original in themselves but radical in so far as the revolutionary interpretation and use that Gandhi made of these in his private and public life.

Being an activist primarily, Gandhi conceived some definite economic, social and political programmes and gave them a practical shape in his dexterous and multifarious career as a freedom fighter, statesman, social reformer and a leader of the masses. Besides being the chief architect in the Indian struggle for freedom, Gandhi evolved the unique way of *satyagraha* (soul force or truth force), a highly effective method of civil disobedience and non-violent resistance that was intended to be an alternative to violence and designed to bring about positive social and political change.[3] His entry into the scene of Indian struggle for independence heralded a new era which was characteristic of moral idealism becoming the basis of successful political leadership. Not only was he responsible for the resurgence and independence of India but was also instrumental in revitalization of Afro-Asian political consciousness and their freedom from colonial rule.[4] In the course of his political activism, he strove to release the masses from the bondage of servitude and despondency and emphasized upon character building and cultivation of a spirit of brotherhood or fellowship. He advocated the renunciation of passivity, lethargy and fatalistic postures and emphasized upon the substitution of these with action, determination and courageous self-reliance. Finally, through the grandeur of his spiritual strength and courage, he ably guided the masses in their struggle.

Endowed with an inquisitive, discerning and creative mind, Gandhi experimented with many things in his life and tried to learn his lessons from these. Declaring himself to be a "seeker of truth" he made its pursuit the determining factor of all his thoughts and actions. As a result of such a heuristic approach not only did his vision of life become a broad and open ended one, but also a greatly flexible one, which creatively adjusted itself with the streaks of truth that trickled down to him through his experiences of the changing conditions and ideas flowing from outside. He was not hesitant to alter his views and did not worry about being inconsistent in the process. Through such a recourse of being consistent only to the point of living up to the truth that he experienced from time to time, relative truth as he called it, Gandhi envisaged to make steady progress towards the ultimate truth which he equated with God and recognized as the ultimate goal of his life. In the realization of such a moral growth, Gandhi not only allowed for the inevitability of inconsistencies between moral decisions at different times and in different situations, but also for the impossibility of achieving at any time or in any situation the entirety of what one sets out to do.[5] Flexibility and evolutionism, thus, became important traits of his philosophy as well as activism.

The concessions of flexibility and evolutionism, Gandhi emphasized, should not be perverted or usurped. In order to circumscribe these possibilities of misuse and to ensure conformation to "truth", Gandhi emphasized upon not only an uncompromising consistency in the pursuit of the ideal or the noble, but also a steadfast consistency in the adoption of noble means to realize the noble ideals. This understanding of Gandhi had a widespread ramification in his social, economic and political thought.

In the domain of politics, Gandhi's views challenged the conventional views on the nature and domain of politics. He not only conceived a broader notion of political power, but also assailed all dichotomous distinctions made between private and public morals, religious values and political norms and ethical principles and political expedience.[6] Politics, in modern times, he recognized, had pervaded all aspects of individual life; as such it had become indispensable to the individual. However, a politics bereft of the quintessence of religion or *dharma*, he contended, was not only as useless as a corpse but also fatal to man's quintessential existence. Consequently, he emphasized upon the introduction of religion into politics, or "spiritualization of politics" as he called it. The two became inseparable for Gandhi. This inseparability meant subordination of politics to ethics and organizing the former on principles deduced from the latter. It also meant that politics should become a means for articulating and reflecting the basic value commitments essential for human existence.[7] Within the ambit of such a broad notion of "spiritualization of politics" his ideas on state and government, political power, political obligation, rights, liberty and protest assumed specific connotations.

Gandhi's proscription of all things unnatural to man's essential existence extended to include the state and its agent, the government. Recognizing state as an external imposition on man, he decried it for its soulless and mechanical nature. The history of the actual functioning of the hitherto existing states testified his fears about the state acting as a hindrance to the all-round development of the individuals inhabiting it. These aspects of the state, together with his optimism about individuals making limitless progress in the vista of perfection, made Gandhi prefer, as an ideal, a stateless society. In this ideal set-up he recognized all individuals to possess such moral and mental development which enabled to regulate their life in such a manner that they not only pursued enlightened goals but also, while doing so, refrained from hindering similar progress and felicity of their fellow men. This was recognized by him as *Ramrajya* or "The Kingdom of God on Earth".

However, this ideal being the more distant scene, and the national life in the more immediate and near scene being imperfect, Gandhi acquiesced in the existence of a state. Even in its existence as a necessary evil, while circumscribing its functions to the barest minimum, Gandhi was emphatic about this functioning to be in conformity with the principles of truth and non-violence and the concomitant notions of justice, rights, liberty and dignity of the individuals inhabiting it. The state, he recognized, should not interfere in any way detrimental to the individual's moral progress; it should, on the contrary, provide the congenial conditions for such a progress. The state's goal, he emphasized, ought to be *sarvodaya* or the uplift, welfare and good of all who live within its domain. In the process, he recognized certain protective, prohibitive, economic and international functions of the state. These, thus, became the various manifestations of the essential obligations of the state to its citizens or the *raison de' etre* of its existence.

However, this obligation of the state to the citizens was only a part of his overall speculation on political obligation. His views on the reciprocity of the obligations of the citizens to the state and the citizens *inter se* completed this speculation of Gandhi.

Towards a state purporting *sarvodaya*, and through it, *Ramrajya*, Gandhi recognized certain obligations of the citizens. Active cooperation with it in the event of it being threatened by disintegrative forces operating from within or outside it, willing obedience to all the good laws; tolerating some of its laws that were inconvenient; maintaining public peace, contributing to its financial stability; expressing and conveying an assurance of the citizens; loyal and respectful attachment to it, etc. were some of the obligations of the citizens to the state recognized by Gandhi. So far as the obligations of the citizens *inter se* conceived by Gandhi, it may be said that these were reflective of an emphasis on a general conformity with the principle of "unity of life", which in turn implied the inculcation of ethical values accompanied by altruistic orientation in the conduction of activities related to citizens' day-to-day life.

Speculating on political obligation, Gandhi inevitably envisaged into the vistas of rights and duties of the citizens. However, on account of his idealizing the *nishkamakarmayogi*, Gandhi accorded primacy to duties instead of rights. It was his belief that if the citizens performed their duties well, rights would not only automatically follow but also be quickly and effectively realized. Thus, for Gandhi, the true source of rights was duties. In his political activism, thus, certain rights were regarded by him as concomitants of an honest discharge of political obligation or duties. Among the political rights that he advocated and fought for in the course of his public activism were those of participation in one's governance; of voting or choosing one's representatives; to warn, protest and disobey a bad government; and, in case of all subjected nations, to free the country from the servitude of a foreign nation.

The notion of freedom assumed radical implications in the treatment of Gandhi. His notion of freedom transcended beyond the common understanding of freedom from external impediments or that of legal impositions. The freedom that he sought was that of self-actualization in the transcendental sense while being a part of the phenomenal world. Distinguishing between external freedom and internal freedom, he recognized that real freedom implied one's own rule over the self, *swaraj* as he called it, in accordance with certain principles that underlie the quintessential existence of man; such a freedom, therefore, could not come from any external agencies or conditions, but only through an inward change brought about by an inward prayer and a definite and living recognition of the presence of the mighty spirit residing within.[8] This pursuit, he recognized, could not be an ascetic endeavour because the phenomenal world, on account of it being inherent with innumerable relative truths, served as the indispensable means for self-actualization in the transcendental sense.

These two conditions of leading a life symbolic of the true-self of one's existence and living it within the empirical world, Gandhi contended, could only be satisfactorily met when the individuals achieved a mastery over their senses so much so that the glittering attractions of the earthly things lost their hallucinating power on them and they remained, consequently, undeterred from the quest of the transcendental truth or God, which according to Gandhi is the culmination of self-perfection process. In the pursuit of such a goal, Gandhi was emphatic about eradicating all external impediments, individual as well as institutional.

Gandhi's recognition of freedom from foreign rule as a precondition for the attainment of self-rule or *swaraj* could be seen as a logical consequence of his denouncement of any impediments on the individuals' pursuit of the transcendental truth or God. Therefore, he recognized it to be the birthright of any subjected nation to gain freedom from foreign yoke. Foreign rule, by its very nature, Gandhi recognized, was detrimental to the enjoyment of self-rule. Consequently, he contended that howsoever efficient a foreign government might be, it could not become an excuse for self-rule or *swaraj*; anarchy under "Home Rule" was thus preferred by him to that of any orderly foreign rule.[9] Therefore, he viewed it to be the duty of the British to grant India its independence and through the adoption of *satyagraha* tried to actualize it. Thus, it has been rightly remarked, "Gandhi launched *satyagraha* movement to convince the British to perform their duties of not taking away the rights of Indians to be free. Instead of forcing the British to concede the rights of Indians, Gandhi tried to remind the British of their duties to concede freedom to India."[10] However, Gandhi denounced all tyrannical rules, be it a foreign or indigenous one, which perpetuated diabolic designs and coerced the individuals to acquiesce in its acts. He conceived it to be the sacred duty of the individuals to resist such a rule and be prepared to undergo any amount of suffering to check and influence it to renounce its unrighteous goals.

Gandhi justified the citizen's right to not only warn and criticize the state when it embarked on a wrong course but also to protest it effectively so as to influence it to renounce its wrong designs and to work for the redress of the grievances that had so arisen. In carrying on this protest, Gandhi advocated an initial recourse to all the available means within the constitutional prescription. Thus, he recognized the recourse to petitioning, pleading and praying to those manning the administrative positions in order to influence them to take the desired step in the direction of ameliorating the grievances of the citizens.

When the recourse to constitutional means failed to secure the necessary effect, Gandhi advocated the need to supplement these efforts by that of an agitation, the intensity and tactics of it being determined by the need of the hour or situation. However, in all such protesting, Gandhi was emphatic about an overarching conformity with truth and non-violence. He also insisted that all acts of defiance of law should be done in a civil manner. Before the act of defiance or disobedience was actually resorted to, Gandhi emphasized that the citizens should prove their law-abiding quality to the state. Moreover, this obedience, he recognized, was a prerequisite for the citizen to get convinced about the unjust or evil nature of the law through his personal experience of it while initially rendering obedience to it. All these nuances of protest was superscribed by his philosophy of *satyagraha* and was an important contribution of Gandhi in the field of political theory.

The speculation on the principles that should form the basis of a good government and those principles that justify an action to check or change a government or a system that does not measure up to the idealized principles has been a fundamental issue in the history of political theory. Protest has generally been used to refer both to a serious verbal objection or remonstrance as well as to a conceptually distinct mode of behaviour. It has been defined as an expression of objection, disapproval or dissent with reference to certain goals pursued by those in authoritative positions which the protesters deem as unjustifiable. In their immobilized capacity before taking recourse to a protest, the protesters are unable to prevent the authorities from pursuing such a goal; but through their protest, which involves optimum mobilization of their internal and external resources, the protesters seek to challenge and check the authorities from pursuing these unjust goals and seek the redress of their grievances.

As a concept, protest has a definite historical context that lends to it a specific meaning; but like many other concepts it has not remained frozen in time and has been used in different contexts with slightly varying implications and emphasis. However, at the core of these enunciations lies a general recognition of a de-emphasis of institutional basis of authority. While conceding the fallibility of the institutions, including the state and the government, these usage of protest recognize not only the right of private judgement of the individuals coming within the domain of these institutions, but also the justification of the appropriate actions taken thereof to check the follies and for seeking the redress of grievances that have already arisen. As such political theory is abundant with such a speculation on protest. William Godwin, Henry David Thoreau, Albert Camus, Georges Sorel, etc., are some of the thinkers who have made significant contribution in this regard.

William Godwin,[11] the famous British anarchist, recognized that individuals were not obliged to conform supinely to whatever norms that were handed down to them by their superiors, tradition or hypostatised institutions. When faced with a dilemma as to how to act in such a given situation, Godwin advocated the need to apply directly the "test of utility". This right of "private judgement", Godwin contended, was an inviolable right of the individual as it was indispensable for the individual to perceive the "moral truths" given with the *telos* or essential existence of mankind. Godwin conceded the state as a necessary existent acting as a bridle on corrupt human nature and thus condescended in its existence to discharge the requisite responsibilities. To such a state he also recognized the prudential discharge of obedience by the citizens. However, conceding the possibility of the state transgressing its assigned functions and creating impediments in the individuals' practice and realization of "virtue", Godwin recognized the need for the right of resistance to be given to the individuals. Such a resistance, he emphasized, should not be manifested in a recourse to revolutionary methods as it circumscribed truth. Recourse to rational persuasion, he recognized, was the only appropriate means as it would permit truth to emerge and permeate the wider society and ultimately influence the state to renounce its evil designs.

One of the names mentioned by Gandhi while recounting the influences on him was that of Henry David Thoreau.[12] Thoreau was an ardent champion of individual liberty. Refuting the notion of the state possessing superior wisdom or sanctity vis-à-vis the individual, he contended that the state could not force its subject citizens to obey any of its laws that were baser than the law of the individual's self. A state coercing the individual to do so, Thoreau emphasized, should be effectively resisted by way of civil disobedience by the individuals who *in foro conscentiae* were convinced about the diabolic designs of the state. In protesting such a state, Thoreau wanted the conscientious individuals to be brave and unmindful of the consequences that might follow their act of defiance to the state. Through such a courageous protest, Thoreau claimed, not only would the dignity and sanctity underlying the individual's quintessential existence be upheld, but also the state would be effectively checked and forced to renounce its unrighteous goals.

The theorists of protest do not belong to a single ideological fold. In existentialism also we find sources of protest. One of the leading lights of existentialism was Albert Camus[13] who sought to not only highlight the absurdities facing human life in general, and the war-prone world in particular, but also, more importantly, to advocate a resistance to all these absurdities and thereby usher in a new renaissance of man, who, he regarded, was the only existent to have a meaning in this otherwise meaningless world. While this resistance at the metaphysical level was against the ultimate oppressor "death", at the temporal level it was a protest against every such force which threatened to obliterate or extenuate the individual's importance, his freedom and happiness.

According to Camus, there existed no justification for the perpetuation of injustice and exploitation against mankind. Any authority, including the state, he contended, when it became cruel, capricious and destructive, should be resisted. The ideal rebel, Camus recognized, refused to obey orders which he believed to be intrinsically wrong. Through this act of refusal the rebel affirmed his faith in the values which he recognized as sacred and inviolable and bore witness, as a man of principle, to the reality of moral values by his conduct. However, Camus did not prefer a recourse to revolutionary or violent methods for protesting the usurped and unjust authority. He, instead, advocated moderation or *mesure* while seeking to avoid the extremes of amoral revolution and passively immoral quietism. Making a distinction between the evil and the evil-doer, he recognized the need for the continued existence of the evil-doer in order to facilitate correction, modification or reform in him. Therefore, Camus recognized a non-violent persuasion and appeal, rather than violence and annihilation, as the appropriate method of resistance.

Another French thinker was Georges Sorel[14] who advocated a new theory of protest. Sorel was a Marxist-turned revisionist who contended that violence was concealed within the socio-political and economic structure of modern state. All claims and efforts towards a peace through rational discourses and conciliation in such a state, he recognized, was a facade of the bourgeoisie class to hide their real exploitative and unjust nature and to avert any eventual proletariat retaliation against their privileges. Renouncing faith in reason's capacity to solve the structural violence's inherent in the bourgeois state, Sorel advocated the recourse to irrationalism in pragmatic politics. He advocated a mystical faith in the proletariat-will making its way through conflict and violence to the ultimate realization of a new order free from the oppressive forces of capitalism.

Sorel contended that every conciliatory effort in the existing bourgeois system was an endeavour to protect and promote the existing unjust and exploitative arrangement. Consequently, recourse to violence became inevitable. This violence, chiefly perpetuated by the working class, Sorel claimed, also released some of the noble sentiments inherent in both the parties involved in the conflict and ultimately gave rise to a more vibrant and righteous order. In mobilizing the working class Sorel recognized the need for a recourse to irrationalism and myth to deliver a catastrophic defeat and destruction of the exploitative structures, processes and institutions of the state. It was in this context that Sorel conceptualized the notion of "general-strike". This violence inherent in the "general-strike", Sorel contended, was pure and had to be essentially distinguished from others that might be pursued for the narrow goals of its users. He also contended that this violence, on account of its inherent creative potential and purity, was superior in quality to the conciliatory attempts that sought to reconcile differences by patchwork. Thus, Sorel's theory of protest sought to idealize the aggressive and heroic action of the oppressed which is performed with the sense of impersonal consecration to the idealized goal of the liberation of the oppressed community form the clutches of oppression.

Before Gandhi commenced his political activism in India, there were already numerous individuals protesting the colonial regime of the British for its consistent neglect of the aspirations of Indians and violation of certain principles which they believed should largely inform the functioning of the government. Broadly, these protests may be classified under the heads of moderate and militant protests. While each fold had many proponents, each unique in certain respects, yet in their essence they had certain common traits. The most prominent personalities whose views on protest largely included the general traits of their fold were Gopal Krishna Gokhale as the exponent of moderate protest and Bal Gangadhar Tilak as that of extremism in protest. As senior contemporaries of Gandhi, and having tremendous popularity, both Gokhale and Tilak bequeathed to Gandhi, in their own limited way, their views on the nature and method of protesting the colonial regime. However, given the limitations of their protest, and his own convictions and views, Gandhi was influenced to borrow with a critical spirit from these and continuously improvise them to make the protest against the colonial regime more effective. In the process, many of the interpretations and improvisations that he made assumed radical implications.

In Gokhale's recognition, the hallmark of any good government was its strenuous endeavour for the welfare of its people, identification with the needs and aspirations of its subject citizens; facilitating public participation in administration; and, in its functioning, the inculcation of the notions of trust, conciliation and justice. Political governance, he recognized, transcended beyond legal connotation; it was a great moral responsibility and trust reposed on those who held the reigns of the government. Therefore, it should be spiritualized by way of imbibing such principles of ethics like that of truthfulness, non-violence, honesty, altruism, etc., in its functioning. To a state conforming to these principles, Gokhale became a great champion of loyalty.

However, this notion of loyalty for Gokhale neither implied an uncritical adulation for those holding the reigns of power, nor of a passive acquiescence or subservience to the unjust and oppressive rule. Instead, to an unrighteous, oppressive and unjust rule, Gokhale recognized the need for an active protest; and while doing so he was emphatic about the appropriate nature that this protest should assume. He denounced revolutionary and violent tactics for resisting the unrighteous and usurped authority. Instead, he advocated moderation and pragmatism. These were the underlying notions in his concept of "constitutional protest" through which he sought to not only check and reform the unjust government but also to preserve the freedom and integrity of the citizens and thereby uphold the spiritual values which their conscience perceived as inviolable.

Tilak,[15] in contrast to Gokhale, was more militant in his views and activism. For Tilak, a general conformation to the principles of freedom, equality and justice concomitant with an endeavour to work for the decent and dignified existence of the subject individuals, largely determined the justification of any government's existence. A government flouting these principles, he recognized, should be actively resisted by the individual; it was his principal and moral duty. The aim of such a resistance should be to force the government to conform to the idealized principles and take the necessary steps towards the redress of grievances that had arisen as a consequence of government's negligence or transgression of the vital principles. One such principle was freedom. This freedom, *swaraj* as Tilak called it, was the elan vital or *chaitanya* of a nation and indispensable for the existence and all-round development of the individuals. Therefore, he recognized *swaraj* as the birthright of every individual and emphasized upon achieving it at all costs.

The nature of resistance for *swaraj*, Tilak recognized, was largely determined by the prevailing conditions in a given political system. Thus, to a regime responsive to constitutional agitation, Tilak accorded recognition to such means of protest like that of requests, petitions, persuasions and passing resolutions. However, to a government unresponsive to such constitutional agitation, Tilak recognized the need to resort to any extra-constitutional means to effectively realize their goal. The only thing about which he was emphatic about was the purity of the goal itself. Thus, in his speculation on protest, some scholars claim, he adhered to the doctrine that "the end justifies the means". Consequently, in his public activism, Tilak is alleged of inciting violence against the colonial rule of the British.

The apparent inefficacy of existing protest to check the oppressive regime of the colonial rule, and to realize the cherished aspirations of the Indians, made Gandhi recognize the need for a more effective protest that would help in transcending the prevailing impasse. As he delved into the various nuances of his theory of protest – *satyagraha* – he became more and more confident about its efficacy. The results of his various campaigns further testified his faith in its efficacy. Thus, he recognized it as the surest way to successfully realize any noble goal under any prevailing circumstance. This confidence of Gandhi in *satyagraha,* as well as its exposition by him, was characterized by an evolutionary feature, which was a hallmark of his total philosophy and growth from "Moniya to Mahatma".

Having decided to choose law as a career, Gandhi had to undergo numerous travails from the very beginning – making it to England to study law; and then again in England for completing this study. Finally, when he returned to India, his complexes and scanty knowledge of Indian law stood in his way of practising at the bar. He felt very weak to plead his first case at Bombay. He even unsuccessfully ventured to become an English teacher. However, being adept in drafting applications and memorials, he finally settled for this work instead of the lawyer's and shifted back to Rajkot. The Dada Abdulla and Co. offer came as a welcome break for Gandhi from the drudgery of the drafting work.

However, before he left for South Africa to take up the case, Gandhi had no knowledge of the racial stigma attached to the coloured man's life. Within a few days of his arrival, he was subjected to numerous indignities. The "creative experiences" of these indignities heaped on him made him a determined man to protest and remove the racial prejudice and all its concomitant evils, not for his personal self but for the larger Indian community that was subjected to such indignities. Gradually, from a lawyer enjoying good practice and concerned with the material prospects of his self and all his near and dear ones, he started transcending into the realm of public activism to uphold the dignity of the Indians in particular and the individuals in general, and into altruistic concerns, within the fold of which an increasing lot of people from a wider section of the society came to be included. Simultaneous with his role as a public activist it also dawned upon him that to effectively discharge this role he had to perfect his self – to transcend from the concerns of the self and the physical, into one seeking the welfare of a wider society and the spiritual.

As he drifted into the realm of spiritual evolution and became deeply involved in the struggle against racism, he embarked into the vista of a maturing political philosophy. He denounced racial prejudices on moral grounds and, as a public activist, openly aired his views on the native governments in South Africa. He was critical about their discriminatory and unjust policies and sought to mobilize the Indian community against this evil. He made optimum use of all the available means for ventilating grievances and seeking their redress. As the native governments were adamant in their stance, a confrontation between the Indian community led by Gandhi and the native governments became inevitable. This tussle culminated in the birth of *satyagraha* or Gandhi's theory of protest.

In South Africa this method of protest was just a seedling, but in the course of Gandhi's political activism in India it gradually matured into a mighty tree with numerous limbs having their offshoots thrust deep down into the earth like the banyan.[16] A concomitant evolution was Gandhi's speculation on the principles that should inform the functioning of a good government. As his political philosophy matured, it started to more steadfastly conform to the idealized vision of his spiritual enterprise. Consequently, he recognized that if there existed a few principles, the conformation to which justified the existence of a given government or state, then to the extent that the government or state transgressed these principles, it should be protested to bring it back to conform with these principles and seek the redress of the grievances that had so arisen on account of such transgressions. However, in protesting such an unjust and unrighteous state and government, Gandhi recognized that there were certain principles, conformation to which justified the protest so undertaken. The progressive speculation on the principles of a good government and that of a justified protest was concomitant with his gradual transformation from a loyalist to a non-cooperator of the British rule in India.

Quite a few interpretations have been made regarding the real meaning, intention and significance of Gandhi's confrontation with the British Empire. For academic purpose these views can be broadly classified under the broad categories of (i) occidental interpreters, and (ii) oriental interpreters.

The major occidental studies are those of Judith M. Brown,[17] Maureen Swan,[18] L.I. Rudolph and S.H., Rudolph[19] Antony Copley[20] and P.H.M. Van Den Dungen.[21] These studies highlight and examine the various facets of Gandhi's rise to the status of a mass leader. Recognizing Gandhi as a leader seeking to create his constituency of support and making optimum use of the opportunities provided by the prevailing political conditions, these studies portray Gandhi virtually as a great manipulator who sought political power to pursue some of the ideas that he constructed on account of his idiosyncratic views. His loyalty to the British rule, these studies contend, was a dynamic one and his transformation into a rebel has to be understood in the context of British response to Gandhi's vision and activism. There are also a few contemporaries of Gandhi like H.S.L. Polak[22] and C.F. Andrews[23] who have thrown light on Gandhi's transformation from a loyalist to a non-cooperator with the British rule; but these works are limited in the sense that they consider this transformation as a sudden phenomenon and explain the causative factors as those events happening between 1918 and 1920.

A few oriental scholars like B.R. Nanda,[24] Pyarelal,[25] R.R. Diwakar[26] and Bhikhu Parekh[27] have also endeavoured to explain Gandhi's transformation from a loyalist to a rebel of the British rule. The studies regard Gandhi basically as an ethico-religious person deeply rooted in Indian tradition, but making revolutionary interpretations and usages of these traditional values to seek solutions to the various maladies affecting his contemporary society. They recognize Gandhi as a conscientious rebel against the excrescences committed upon the pure and pristine tradition of Indian civilization which he held to be a true civilization in the real sense of the word. Gandhi is recognized by these studies as a part of the saintly tradition of India and his enunciation and practice of *satyagraha* is treated as a way of life and a tool for resolution of various types of conflicts by adhering to certain fundamental principles and adopting a distinct set of means for doing so. Recognizing the colonial exploits of the British rule as a serious malady affecting Indian society, a fact not obscure to Gandhi, these studies seek to explain Gandhi's confrontation with the British rule in the context of his overarching ethico-religious approach to life.

Among the oriental scholars a mention may be made of Raghavan N. Iyer,[28] Ramashray Roy,[29] Buddhdev Bhattacharyya[30] and V.R. Mehta[31] who have treated Gandhi as a political thinker who has enunciated certain concepts and attempted theorization and has, therefore, universal relevance. Continuing in this tradition, these studies seek to highlight the various facets of Gandhi's protest. Recognizing *satyagraha*, which is Gandhi's theory of protest, as an important part of his overall political philosophy, they try to highlight the various nuances and facets of Gandhi's protest as it evolved in his long chequered career as a public activist juxtaposed in a colonial set-up reigned by the British. However, the relevance of Gandhi's protest against the colonial rule is not limited to India or any other nation subjected to the British rule. The British rule may be recognized as just one of the many possible manifestations of an unjust and unrighteous rule available anytime and anywhere in the vast arena of the nation-state system existing today. Hence, Gandhi's theory of protest, though located in the historical context of the colonial rule of the British, transcends the notion of a limited relevance to a colonial set-up or Indian setting alone. In this capacity it is comparable to many other theories of protest that exist in political theory. This study, therefore, also tries to delve into the vistas of comparison and determination of the appropriate fold or tradition of protest into which Gandhi's theory of protest may be placed.

Notes

1. Thomas Weber, *Gandhi as Disciple and Mentor*, Cambridge University Press India Pvt. Ltd., New Delhi, 2007, p. 12.
2. Bhikhu Pareek, *Colonialism Tradition and Reform: An Analysis of Gandhian Discourse*, Sage Publications, New Delhi, 1989, p. 10.
3. Anand Kumaraswamy, *Gandhi on Personal Leadership: Lessons from the Life and Times of India's Visionary Leader*, Jaico Publishing House, Mumbai, 2006, p. 14.
4. V.P. Varma, *The Political Philosophy of Mahatma Gandhi and Sarvodaya*, Ms. Laxmi Narain Agarwal, Agra, 1980-81, p. 19.
5. Raghavan N. Iyer, *The Moral and Political Thought of Mahatma Gandhi*, Oxford University Press, Delhi, 1973, pp. 65-6.
6. Ibid., p. 40.
7. Ramashray Roy, *Self and Society: A Study in Gandhian Thought*, Sage Publications, New Delhi, 1985, p. 170.

8. *Collected Works of Mahatma Gandhi*, Publication Division, Ministry of Information and Broadcasting, Government. of India, New Delhi (hereafter cited as CWMG), Vol. 34, p. 506.
9. M. K. Gandhi, *Hind Swaraj*, Navajivan Publishing House, Ahmedabad, 1990, p. 87.
10. R.P. Mishra, *Rediscovering Gandhi*, Vol. 1, *Hind Swaraj: Gandhi's Challenge to Modern Civilization*, Concept Publishing Company, New Delhi, 2007, p. 70.
11. The important work of William Godwin is *An Enquiry Concerning Political Justice*, I. Krammick (ed.), Penguin Publication, Harmondsworth, 1976.
12. The most celebrated work of Henry David Thoreau is *On the Duty of Civil Disobedience*, in Reform Papers, Princeton University Press, Princeton, New Jersey, 1973.
13. The important works of Albert Camus are:
    (i) *The Rebel*, Trans. by A. Bower, Knopt Publications, New York, 1956.
    (ii) *The Outsider*, Trans. by Justin O' Brien, Penguin Publication, New York, 1960.
    (iii) *The Plague*, Trans. by Stuart Gilber, Penguin Publication, New York, 1960.
    (iv) *The Myth of Sisyphus*, Trans. by Justin O' Brien, Penguin Publication, New York, 1975.
    (v) *The Fall*, Trans. by Justin O' Brien, Penguin Publication, New York, 1963.
14. Georges Sorel's important work is *Reflections on Violence*, Trans. by T.E. Hulme and J. Roth, The Free Press, Glencoe, Illinois 1950.
15. Tilak's celebrated works are:
    (i) *The Orion*, Ms. R.A. Sagoon, Bombay, 1893.
    (ii) *The Arctic Home in the Vedas*, Kersari Office, Pune, 1903.
    (iii) *Srimad Bhavadgita Rahasya*, Lokmanya Tilak Mandir, Pune, 1955.
16. Bhabani Bhattacharya, *Mahatma Gandhi*, Arnold Publishers (I) Pvt. Ltd., Delhi, 1977, p. 8.
17. Judith M. Brown's works on Gandhi are:
    (i) *Gandhi's Rise to Power: Indian Politics 1915-1922*, Cambridge University Press, Cambridge, 1972.
    (ii) *Gandhi and Civil Disobedience: The Mahatma in Indian Politics*, 1928-34, Cambridge University Press, Cambridge, 1977.
    (iii) *Gandhi: Prisoner of Hope*, Oxford University Press, New Delhi, 1990.
18. Maureen Swan, *Gandhi: The South African Experience*, Ravan Press, Johannesburg, 1985.

19. The works of L.I. Rudolph and S.H. Rudolph on Gandhi are:
    (i) *The Modernity of Tradition*, Chicago University press, Chicago, 1967.
    (ii) *Gandhi: The Traditional Roots of Charisma*, Chicago University Press, Chicago, 1983.
    (iii) *Post-Modern Gandhi and Other Essays: Gandhi in the World and at Home*, Oxford University Press, New Delhi, 2006.
20. Antony Copley, *Gandhi Against the Tide*, Oxford University Press, Calcutta, 1993.
21. P. H.M. Van Den Dungen, *Gandhi in 1919: Loyalist or Rebel*? in R. Kumar (ed), *Essay on Gandhian Politics: The Rowlatt Satyagraha of 1919*, Oxford University Press, New Delhi, 1993.
22. H.S.L. Polak et al., *Mahatma Gandhi*, Jaico Publishing House, Delhi, 1962.
23. C.F. Andrews, *Mahatma Gandhi's Ideas*, George Allen and Unwin Ltd., London, 1949.
24. B.R. Nanda's works on Gandhi are:
    (i) *Gandhi and His Critics*, Oxford University Press, Delhi, 1985.
    (ii) *Mahatma Gandhi: A Biography*, Oxford University Press, Delhi, 1989.
25. Pyarelal's works on Gandhi are:
    (i) *Mahatma Gandhi: The Last Phase*, 2 Vols., Navajivan Publishing House, Ahmedabad, 1956-58.
    (ii) *A Pilgrimage for Peace*, Navajivan Publishing House, Ahmedabad, 1959.
    (iii) *Towards New Horizons*, Navajivan Publishing House, Ahmedabad, 1959.
    (iv) *Mahatma Gandhi: The Early Phase*, Navajivan PUblishing House, Ahmedabad, 1965.
26. R.R. Diwakar's works on Gandhi are:
    (i) *Satyagraha: Its Technique and History*, Hind Kitabs, Bombay, 1946.
    (ii) *Satyagraha in Action*, Signet Press, Calcutta, 1949.
    (iii) *Gandhi's Life, Thought and Philosophy*, Bharatiya Vidya Bhavan, Bombay, 1963.
    (iv) *Gandhi: The Spiritual Seeker*, Bharatiya Vidya Bhavan, Bombay, 1964.
    (v) *The Saga of Satyagraha*, Gandhi Peace Foundation, New Delhi, 1969.
27. Note 2.
28. Raghavan N. Iyer's important works on Gandhi are:
    (i) *The Moral and Political Thought of Mahatma Gandhi*, Oxford University Press, Delhi, 1973.

(ii) *The Essential Writings of Mahatma Gandhi*, Oxford University Press, 1993.

29. Ramashray Roy's works on Gandhi are:
 (i) *Gandhi: Soundings in Political Philosophy*, Chanakya Publications, New Delhi, 1984.
 (ii) *Self and Society: A Study in Gandhian Thought*, Sage Publications, New Delhi, 1985.
 (iii) (ed.), *Contemporary Crisis and Gandhi*, Discovery Publishing House, New Delhi, 1986.
30. Buddhdev Bhattacharya, *The Evolution of Political Philosophy of Gandhi*, Calcutta Book House, Calcutta, 1969.
31. V.R. Mehta's works on Gandhi are:
 (i) *Ideology, Modernization and Politics in India*, Manohar Publication, New Delhi, 1983.
 (ii) *Foundations of Indian Political Thought*, Manohar Publication, New Delhi, 1992.

2

Protest: A Conceptual Analysis

The ever increasing demands of the individuals and either the unwillingness or the inability of those in authoritative positions in the society to satisfy all these demands have created a situation in which every society at a given point of time is confounded with the problem of resolving tensions generated by sources of deprivation, disprivilege and injustice. Whatever be the level of integration reached by a society, when the relatively disprivileged and deprived individuals become conscious of the unjust and arbitrary differences created during the process of value allocation by the political system, they organize themselves for challenging the existing arrangement.

Challenges to the political system may take various forms – from a milder and relatively less violent ones that seek to ameliorate specific grievances within the existing system, to a more militant, aggressive and violent ones that seek to remove those in authoritative positions or to change the existing system itself. While under the former category one can include the movements of dissent, protest and reform, under the latter category one can include the movements of revolt or rebellion and revolution. However, these forms of political challenges are not exclusive categories. Only a thin line separates them and what may seem to be a dissent or protest movement in an early stage may assume the proportion of a rebellion or revolution later on. One cannot rule out the possibility of many of these operating simultaneously over a given issue. To quote Gusfield J.R., "We must not imagine that meanings are fixed and unchangeable, nor that movements do not grow, change and confront new situations... To understand the history of a movement we need to see it as it meets opposition, resistance and contradiction, and how these encounters in turn affect the interpretation of the movement by society and of the social order by the adherents of the movement. Such encounters are crucial to the reinforcement or reformulation of belief, strategy and loyalty."[1] Nevertheless, it may be said that to know the meanings implied by a particular concept or word comes in as handy since it not only helps one to evaluate a movement of political challenge and the likely consequences but also to conceive the likely attitude and reaction of the common man as well as of those in authoritative positions upon whom the success or failure of a movement greatly depends.

Concepts do have a historical context that lends to them a definite or particular meaning. Nevertheless, one cannot overlook the fact that meanings of a word or concept do not remain frozen in time and have been used in different context with slightly varying implications. The concept of protest is no exception to this general rule. Therefore, while conceptualizing or examining the credibility of a movement as a protest, it must be borne in mind that one need not be imprisoned by the historical meaning that protest connotes and, instead, take into consideration the changing context of protest also. Historically speaking, protest movements have been associated with the Reformation era of the 16th century Europe in which under the leadership of Martin Luther the Western Church protested against Roman Catholicism. To quote C. Badrinath, "To elaborate, until Martin Luther appeared on the scene the word protest carried with it no negative meaning. The Greeks did not have that word, in Roman Law to protest meant to make an assertion, 'to put forth a case'. Even after Luther this usage continued, for example in English literature, Shakespeare's 'the lady doth protest too much', is an instance. Even today, phrases like 'I protest my innocence' is a common usage. The movement started by Luther on the day he nailed his famous theses on the door of the Catholic Church and the theological and political events that followed gave that special meaning to the word 'protest'."[2]

Protest in Protestantism

So far as the principle of protest developed by "Protestantism"[3] is concerned, it may be said that it has been used as a means for the evaluation of not only the beliefs and institutions existing in any society, but also of judging one's own movements and thoughts. The guiding factors in this judgement, as enunciated by "Protestantism", may be cited as the following principles:

1. "Justification by grace through faith", which implies that man can achieve salvation only if he has the grace of God. This grace can be had only through a firm faith and reverence for Him rather than appeasing or pleasing Him by making generous donations for his agents;
2. "Priesthood of all believers", which implies the notion of equality of all followers of the faith; and lastly,
3. "De-emphasis of institutional basis of authority", which asserts that the final authority resides in the "word of God", but since no single interpretation of it can lay claim to infallibility, every individual possesses the right of private judgement and action thereof.

The Protestant preachers continued to advocate its adherents to follow Christ, who, apart from being a model of simple and virtuous life, also came to be regarded as the one who voiced against the powers of false religion and its practitioners and the established evil forces in the civil society. In such a following of the true faith, it has been advocated that the believers should be prepared to suffer to any extent, even to that of death, at the hands of civil authorities or men of opposing faiths.

The principle of protest as enunciated by "Protestantism" seems to have an overall ethical or moral pervasiveness and there seems to be hardly any reference to the use of, or indulgence in, violence. The "way of Christ to the Cross" which is symbolic of virtue, non-violence, love, tolerance and altruism seems to be the idealized form of every protest. Nevertheless, so far as the operational aspect of "Protestantism" is concerned, it may be pointed out that there exist wide variations from such idealized principles. Yet, all these movements of challenge have gone in the annals of history under the broad category of "Protestant movement" or "Protestantism". Similarly, one finds in other social sciences such expositions, analyses and evaluations of protest movements. This changing context can be explained by the fact that generally individuals confer meaning to events or things by selecting and excluding those aspects of it which they consider as significant, which itself is dependent on factors like individual's knowledge or understanding, experiences, interests and his position and capacity (individual, group and official) in the society. On account of these factors, the interpretation of a movement as protest or the judgement of the credibility of protest movement varies from individual to individual, from individual in his single capacity to that of his group capacity, and from the individual in his private capacity to that of his official capacity.

Among the various usages of the concept of protest, we may say that it has been used either generically to refer to any form of verbal or active objection or remonstrance, or used technically to refer to a conceptually distinctive set of behaviours.[4] The *Random House Dictionary* defines it as an expression or declaration of objection, disapproval or dissent, often in opposition to something a person is powerless to prevent or avoid.[5] Similarly, the *International Encyclopedia of Psychiatry, Psychology Psychoanalysis and Neurology* states, "Social protest refers to a more or less vigorous group behaviour brought about when individuals have failed to achieve goals they deem justifiable and when they have exhausted all conventional means of satisfying their grievances. The protest may be such by its very nature it is instrumental in correcting the injustice. In many cases, however, the protest may follow by frustration-aggression model which suggests that when persons are thwarted in the attainment of goals they sometimes behave in ways not rationally related to goal attainment."[6] As such, protest constitutes a formative part of a confrontation, resistance or opposition arising out of a deeply felt disquiet feeling on account of the public officials' indifference to real values and the human needs of the protesting subjects. An element of non-conformism, challenge or defiance of the rules prescribed by those who make authoritative allocation of values in the society forms an essential ingredient of a protest movement. Through their actions, the protesters seek to draw the attention of the authorities in the society towards their grievances and influence them to take steps for the amelioration of these grievances. To quote Ralph Turner, "The principal indicators of a protest definition are concerned with identifying the grievances as the most adequate way of accounting for the disturbance and the belief that the main treatment indicated is to ameliorate the unjust condition."[7] Robert Fogelson too identifies protest as attempts that seek to draw the attention of those in authoritative positions towards the protestors' widespread dissatisfaction with their unjust and dispriviledged position in the existing system.[8]

Protest may represent not only an active challenge to the establishment seeking to motivate it to act in a particular way as desired by the protesters but also may be a challenge that seeks to restrain the authorities from acting in a particular way that is not conducive to the interest of the protesters. It is in this capacity "a form of public check on the exercise of authority."[9] To quote S.C. Mishra, "The protest is thus felt to be not only against a manifest injustice, an oppressive act or a series of acts by the rulers, but it also denies the validity of rulers' acts."[10] Both in its capacity as a means for seeking the authorities to take particular step or to restrain them from a particular act, protest only serves as a communication medium that seeks not to dislodge those in power but rather a continuation with them in the existing arrangement to the extent that the protesters' needs are satisfied. Turner observes, "In contrast, protesters – even when they resort occasionally to desperate means – need not reject the values of those whom they protest. They may share the same values and seek only their share of what others already have. Therefore, the belief in widespread protest calls into question the mechanics of society's operation but not necessarily the value consensus."[11] In a way the protesters are thus like the revivalists or reformers who do not as such question the system but desire the extirpation of its corrupt part and the purgation of the illegitimate practices from the system so as to revivify the system back to its idealized, pure and pristine state.[12]

Protest should have a content in terms of its positive content and criticism and for this it has to be based on dissent as an ideology.[13] Without this it becomes deviance, not protest. Dissent may be defined as the inner urge for an alternative socio-political or economic order promising a more just and dignified life. Such an urge may be activated not only by the perceived inequities and injustices of the existing socio-political or economic order but also on account of a spiritual quest which often begins within the dissenting leaders who feel deeply disturbed on account of the authority's indifference to real values and the human needs of the subjects. It questions the illegitimate acquisition of privileges and the power and wealth which rulers have acquired by virtue of their hold on the levers of privileges. Dissent primarily remains at the ideational level. However, it has the potential to form into independent belief system or an ideology viable in its own right. When dissent assumes the shape of a thoroughgoing public attack on the privilege system, it assumes the proportion of a protest movement. Its leader or leaders acquire a charisma, a holiness not only because of their disdain for the worldliness for which they attack the existing beneficiaries, their critique of the existing system, but also because of their insistence on a real and existential faith and their own lives in which they live their faith.[14] M.S.A. Rao, while describing this relationship between dissent and protest says, "Protest is a formal declaration of dissent and represents a more confirmed state of opposition and conflict."[15] Thus, an act of defiance or challenge or non-conformism is an important aspect of protest movement and this non-conformism may be either on account of psychological reasons within the individual or because of his dissatisfaction with individuals' behaviour (especially the elites) which is generally in contrast to the prescriptive values of the society in which he lives.

Protest is generally very specific in nature and centres around specific issues. However, at times, it may have a generalized objective too. To quote David Bayley, "Coercive public protest may have a specific or a generalized object."[16] Protest serves as a means of communication channel to convey to the public authorities the grievances of the protesters and is potentially effective means for influencing government decisions and policies. However, in order to resort to protest, it is essential that the protesters are conscious of experiencing some sort of injustice, deprivation or disprivilege. If individuals suffering from different kinds of inequities or injustice do not complain about their condition and accept everything as providential, then, the chances of a protest movement are virtually absent. Thus, the individual's sharing of a sense of deprivation and disprivilege or a conviction of some wrongs or injustice being done to him may be said to be the starting point of any protest. To quote Y.B. Damle, "Nevertheless, the mere existence of deprivation, disprivilege and injustice does not warrant a movement towards changing existing social arrangements. What is essential is the awareness of such differences and an awakening of consciousness in certain sections of the society in order to do away with arbitrary differences."[17] Similarly, accordance of an element of divinity to all institutional basis of authority and a sense of fatalism also reduces the chances of a protest movement. A feeling or experience of specific grievances constitutes an indispensable part of a protest movement. Nevertheless, this feeling or experience of the grievances and the consequent reaction to be credible as a protest must be serious and intended to provoke ameliorative action. It cannot be trivial and chronic challenges that are indicative of a reaction style. A challenge to be credible as protest must therefore be based on some shared system of values cherished within the society.

The protesters, as has been opined, are unable to correct the unjust or disprivileged position directly by their personal effort. This is because the protesters do not have enough resources at their command. Despite all the conventional means legitimized by the political system, these individual are not able to improve their conduction. Since the protesters are not capable of improving their condition by independent action, every protest is a request or call to those in authoritative positions to take steps towards the amelioration of the protesters' grievances. The protesters may, as mentioned before, either demand those in authoritative positions to take action in a particular direction or may seek to restrain them from taking some particular action. In essence, all such communications strive to promote the specific interest of the protesters. Thus, protests are effective means for transmitting information about citizens' preferences to officials and this is particularly true concerning preferences about specific policy initiatives.[18] To quote Bayley, "Protests have a very explicit purpose of seeking to affect governmental policy. They are groups indulging in agitational activity which by constituting a threat to public order seek to challenge and change the politics of government."[19] Michael Lipsky too regards protest as a mode of political action oriented towards objection to one or more policies or conditions, characterized by showmanship or display of an unconventional nature and undertaken to obtain rewards from political or economic system while working within the system.[20]

Political challenges are potential process of conflict and may even culminate into real conflict situation. However, the principal goal of the protesters being the amelioration of their specific grievances they primarily make efforts to seek a conciliation. They make efforts to forestall the incipient conflict or to avoid the instance of actual violent confrontation. This conciliatory effort has a basis which considers the intention to do injury as secondary in importance to that of actual redress of the grievance faced by the protesters. Within this effort for conciliation is included the offer not only to stop or refrain from injurious attacks but also to help to correct any harm if already done. Conciliatory efforts not followed by actual subsidence of disruptive activities influences such a political challenge to be interpreted as a rebellion. On the other hand, when there is no prospect of involvement in conflict and no occasion for conciliation, crime or deviance is likely to be the interpretation of the movement.

Protest is not the only means available to the citizens for the transmission of information on idea, emotions, values and attitudes. There are many means of political participation through which the individuals can convey their value preferences and grievances faced by them in their day-to-day life. Thus, the individual or groups may try to contact officials, submit petition requesting the authorities to act in particular manner, try to influence the political parties, form interest groups and canvass their cause through mass media. A movement to be credible as protest must seem to exhibit the fact that its participants have exhausted all conventionally available means of communication and are earnestly seeking the amelioration of their grievances. Thus, protest activities are potentially effective means for influencing government policy and are utilized by individual or groups who feel that the normal political process is not responding to their needs or grievances.[21] Although this has been the general trend, the individual's lack of faith in the efficacy of conventional means and their impatience and desire to achieve quick results have often influenced them to take recourse to protest as a matter of first policy. Explaining this tendency in the protesting individuals, Bayley remarks, "Agitational politics is now a substitute for institutional means of exercising influence and of seeking redress of grievances. Protests are so common that they not only supplement formal procedures but supplant them and render them irrelevant. Protests are not used only when other avenues of accommodation have been exhausted, they have become a court of first resort."[22]

Place of Persuasive and Coercive Tactics and Reference Public

One major factor which contributes to the tendency to engage in protest activities is related to the capacity of the political system to fulfil the value expectation of its subjects. An unjust system of authoritative allocation of values and the awareness of this position of disprivilege, deprivation and injustice tends to give rise to a protest movement. A political system has several information feedback mechanisms through which it gains acquaintance with events occurring in the system. It is rarely the case that those in authoritative positions in the society are unaware of the grievances of individuals who, having generally exhausted all conventional means of ameliorating their grievance, decide to resort to protest. Generally, the inaction of the political system to take ameliorative steps is either due to the unwillingness of the authorities to take the desired steps or due to the lack of resources within the system to be able to remove these grievances. The apathetic attitude to those in authoritative position towards the grievances faced by the protesters is generally due to the fact that the protesters in their independent capacity do not constitute a potentially influential force in the political calculation of such people in power. Since the protesters do not have anything worthy of interest for these people in power or public office, there is not enough motivation for them to take action for the amelioration of interest of the protesters. When ethical or moralistic consideration become secondary to such consideration of the tangible gains accruable through the bargaining or "give and take" process in politics, the aggrieved individuals find themselves in an uncomfortable position. This problem of the protesters is designated by James Q. Wilson as the "problem of the powerless".[23] Faced with such a situation the aggrieved individuals are in a state of dilemma as to how to motivate those in authoritative position to take ameliorative steps. This dilemma is resolved by a two-pronged strategy:

1. adoption of a combination of persuasive (appeal) and coercive (threat) tactics which tend to stimulate sympathy or fear respectively in the public officials and influence them to behave in the manner as desired by the protesters; and
2. giving publicity to their grievances and, through their appeal and threat tactics, try to rope in the support of influential people outside the protesting groups, who, by virtue of their influential or resourceful position, are able to influence the decisions or actions of those in public office.

The activities of the protesters range from relatively persuasive to relatively coercive strategies. Through the persuasive tactics the protesters repeatedly and emphatically advertise their powerlessness and aggrieved position and try to gain the support of wider public for their cause. This in turn helps them to stand in good stead during the bargaining process vis-à-vis the government officials. The relatively persuasive tactics are verbal and written communications, petitions and proclamations, some forms of strikes and fasts, holding public meetings and carrying out processions, campaigning through mass media, etc. The persuasive tactics are generally non-violent in nature.

The coercive strategies, on the other hand, by virtue of its predominant threat content instils in the authority, as well as the public, a sense of fear of disruption of normal life and prevalence of chaotic situation where the insecurity of both life and property largely looms in the air. Out of fear of such a chaotic situation the wider public who exercise some control on the government influence it to take steps towards the amelioration of the protesters' grievances. The government itself may take ameliorative steps to prevent events getting out of hand. Some of the coercive tactics are rioting, gang beatings, some forms of strikes and *hartals*, crowd behaviour, looting and arson. The coercive tactics are generally imbued with an element of violence. Violent protest may itself be classified into three categories:

1. Violence of remonstrance;
2. Violence of confrontation; and
3. Violence of frustration.[24]

Generally, the protesters make use of both the appeal and threat strategies and therefore the nature of movement varies to the extent that the combination ratio of appeal and threat contents changes. Threat content, when predominating, obliterates the appeal content and makes liable the political challenge to be interpreted as a rebellion or revolt. Appeal content, although required to be a salient feature in any protest movement, is in itself a weak attention drawer and seldom serves as a positive factor in the interpretation of a movement as protest. Therefore, an optimal combination of threat and appeal is necessary for the probability of seeing a disturbance as protest. When the threat component falls below the optimal range, the most likely interpretation is deviance; above the optimal range, preoccupation with threat makes rebellion the probable interpretation.[25] An optimal balance between appeal and threat tactics greatly determines the effectiveness of a protest movement and its ability to overcome the widespread disapproval or opposition it engenders; as and when the rhetoric or tactics of protest become increasingly militant, the effort may be to discourage potential public support.[26]

It is this consideration of an optimal balance between appeal and threat as well as a similar principle of "cost-benefit optimization" that distinguishes a protest from other forms of political challenges and from violence itself. Eisinger, while highlighting the difference between protest and other forms of verbal objection and politically inspired collective violence, emphasizes the following:

1. Protest is a collective act carried out by those concerned with the issue and not by their representatives. As a mass action it relies on the resources which the aggrieving groups can command.
2. Protest is a device by which participants making demands in the political system try to maximize the impact of their meagre resources while simultaneously striving to minimize

the cost which they might have to incur during the process of such demand making.

3. Reliance on implicit threat of violence rather than an explicit intention to do physical harm through open threats or actual violent behaviour. In other words, it harnesses aggressive impulses by controlling and, to some extent, masking them in order to distinguish it from ordinary violent activities and, thereby, to gain a slim element of legality and even legitimacy.

Thus, the protesters manipulate the fear of disorder and violence but simultaneously they protect themselves from paying the potentially high cost (denial of legality and legitimacy) of acknowledging such a strategy.[27] Similarly, Turner observes, "Any evidence of covert planning, conspiracy or seriously intended threats of violence before the event would weaken the credibility of protest interpretation.... To be credible as protest, indications of the use of riots (violence) feuds or enjoyment of violence and destruction must be subordinated to naive anger and desperation."[28]

Coming to the second strategy of protesters to seek the support of the wider public for their struggle and goals, it may be said that this effort becomes indispensable for the protesters on account of their non-resourcefulness to enter into a bargaining process with those holding authoritative positions in the society. Since they themselves do not have anything worth of interest for those in the authoritative positions in the society, the protesters seek to influence and gain support of some third parties who are resourceful to influence the decisions of the authorities in the political system. These third parties may be termed as the authority's "reference public". The reference public makes its own felicific calculations before extending support or joining the protesters. They are likely to join the protesters only if the cost incurable by such close association is likely to be much lesser than the gains accruable from close identification with it or if the loss likely to be incurred by remaining aloof, apathetic or neutral is likely to be greater than the gains accruable from close identification with the protesters. Also, it is more likely that the more the convergence of goal orientation between the protesters and reference public, the more the chances of close cooperation.

In this capacity, therefore, protest may be described as a process characterized by reciprocal relations in which protest leaders frame strategies according to their perception of the needs of many other actors.

From the above examination of the various aspects of protest, it is clear that protest as a challenge to the political system is a milder and relatively less violent form and seeks to ameliorate specific grievances that the protesters face within the given political system. Being conscious of their exploited condition, the protesters question the mechanics of their society's operation. They try to communicate to those in power their difficulties and influence them to take actions to further their specific interests. In conducting their activity, the protesters have to encounter quite a few hindrances like effectively influencing those in power to take actions for the amelioration of their grievances; generating public opinion in their favour; abstention from violence as much as possible, or in the outbreak of it, at least minimize its costs; generate internal resources and make its optimum use for receiving maximum benefit; etc. The presence of these elements gives to protest its distinctiveness vis-à-vis other forms of challenges to the political system like dissent, reform, deviance, rebellion, revolts and revolution.

Notes

1. J.R. Gusfield, Development of Collective Meanings, in *Protest Reform and Revolt: A Reader in Social Movements*, J.R. Gusfield (ed.), John Wiley & Sons Inc., New York, 1977, p. 311.
2. C. Badrinath, Dissent Protest and Reform: The Historical Context, in *Dissent Protest and Reform in Indian Civilization*, S.C. Malik (ed.), Indian Institute of Advanced Study, Simla, 1977, p. 42.
3. For details see the article on "Protestantism" by William F. Hordern in the *Encyclopaedia Americana*, International Edition, Grolier Incorporated, Danbury Connecticut, Vol. 22, 1991, pp. 679-93.
4. Peter K. Eisinger, The Condition of Protest Behaviour in American Cities, *American Political Science Review*, Vol. 67, 1973 (March), p. 13.
5. As quoted by Ralph N. Turner, The Public Perception of Protest, *American Sociological Review*, Vol. 34, No. 6, 1969, p. 816.

6. *The International Encyclopaedia of Psychiatry, Psychology, Psycho-analysis and Neurology*, Benjamin B. Wolman (ed.) Aesculapius Publishers, New York, Vol. 9, 1977. pp. 106-07.
7. Note 5.
8. For details see Robert M. Fogelson, Violence as Protest, in *Urban Riots: Violence and Social Change*, Robert H. Connery (ed.), Academy of Political Science, New York, 1968, pp. 25-41.
9. Note 2, p. 45.
10. S.C. Mishra, *Dissent Protest and Reform: A Note on Definition*, Note 2, p. 55.
11. Note 5, p. 820.
12. S.C. Mishra holds a different opinion and is ready to make an intepretation of a movement as protest even if it challenges the rulers or the existing system and aims to overthrow or change them. For details see S.C. Mishra, Note 2, pp. 54-5.
13. Note 10, p. 54.
14. Ibid.
15. M.S.A. Rao, *Themes in the Ideology of Protest Movement*. Note 2, p. 57.
16. David H. Bayley, Pedagogy of Democracy: Coercive Public Protest in India, *American Political Science Review*, Vol. 56, 1962 (September), p. 663.
17. Y.B. Damie, *Protest Dissent and Social Reform: A Conceptual Note*, Note 2, p. 28.
18. Dennis S. Ippolito et al, *Public Opinion and Responsible Democracy*, Prentice-Hall Inc. Englewood Cliffs, New Jersey, 1976, pp. 237-38.
19. David H. Bayley, *Public Protest and Political Process in India*, Note 1, p. 298.
20. Michael Lipsky, Protest as a Political Resource, *American Political Science Review*, Vol. 32, 1968 (December), p. 1145
21. Note 18, p. 233.
22. Note 19, p. 304.
23. James Q. Wilson as quoted by Michael Lipsky, Note 20.
24. For a detailed examination see David H. Bayley, Note 19, pp. 299-300.
25. Note 5, p. 821.
26. Note 18, p. 235.
27. Note 4, p. 14.
28. Note 5, p. 819.
29. Note 20, p. 1146.
30. Ibid.

3

Protest Theories of the West

Speculation on the principles that justify the existence of a particular form of state or that which should form the basis of a good government has been a fundamental issue in the history of political theory. A concomitant part of this speculation has been the enunciation of certain principles on the basis of which an action to alter or change the existing form of state or a government that does not measure up to the idealized principles may be justified. Basically a notion western in origin, protest emerged as a concept in the 16th century Reformation era and symbolized the struggle of the European Church against the Roman Catholic Church. In course of time movements symbolizing challenges to the established political regimes by certain individuals or groups also came to be referred as protest movements. Thus, from a concept originating in the religious arena, protest came to have a political context too. In this context, the speculations on protest make a clear distinction between the individual and the state or its agencies and, while recognizing certain realms or rights of the individuals as inviolable by the state or the government, concede to the individual the right to check the diabolic designs of the state and seek the redress of the grievances that arise on account of such excrescences by the state or the government. These speculations on protest have focussed on several aspects of protest like that of the means to be adopted, the principles to which these must conform, the effective way to mobilize the available resources, etc. Amongst the seminal contributors to these speculations on protest, a mention may be made of

William Godwin, Henry David Thoreau, Albert Camas and Georges Sorel.

William Godwin (1756-1836)

William Godwin was a prominent British thinker who, starting from the commonplaces of 18th century philosophical beliefs, elaborated the most complete and worked out statement of rational anarchist belief.[1] As one of the principal architects of rational anarchist system of thought, he attempted to carry through the philosophy of anarchism to its logical conclusion and defend it on the basis of the principles of natural justice, utility and rights of man. Attempting to synthesize the principle of utilitarianism with that of perfectionism,[2] Godwin, in his most celebrated political work *An enquiry Concerning Political Justice,* contended that the happiness accrued on account of virtuous or just actions was entirely incidental to the practice of virtue and was in consistency with the *telos* or essential nature of human existence.

Godwin contended that the state or the government, in all their forms, tended to commit excrescences on either or both of these principles. He therefore said, "It is earnestly to be desired that each man should be wise enough to govern himself without the intervention of any compulsory restraint; and, since government, even in its best state, is an evil, the object principally to be aimed at is that we should have as little of it as the general peace of human society will permit."[3] Godwin was averse to such influences from outside like that of the state because it, he believed, tended to restrict the freedom of the individual to act in the manner he deemed to be appropriate and coerced him to passive obedience. Moreover, he contended, it was accompanied by such undesirable side effects like expense, taxation, corruption and patronage.[4] Government, he contended, while asserting its authority over the judgement and understanding of its subject citizens, corrupted the formation of opinion and pursuit of truth among its citizens. Worse still, he claimed, was the tendency among individuals who, hankering after rewards from the state, renounced the use of their critical judgement and rendered blind obedience to it. This, in turn, he contended, not only bound them further into condemnable servitude but also led them further away from such noble values like moral truth, justice, virtue, and genuine felicity. Godwin recognized an imminent need to bring about a change in the existing affairs of such a state or government which transgressed its originally prescribed limit of being a necessary existent acting as a bridle on corrupt human nature and, in the existing conditions, sought to use force and fraud to exploit individuals. He was optimistic about human beings' capability to gradually emancipate themselves from the arbitrary interference and coercive impositions of such a state.

The state's or the government's functioning vis-à-vis the freedom to exercise private judgement for the realization of moral truths, he recognized, should always be critically evaluated. He recognized that the individuals should courageously say to the government that sought deference to political authority, "It is yours to shackle the body and restrain our external actions. But do not seek to enslave our minds... Obedience and external submission is all you can be entitled to claim; you can have no right to extort our deference, and command us not to see and disapprove of your errors."[6] Thus, Godwin advocated the dissenting individuals to practise critical obedience rather than blind adulation.

Godwin did not favour inactivity on the part of the dissenting individuals while corruption and evil prevailed at large in the functioning of the state. Alternatively, he suggested that argument and persuasion were the most appropriate means of bringing about a change in the sentiments and dispositions of individuals. This, he contended, would consequently bear upon the corrupt state to mend its ways. Truth always emerged, he contended, in a free and unrestricted discussion; the best argument or perfect reason would always be vindicated in the ultimate analysis.

Godwin's rejection of coercive tactics in the act of resistance to the corrupt state was also based on his recognition that men as mortal being were fallible and therefore no individual could be absolutely certain about the correctness of his conviction about moral truths. Hence, he emphasized, the individual should not impose his opinions on others but has an open approach towards those individuals who held a different view from his own. This, Godwin contended, would enable the individual not only to have a feel of the opponent's views and feelings about a given situation but also, thereby, make a broader interpretation of the issues involved.

The rejection of force by Godwin was also on account of the fact that he believed every evil or vice to possess certain causative factors behind it. He therefore claimed that when the reason behind such vices was understood and the causes of the evil removed, the evil would vanish automatically.

Thus, in conclusion, we can say that Godwin's account of resisting the corrupt state was fully consistent with the basic principles which acted as the guiding force of his whole philosophy. "These principles", comments Mark Philip, "are much more those of liberalism than of revolutionary republicanism. Indeed he provides us with an account of nonviolent change and transition which is in many ways more conservative than Locke in its implication for the justification of violent political action."[7]

Henry David Thoreau (1817-1862)

Thoreau may be regarded as one of the principal proponents in the history of American political speculation to enunciate the essential premises on which the state may be resisted. Belonging to the transcendentalist tradition of Emerson, Coleridge, Carlyle, etc., Thoreau attempted to synthesize the idealism of English and German thinkers with American individualism. Being critical of the facade of the industrialized western civilization and its progress, he decided to live in the "woods" amidst the simplicity of nature and away from the evils of materialistic civilization. In his days in Concord, Massachusetts, he had refused to pay taxes on a few occasions and once even protested publicly and went to prison to uphold and assert his freedom to follow such values of self-reverence, self-knowledge and self-determinism which he held close to his heart. His essay *On the Duty of Civil Disobedience*, written in 1849, makes a full-scale defence of these values.

As an ardent champion of individual liberty, Thoreau resisted those coercive tendencies of the state that fatally affected the individuality and freedom of the individual. He said, "I was not born to be forced. I will breathe after my own fashion."[8] The state, he recognized, had neither a superior wisdom nor an ethical sanctity when compared to the individual. The only aspect in which it was superior to the individual was the realm of physical strength. Since it had neither a superior wisdom nor a greater ethical sanctity than the individual, Thoreau contended that the state could not force its subject individuals to obey any of its laws that were baser than the law of the individual self. He therefore recognized that it could not have a carte blanche right over the individual and should have the sanction and consent of the governed for its power and authority. Neither on grounds of sympathy nor for fear of suffering punishment, Thoreau recognized, should the individuals agree to obey the unjust command of the state or implement its diabolic designs.

Like many other thinkers and public men who have denounced and decried the coercive tendencies of the state, Thoreau too opined that the state in contemporary era by virtue of its extended scope performed a wide range of activities. Often on the pretext of such narrowly defined interests like social order and security it subjected individuals to render obedience to a variety of coercive decrees that violated the integrity, dignity and the very essence of individual beings. The individuals, on their part, consciously or otherwise, willingly or unwillingly, by obeying such decrees, have protected and promoted such felicific calculations that were more reflective of their baser self. Such habitual obedience to the state, Thoreau recognized, would ultimately prove disastrous because such acts when progressively practised and tolerated would make the individuals indifferent to the performance of such acts, and more progressively, the recognition of an element of sin or evil in such acts would disappear. When individuals on a large scale indulged in such activities, Thoreau recognized, they would destroy the very moral fabric or the essence of human existence. Therefore, he held the view that dissent without disobedience was consent, and, therefore, culpable.[9]

Having recognized the right of the individuals to resist unjust laws of the state, Thoreau delved into one of the most debatable aspects of protest, namely, whether one should obey an unjust order until one succeeded in convincing and motivating those in authoritative position to amend them, or whether to violate the unjust law at the first instance and make efforts for its amendment subsequently. Thoreau did not favour any such doctrine of resistance which, on the pretext that a remedy through a resistance to the state is liable to be worse than the evil, advocated the individual to have patience until they had persuaded the majority to alter them. He believed that it was better to protest the unjust law at the first instance than allowing the injustice to continue. The inconveniences that might arise on account of protesting the unjust state in the first instance, Thoreau believed, were likely to be far less undesirable than allowing the unjust state to perpetuate its unjust or evil designs. He therefore remarked, "If a thousand men were not to pay their tax-bills this year that would not be a violent and bloody measure, as it would be to pay them, and enable the state to commit violence and shed innocent blood. This is in fact the definition of peaceable revolution if any such is possible."[10] Thoreau, therefore, wanted the conscientious individuals to be brave and unmindful of the consequences of protesting the unjust state. He did acknowledge the possibility of a violent and bloody reaction from the state in the event of disobeying its orders; but such physical injuries, he recognized, were far less inconsequential when compared to the wound caused to the conscience of the individual by submitting meekly to the unjust command and thereby giving a fatal blow to the essence of human existence. So, he said, "Through this wound a man's real manhood and immortality flow out, and he bleeds to an everlasting death."[11] Believing the strength of wisdom and truth to be greater than the combined strength of all evils, Thoreau recognized that it was a sufficient ground for the individuals convinced about the diabolic goals of the state to resist it. Having the voice of conscience or God on their side, rather than the support of the majority, Thoreau believed, was enough for the righteous individuals to protest the unjust state.

Thoreau, unlike Green, was not willing to advocate the individual to conform to the unjust commands of the state until he had succeeded to get the unjust command annulled through legal measures provided by the state. He held the state, rather than the protesting individual, responsible if any recourse for a remedy through resistance to the unjust state resulted in a worse situation than the injustice perpetuated by the evil law. The state, he recognized, should anticipate and provide for reform, rather than resist attempts made by individuals to remedy the unjust condition. It should give due recognition to the integrity and wisdom of the individuals and should always encourage its citizens to be on alert to point out its fault and the prospects of better performances, rather than treating these individuals as its enemies. Thus, Thoreau said, "But it is the fault of the government itself that the remedy is worse than the evil... Why is it not more apt to anticipate and provide for reform? Why does it not cherish its wise minority? Why does it cry and resist before it is hurt? Why does it not encourage its citizens to be on alert to point out its faults and do better than it would have them? Why does it always crucify Christ, and excommunicate Copernicus and Luther, and pronounce Washington and Franklin rebels?"[12]

The individuals, Thoreau recognized, generally tended to depend upon the state to protect and promote their interest related to life, family and property. Those who had renounced their conscience tended to blindly support and owe allegiance to such institutions which helped them to pursue and promote their selfish interest. Only through such subservience, Thoreau contended, these individuals were able to conceal many bitter and embarrassing questions related to their mean pursuits and avoid public disgrace. Thoreau denounced such an immoral attitude and wanted every individual to lead a simple and honest life. He regarded it to be much easier for honest individuals who were largely self-reliant to resist every attempt that tended to perpetuate evil and coerce the individual to be a participant to this endeavour. This was because, Thoreau argued, the most important consideration for such simple and righteous individuals was to live and uphold the values that they cherished most. The material considerations, of which they possessed very little, occupied only a relegated importance. Such being their approach to life, the relative cost of suffering the penalty for disobedience to the unjust state for them was much lesser than that of obeying the unjust command and thereby fatally injuring the values that they held in great esteem. Therefore, Thoreau advised, "If a man is thought-fee, fancy-free, imagination-free, that which is not ever for a long time appearing to be to him, unwise rulers or reformers cannot fatally interrupt him."[13]

It would perhaps be more appropriate to consider Thoreau as a thinker who conformed more to the liberal tradition demanding better governance from the existing political arrangement than as one belonging to the anarchist tradition demanding an immediate end to the existence of the state and its governance of man. The initial denouncement of the coercive tendencies of the state and the government and the advocacy of resisting all such coercive and unjust authority in Thoreau's essay *Civil Disobedience*, became in its concluding part, an effort to picturise the qualities of a more free and fair state, to which, Thoreau said, he was ready to obligate himself. This state, Thoreau perceived, was one which recognized the individual as a higher and independent power; derived its authority and power from the sanction and consent of the governed individuals; gave the individual the due recognition of being a more sacrosanct entity than itself; treated them as the basis of its existence and functioning; and lastly, was just to all individuals and harboured no feeling of ill-will even towards those wise, simple and honest individuals who lived aloof from it and recognized no need to depend on it for their sustenance; instead, it treated them as its friend and sought their wise advice in times of need. To quote Thoreau, "There will never be a really free and enlightened state until the state comes to recognize the individual as higher and independent power from which all its own power and authority are derived, and treats him accordingly. I please myself with imagining a state at last which can afford to be just to all men, and to treat the individual with respect as a neighbour; which even would not think it inconsistent with its own repose if a few were to live aloof from it, not embraced by it, who fulfilled all the duties of neighbours and fellow men".[14]

Albert Camus (1913-1960)

Albert Camus was a well-known French existentialist. He was a vehement critic of the contemporary world which, he recognized, had grown indifferent to the general decline in human values and consequently also to evils inhabiting its various domains. His entire life as a moralist and philosopher of revolt was therefore given to finding some sense that could be attributed to this indifferent world.[15] Both, through his literary work – *L'Homme Revolte, Le Mythe de Sisyphe, L'Etranger, Caligula, La Peste*, etc. – and his journalistic enterprise with *Alger-Republicain, Le Soir-Republicain* and *Combat*, Camus endeavoured not only to highlight the absurdities facing human life in general and the war-prone world in particular, but, more importantly, also to advocate a resistance to all these absurdities and thereby usher in a new renaissance of man, who, he regarded, was the only existent to have a meaning in this otherwise meaningless world. He consistently stood forth in defence of human freedom and dignity against all forms of oppression. Through such picturisation of noble and heroic character like Sisyphus, Dr. Rieux, Mersault, etc., he testified to the strength of human beings to face the most dispiriting truth without cracking.[16]

Authority, when it became cruel, capricious and destructive, Camus recognized, should be resisted. Camus contended that there could not exist any justification for the perpetuation of evil against mankind. Every evil ought to be resisted. This resistance implicit in Camus' enunciation of *La revolte and L' Homme revolte* is unique in its meaning of rebellion and rebel which are the English translation of Camus *La revolte and L' Homme revolte* respectively. Thus, Cranston writes, "It is a curious thing about Camus that despite his being one of the best prose stylist of his generation, he had a certain partiality for words which suggest something different from what he meant to say and often something more extreme. *L' absurde* is one such word. *La revolte* is another. *La revolte* is usually translated into English as rebellion and *L'homme revolte* as the rebel, both terms commonly connected with the ideology of violent change. And this is precisely what Camus is not upholding."[17] Camus wrote at the beginning of his *Remarque sur la revolte*, "What is an *homme revolte*? In the first place he is a man who says "no". But in refusing he does not renounce. He is also a man who says "yes".[18] The rebel's "no" implied his refusal to obey orders beyond a certain point which he believed to be intrinsically wrong and, thereby, affirmed his faith in something which he considered to be sacred and inviolable. Similarly, the rebel's "yes" referred to his belief that an individual, through his act of resistance, was capable of creating his own moral values and as a man of principle bear witness to the reality of moral values by his conduct. Through such pamphlets like *Reflexions sur la' guillotine* and such plays like the *L' Etat de siege*, Camus endeavoured to defend the individual against the abstractions and terrors of the totalitarian states.

The theory of *la' revolte* which Camus, enunciated in *La Homme Revolte,* was directly opposed to one of revolution. Revolution, he believed, sought to annihilate the real in order to actualize the ideal. This annihilation, due to its destructive potency, provides little scope for reform on account of the fact that things once annihilated or destroyed cannot be reformed. As opposed to such a revolution, Camus' theory of *la' revolte* sought to modify, to correct and reform the existing reality. It sought to preserve things in order to make improvements in the condition of man's life on earth. Thus, Richard Cox, pointing to Camus' pure *revolte's* endeavour to strike a balance between the two extremes of absolute negation and absolute affirmation, says that Camus' notion of *La' revolte* strives to achieve unity and order by accepting as inevitable the historical forms and conditions – the "reality" which it finds around it; but it transforms that reality by revolting against it through the process of artistic creation.[19] Thus, the *La homme revolte* is essentially a precursor against unhappiness and oppression; one who does not resign himself simply to ignore and live with the injustice of society but undertakes the difficult task of finding a middle way between amoral revolution and passively immoral quietism.[20] The enunciation of such a revolt which is guided by a sense of limits of *mesure* or moderation presents, R.W.B. Lewis opines, an ideal of a well-balanced rebellion.[21]

Reflecting on the ineffectiveness of a recourse to violence as a means of rebellion, Camus said, "When violence answers violence in a growing frenzy that makes the simple language of reason impossible, the role of intellectuals cannot be, as we read every day, to excuse from a distance one of the violence and condemn the other."[22] He also said, "It seemed to be both indecent and harmful to protest against tortures in the company of those who readily accepted Melouza or the mutilation of European children; just as it seemed to me harmful and indecent to condemn terrorism in the company of those who are not bothered by torture."[23] Camus, therefore, could not accept the wanton indifference of those who encouraged, no matter in how sophisticated form, the idea of revolution accomplished through a violent seizure of power. The prospect appeared to him to be not only unrealistic on account of the superior power of modern states but also unjustifiable as it tended to heap murder upon murder and created terror without end and, thereby, threatened the very existence and felicity of human beings. Consequently, he recognized that violence ought not be answered back in violence; instead, one should endeavour to elicit humane reactions from the opponent by speaking to him in the language of common humanity. Such a critical reflection on the recourse to violence, it may be contended, also guided one to find the necessary corollaries in Camus' *La revolte* the emphasis on purity of means, sincerity of purpose and a great regard for non-violence.

In his recognition it was not the end that justified the means, but the means that justified the end.[24] Since only pure means could produce pure and noble ends, the rebel, Camus emphasized, only took recourse to just means in his act of rebellion. Similarly, Camus believed, writes Maurice Cranston, that sacrificing oneself tantamounted to conferring a certain dignity on the end; while sacrificing others for a noble ideal tantamounted to robbing that ideal of its nobility.[25]

However, Camus, despite his great regard for non-violence, conceded that absolute non-violence was as impossible as absolute freedom.[26] Force, he conceded, was necessary to combat violence. However, the *homme revolte*, he recognized, would only recourse to this for limiting it rather than codifying it. Thus, while assailing senseless retribution of violence by violence, Camus seemed to acquiesce in only that violence or force which was needed to suppress violence. As already pointed out, it is not that Camus did not have a high regard for non-violence; on the contrary, to such persons who conformed to the belief of total non-violence, as in the case of Tarrou in *La Peste*, and to the belief as such, Camus did have a great regard, but was not able to share their point of view on account of the fact that for him, as for Dr. Rieux in La *Peste*, there was cherishment neither for heroism or holiness through such deeds, but to remain basically a man doing the duties of his station in that capacity, i.e., identification of his self with his fellow individuals and seeking to serve them through his limited capacity and thus making them happy.

Georges Sorel (1847-1922)

Georges Sorel, a Marxist-turned-revisionist, was a French philosopher and social theorist who, through his revolutionary ideas, infused vigour and vitality to the anarcho-syndicalist movement. His greatest contribution to modern political thought through his seminal work – *Reflexions sur la violence* – has been the championship of violence as a means for the effective realization of goals conceived by any serious political opposition or challenge. Representing an era that had been deeply disgruntled by hitherto efforts that strove to raise rationalism to the high pedestal of being the only genuine means for explaining and controlling every aspect of human behaviour and cosmic phenomena, Sorel introduced this cult, i.e., of renouncing faith in reason and, instead, taking recourse to irrationalism, into pragmatic politics with a simultaneous advocacy of a mystical faith in the proletariat-will making its way through violent combat and, thereby, realizing a socio-political order that was free from the various forms of bourgeois oppression and exploitation.

Violence being inherent in the apparently peaceful structures of the exploitative state, Sorel contended, every conciliatory effort tended to only maintain more or less the same status quo which was in favour of the exploitative class. In a decadent bourgeois society, he recognized, there could not be unanimity regarding the opposing class having fulfilled its respective social duties. He thus, said, "While the employer will be always convinced that he has done the whole of his duty, the worker will be of a contrary opinion and no argument could possibly settle the matter: The first will believe that he has been heroic and the second will treat this pretended heroism as shameful exploitation."[27] Resolution of conflict out of genuine considerations for the opponent class, thus, Sorel believed, was not only impossible but also a facade. The mere claim of it and the consequent results, in Sorel's recognition, was very absurd.[28] Thus, James Joll comments, "All Sorel's doctrine is based on the assumption that the intellectuals are misleading the masses, debauching them with false ideas and cheap sentimentality, making them believe that unrealizable things are possible in order the better to lead them by the nose. Intellectuals impose a pattern on the world that does not correspond to reality."[29]

Prejudice against violence, Sorel contended, existed on account of the fact that its hitherto use, especially in revolution, had been not only for the limited purpose of promoting narrow interests of those who seized power through its exercise but also on account of the fact that it had been carried to excess. Hitherto revolutionary violence, he recognized, had only changed hands; the narrow purposes for which it had been put to use had not changed even a bit. All such violence was recognized by him as political violence. In contrast to this, a proletarian act of violence, Sorel recognized, would not only make a clear distinction between the men who do the evil and the evil itself but also, while having no hatred or revenge against such men and desisting from all acts of savagery against them, would seek the destruction of the evil by striking at its roots.

Proletariat violence, Sorel went on to advocate, should assume the form of a "general strike" as the preferred way of precipitating the creative forces that would bring about radical changes in the existing exploitative bourgeois state. The "general strike", like all great military battles, Sorel contended, perceived a goal which would seek the catastrophic defeat of the opponent and, from the top to the bottom and from the elite to the rank and file in the proletarian class, would instruct and train for the greatest of sacrifices. The "general strike", he recognized, encompassed the whole of socialism in its abiding scheme of things and ensured single and clear interpretation of the cherished ideals and goals. It made crystal clear, Sorel claimed, the division of society into two distinct and antagonistic classes and, thereby, simplified the task to be accomplished through revolutionary violence. The "general strike', as recognized by Sorel, was also a means to exacerbate the tension between the two antagonistic classes and sought to avoid all deceptive compromises or reformist and patchwork schemes. It, while regenerating the inherent virtues of their class in the "industrial captains", rallied the proletariat to a relentless, passionate and organized resistance against the bourgeois and the prevailing exploitative conditions. Thus, he said, "Strikes have engendered in the proletariat the noblest, deepest and most moving sentiments that they possess; the general strike groups them all in a coordinated picture, and by bringing them together, gives to each one of them its maximum intensity."[30] Through its training, disciplining and arousing of sentiments of class solidarity, Sorel recognized that "general strike" would ultimately facilitate the actualization of the catastrophic revolution and, thereby, a society purged off all bourgeois evils. Recognizing it as an industrial action and that too a direct one by the proletariat class, Sorel contended that its justification or merit lay in the action itself rather than in the immediate results that it might bring about. He thus said, "To examine the effects of violence it is necessary to start from its distant consequences and not from its immediate results. We should not ask whether it is more or less directly advantageous for contemporary workmen than adroit diplomacy would be, but we should inquire what will result from the introduction of violence into the relations of the proletariat with society."[31]

The myth of the ultimate triumph of one's cause or cherished will to victory, Sorel recognized, was always kept alive and propagated by an elite. In the degenerated bourgeois state, he assigned this elite leadership to a select few belonging to the proletariat class, who, through the weapon of "general strike", would mobilize the whole of proletariat class to overthrow the existing order. Devoid of any opportunistic calculations they would facilitate the larger proletariat class to think for itself without the guidance of middle-class intellectuals. Sorel greatly romanticized the clean proletarian elite and regarded them as the heroes of social revolution and contrasted them to the corrupt demagogues of social democracy who hoodwink the poor and blackmail the rich.[32] They, through their guidance of the industrial action or "general strike", Sorel recognized, would train, discipline and organize the proletariats in the endeavour to bring about the catastrophic defeat of the bourgeois class and thereby an end to all the evils that were attached to it.

The violence of confrontation that Sorel advocated in the industrial action was not one which implied a physical attack on persons and property; rather it was an industrial war, i.e. the pressure and compulsion of strikes[33] and was akin to a military war carried out as mechanically and methodically without hatred and revenge as by armies in a campaign.[34] Unlike the middle-class revolutionary violence, the proletarian violence, he recognized, would strike at the very root of power of the bourgeois state and seek its destruction. A violence that sought such a catastrophic defeat and destruction of the exploitative structures, process and institutions, in Sorel's contention, was pure and had to be essentially distinguished from others that might pursue the narrow goals of its wielder. This proletarian violence, on account of its inherently creative potential and purity, Sorel recognized, was also superior in quality to conciliatory attempts that sought to reconcile differences by patchwork and degenerate the intrinsic noble qualities of both the antagonistic classes involved in the class conflict. Peace-keeping through conciliatory tactics being a facade, only the violence of confrontation, as represented in the "general strike", Sorel recognized, was the genuine and efficacious means for any serious political opposition or resistance to exploitative and unjust socio-economic and political conditions.

Such being Sorel's contention and recognition of the ethics of violence, Edward A. Shills, whose comment provides the key to the understanding of Sorel's theory of protest against the unjust and exploitative state, has commented, "In his whole life, and underlying all its concrete political changes, as a conservative moralist, as a Marxian socialist, as a revolutionary syndicalist, as an authoritarian traditionalist and as a sympathetic observer of the Bolshevik Revolution, there is one common theme: The highest good is the heroic (i.e., aggressive) action performed with a sense of impersonal consecration to the ends of a restricted, delimited group bound together in fervent solidarity and impelled by a passionate confidence in its ultimate triumph in some cataclysmic encounter."[35]

Notes

1. James Joll, *The Anarchists*, Methuen & Co. Ltd., London, 1979, p. 16.
2. For a detailed discussion, see Mark Philip, *Godwin's Political Justice*, Gerald Duckworth & Co. Ltd., London, 1986, pp. 80-96.
3. See William Godwin, *Enquiry Concerning Political Justice*, I. Krammick (ed.) Penguin, Harmondsworth, 1976, p. 253
4. See Note 2, p. 2.
5. Note 2, p. 133.

6. Ibid.
7. Ibid., p. 77
8. Thoreau's essay on Civil Disobedience as reproduced (pp. 198-212) in Kenneth M. Dolbeare, *Directions in American Political Thought*, John Willey & Sons. Inc., New York, 1969, p. 207. For a detailed discussion on Thoreau' protest see Naresh Dadhich and B. Arun Kumar, Thoreau's Protest: A Means to Maintain the Ontological Essence of Man, *Gandhi Marg*, Vol. 15, No. 3, October-December 1993, pp. 308-22.
9. Louis Fischer, *The Life of Mahatma Gandhi*, Granada Publishing Ltd., London, 1982, p. 116.
10. Note 8, p. 205.
11. Ibid.
12. Ibid., p. 203.
13. Ibid., p. 210.
14. Ibid., p. 211
15. Edward T. Gargan, Revolution and Morale in the Formative Thought of Albert Camus, *Review of Politics*, No. 25, October 1963, p. 483.
16. See Jeffrey Gordon, Nagel or Camus on the Absurd? *Philosophy and Phenomenological Research*, Vol. 4, No. 1, September 1984, p. 27.
17. Maurice Cranston, Albert Camus, *Encounter*, No. 28, February 1967, p. 49
18. Ibid.
19. Richard H. Cox, Ideology, History and Political Philosophy: Camus 'L' Homme Revolte, *Social Research*, No. 32, Spring 1965, p. 77.
20. See Fred H. Willhoite Jr., Albert Camus' Politics of Rebellion, in *Perspectives on Political Philosophy*, James v. Downtown Jr. and David K. Hart (ed.), The Dryden Press Inc. Hinsdale, Illinois, 1973, p. 329.
21. R.W.B. Lewis, Caligula: Or the Realm of the Impossible, *Yale French Studies*, No. 25, 1960, p. 54.
22. Camus as quoted by Cranston, Note 17, p. 53.
23. Ibid.
24. Camus as quoted by Willhoite Jr., Note 20, p. 329.
25. Note 17, p. 51.
26. See Ibid., pp. 50-51.
27. Georges Sorel, *Reflections on Violence*, Trans. T.E. Hulme and J. Roth, The Free Press, Glencoe, Illinois, 1950, p. 83.
28. For a detailed discussion on the futility of conciliatory methods, see Ibid., pp. 84-92.

29. Note 1, p. 190.
30. Sorel as quoted by Atindranath Bose, *A History of Anarchism*, The World Press Private Ltd., Calcutta, 1967, p. 308.
31. Note 27, p. 308.
32. See Note 30, p. 312.
33. Ibid., p. 311.
34. Ibid.
35. Edward A. Shills in Introduction to the American edition of Georges *Sorel's Reflections on Violence.,* Note 1, p. 18.

4

Theories of Protest in Gandhi's Contemporary India

Before Gandhi launched himself in India as a protester of the British rule there were already in existence quite a few individuals and institutional folds who were making a resolute struggle to secure greater freedom, a more responsive, responsible and just administration and a larger participation of the natives in administration. While some of these struggles displayed moderation in their approach, a few were quite militant in voicing their protest. There were also quite a few militant revolutionaries who took recourse to violence in their confrontation with the British. Two of the most important personalities whose distinct protest largely characterized moderation and militantism while confronting the British regime in India were Gopal Krishna Gokhale and Bal Gangadhar Tilak respectively.

Gopal Krishna Gokhale (1866-1915)

More a political activist and social reformer than being a political philosopher in the accepted sense of the term, Gokhale's exposure to the liberal tradition of the West, his knowledge and close association with the nationalistic sentiments of his Indian predecessors and contemporaries and his personal experiences of both the beneficial and baneful effects of a colonial rule, influenced him to speculate upon both the principles that should form the basis of a good government and those that justified an action to resist or protest the government which did not measure up to these idealized principles. Any good government, in his recognition, had to strenuously endeavour for the welfare of the subject people; identify itself with the needs and aspirations of its subject citizens; facilitate public participation in administration; and, in its functioning, imbibe the notions of trust, conciliation and justice. Conceiving political governance as a great responsibility and trust reposed on those who held its reign, Gokhale recognized it more importantly as a moral responsibility than a legal one. Consequently, he emphasized upon its spiritualization. Although he was a great champion of advocating loyalty to the established order, this loyalty of Gokhale was neither an advocacy of uncritical adulation of those holding the authoritative position in the society nor of a perpetual subservience to the unjust and oppressive rule. Far from being a passive recepiency, his loyalty was synonymous with patriotism.[1] "If Gokhale's response to the British rule was one of loyal acquiescence based on an overriding faith in the integrity and beneficence of that which was best in the British tradition, it was by no means the supine surrender of a sycophant or a mendicant to bureaucratic oppression. On the contrary, his protest against the latter first of all led to his choice of a career in public service, and then sustained Gokhale through a lifetime of hopes deferred and apparent failures."[2] Gokhale's enunciation of loyalty thus did not presume the renunciation of the right to protest by the subject individuals; rather, it delved into the appropriate manner that it should assume. Being emphatic on moderation and pragmatism while taking recourse to protest the state, Gokhale's advocacy of constitutional agitation was thus conceived not only as a means to check and reform the unjust or bad government while staying within the parameters of the existing regime, but, more importantly, also as a means for the subject individuals to preserve the freedom and integrity of their self and to uphold the spiritual values which their conscience perceived as uncompromisable.

In its capacity as a means for seeking the authorities to take a desired step or seeking to refrain them from taking an undesired step, Gokhale's protest served as a communication channel for ventilating grievances and sought not the dislodging of those in power, but a continuation with them, and progressive participation of the protesters in the existing arrangement so as to ameliorate the specific grievances faced by them.

In his capacity as a subject citizen of a nation under colonial rule, he did not reject the values for which the British Empire stood; rather, he was opposed to the so called "un-British" type of rule which prevailed in his contemporary India. He, as a proud citizen of the British Empire, cherished the same values as his British counterpart did in Britain and sought for himself and his countrymen what a British already enjoyed in his native land or in the territory which fell within the domains of the British Empire. Thus, Gokhale said, "I recognize no limits to my aspiration for our motherland, I want our people to be in their own country what other people are in theirs. I want our men and women without distinction of caste or creed to have opportunities to grow to the full heights of their stature, unhampered by cramping and unnatural restrictions."[3] Gokhale's protest, thus, only questioned the mechanics of British Empire's working in India, and not the value consensus that it represented. It being so, Gokhale recognized the immediate goal of his protest as lying within the parameters of "self-government within the empire" and a government extirpated off its corrupt, exploitative and unjust facets.

All such emphases of Gokhale like that of causing the "least or the minimum disturbance of existing ideas,"[4] proceeding along lines which one understands however difficult the progress might be",[5] "one step enough for me",[6] etc., were a part of his recognition of refraining from dislodging those wielding power in the existing political arrangement. Consequently, he admonished every such claim for rebellion and revolution which were voiced by his more militant contemporaries and, instead, preferred a recourse to protest and reform. It also influenced his understanding of the concept of loyalty. Interpreting loyalty from a broader point of view, Gokahle emphasized upon the need for the citizens to cultivate an active sense of loyalty to the existing order. He said, "Now loyalty is an active feeling. It implies not merely refraining from any hostile act against the order to which we are loyal, but also a readiness to rush to its support if its existence is in anyway threatened. If we are loyal in this spirit, we may fight if the situation requires it with a clear conscience any individual measure or any series of measures of particular administration, with all legitimate weapons at our disposal."[7] This feeling of loyalty, he further emphasized, "is not one to be trotted out for official favour or demonstrated at official bidding. It must spring out of our very love for our country and it must be sustained by our clear recognition of what is necessary in our best interest."[8]

Gokhale's political realism also influenced him to advocate protest as an art of the possible, desirable and attainable.[9] Although, as a test of a continuously progressive government,[10] Gokhale identified many of the ever increasing demands of the subject citizens being entertained by the authorities, his political realism influenced him to remark, "... whatever you may ask for, that is not the same thing as what you will get, or will be qualified to get or in practice maintain if you get. Let us therefore not go in pursuit of more idle dreams and neglect the opportunities which the present offers us."[11] Even these demands, he emphasized, could not be realized without a ceaseless endeavour for self-perfection so as to be worthy to realize it, and enjoy it when realized. Therefore, he also emphasized the need for the protesters to be self-reliant and be prepared for great sacrifices in order to realize the cherished goals. Thus, he said, "Political privilege could not be had for the mere asking, and they had cost the other people prolonged struggles."[12] It was not sufficient, Gokhale recognized, for the aspirations of the protesters to be theoretically perfect ones; it was a question of not merely of dreams, but also of muscle and character, of capacity, of organization, of sacrifice.[13] It was with this recognition in mind that Gokhale established the Servants of India Society and conducted its functioning; it was also the chief purpose of his public activism through the Congress platform.

This realism apart, Gokhale was also emphatic about the moral aspects of protest. He greatly emphasized upon the primacy of ethics in the conduction of all affairs of human life. Denouncing the recourse to unethical means as a matter of expediency to realize the envisaged goals, Gokahle advocated a steadfast or uncompromising adherence to the purity of means. Whether it be the manner in which political administration was to be carried out or the act of checking, controlling and influencing those holding authoritative positions in the political systems, the consideration of according primacy to ethics, Gokahle recognized, ought not be renounced at any cost. His advocacy of spiritualization of politics had this idea as its quintessential basis.

A natural corollary of Gokhale's political realism and spiritualism in politics was his advocacy of gradualism and constitutionalism as essential aspects of a protest. He often recalled the statement, "I do not ask to see that distant scene: one step enough for me."[14] Through this approach of gradualism and constitutionalism he sought to prevent chaotic and anarchic situations and causing "minimum disturbance to existing ideas".[15] Since violent struggles against the constituted authority would lead to the undesirable trails of hatred, revenge and misery, as an alternative, Gokhale advocated a "constitutional agitation". A "constitutional agitation" was recognized by him as an agitation by such methods which one was entitled to adopt to bring about the desired changes through the action of constituted authorities.[16] It had both negative and positive aspects. Commenting on the negative aspect, Wolpert has written, "Gokhale defined such agitation to include all techniques short of physical force, rebellion, abiding or abetting a foreign invasion or criminal action."[17] Barring these three resources, all other means were recognized by him as constitutional, the appropriateness of each means being determined by circumstantial factors.[18] Its positive facet lay in its advocacy of such resources like that of prayer, petition, appeal, representation, negotiation, constructive criticism of the policies of the government and use of other peaceful methods within the ambit of all these resources.[19] Not favouring a recourse to a direct confrontation with the government, Gokhale favoured a moral persuasion of those human agents who constituted it and a mutual goodwill, cooperation and conciliation for the amelioration of specific grievances faced by the protesters. Therefore, he said, "... the idea that we should leave the authorities severely alone and seek to attain our goal independently of them is inadmissible and absurd."[20] Wolpert says, "He (Gokhale) rejected the 'violation of law' and 'rebellion' as legitimate means of agitation".[21] Consequently, as T.R. Deogirkar has opined, Gokhale's characteristic contribution to a rapidly changing India was the method of constitutional agitation.[22]

Recognizing the need to awaken the consciousness of the hitherto exploited, but apathetic individuals and, thereby, creating the force of public opinion to influence those in authoritative positions, Gokhale emphasized on the need for consolidation of the protesters. This consolidation implied a very intensive and extensive process of developing the resourcefulness of the protesters. Recognizing the importance of public opinion and united efforts, Gokhale sought, through his public activism, to awaken the public consciousness of the masses towards the various maladies affecting them and transform their apathy into creative and dynamic force to influence the authorities to take action for the amelioration of their grievances. He passionately advocated the individuals to sink their narrow differences and, in a cooperative endeavour, strive to secure the more general, pressing and noble objectives. In his speech on the political situation facing the Indians, which he delivered at Madras on July 25, 1904, he thus said, "We have got to realize that on the one side of us are arranged forces of racial ascendancy, of monopoly of power, and on the other side is a vast mass of ignorance, apathy and moral helplessness. Between these two we have to work, to face, to try to overcome the forces marshalled against us on one side and quicken into life and to move into energetic action the vast mass on the other."[23]

Gokhale also recognized the importance of mobilization of resources from within to effectuate the demands of the protesters. Consequently, he emphasized upon each participant contributing to the protest in his own little, but best way. Thus, he said, "If we all recognize our respective duties in this spirit, we shall be able to turn out present efforts into a great, rousing movement for the political emancipation of this land. In the presence of such a movement all our petty personal differences will sink, all our squabbles will vanish, our faith will shine radiantly, sacrifices will be made to the extent they are necessary and the country will march onwards, will press onwards to the realization of that destiny of which we should dream by night and on which we should muse by day."[24]

Gokhale's political realism influenced him to emphasize upon the cognition of the realities of the existing political conditions before taking recourse to any particular means for the mobilization of masses. Accordance of importance to considerations of appropriateness and efficacy, he recognized, was very important before taking recourse to a particular means of protest. Therefore, for him, all that was constitutional did not necessarily tantamount to be wise or expedient.[25] It was this consideration which influenced Gokhale to favour *swadeshi*, when he finally did so, as a more effective and desirable means for consolidation and goal realization than the recourse to boycott or other extreme means advocated by his contemporary militant nationalists. Thus, Raman Murthi comments, "Differing profoundly from the extremist politician of India, B.G. Tilak, Gokhale viewed things and problems from a practical and rational angle."[26] Thus, Gokhale did not want opposition to overstep certain well defined limits.

These advocacies of Gokhale, i.e., of active loyalty to the existing order, moderation in protest, faith in goodness of those wielding political power, cooperation with them, gradualism, constitutionalism, etc., did not however imply that Gokhale advocated passivity to, or acquiescence in, evil or injustice. Compromise with evil or injustice was not acceptable to him; on the contrary, regarding "blunt speech as a duty if the occasion so demanded,"[27] he advocated the ultimate defiance of the oppressive regime when all constitutional means of agitation failed to prevent it from pursuing an unrighteous course. In his recognition this defiance was to be not only open but also concomitant with readiness to suffer the consequences which the laws of the land prescribed for such a defiance. Emphasizing on the nature and importance of such a defiance, Gokhale thus said, "If we strongly and clearly and consciously feel the grave injustice of a law, and there is no other way to obtain redress, I think refusal to acquiesce in it taking the consequences of such refusal is the only course left to those who place conscience and self-respect above their material or immediate interest."[28]

Bal Gangadhar Tilak (1858-1920)

Tilak was an ardent champion of individual freedom, human equality and justice. A general conformation to these principles, together with a simultaneous endeavour to work for the decent and dignified existence of all the subject individuals, Tilak claimed, largely determined the justification of any government's existence or continuation. Any government failing to adhere to these principles or to realize the welfare of its subject citizens, Tilak contended, should be resisted. The aim of such an act of resistance, he recognized, should be to influence the government to conform to these idealized principles and take the necessary steps towards the redress of the grievances which arose on account of the transgression of these vital principles. The justness, or otherwise, of all such acts of resistance, Tilak claimed, was determined by the prevailing conditions in the given political system.

As a matter of first resort, Tilak preferred the redress of grievances through constitutional means like that of humble requests, petitioning, persuasion, resolutions, etc., but when such means failed to bring back the government on the right track, he advocated a vigorous extra-constitutional agitation which, while exploiting the manifest potentials of all existing circumstantial factors, sought to exert pressure on the government to act in a particular manner as desired by the protesting subjects. Advocating a "responsive-cooperation" to the government, Tilak's protest, while attempting to consolidate on the gains conceded by it, sought to influence it to accede to all the demands that were made by the protesting individuals. This notion of "responsive cooperation" simultaneously recognized such an interaction process between the government and the citizens that, on the one hand, it entailed upon the citizens the duty to cooperate and observe moderation in their actions while making demands to the government that had committed a few lapses in fulfilling the aspirations of the citizens, and on the other hand, conceded the right to the citizens to disobey, or to non-cooperate and take recourse to more stringent actions while seeking to realize their demands from the government that was reluctant, unresponsive and unsympathetic to their cherished aspirations. Whatever be the means advocated to Tilak to secure the redress of grievances of the protesting subjects, there exists in his advocacy a basic recognition of the inherent right of the subjects to make a critical evaluation of the performance of the government and to communicate this to it unequivocally. This, he recognized, should not be considered as a seditious act.

Weaknesses or inadequacies of the government, Tilak recognized, should be expressed without fear of the punishment prescribed for such acts. Conforming to the doctrine that eternal vigilance is the price paid for preserving one's liberty, Tilak emphasized upon the conscious existence of the citizens and recognized the need for the mobilization of this consciousness of the individuals for influencing the government to concede the demands of the protesters. Tilak recognized that the protesters had to make not only fearless and ceaseless efforts for the vindication of the essential principles lying at the core of their grievances but also be prepared to sacrifice even some of the best things held dearly in their life while doing so. Such a resistance to the government that deviated from its ordained moral or ethical functions, Tilak contended, was a bounden duty of the subject individuals.

Although embroiled in an active resistance to the unjust and oppressive regime of a colonial power, Tilak's advocacy of resistance did not limit itself to the mere considerations of freedom from a foreign rule. His nationalistic sentiments influenced him to prefer self-government, however deficient it might be, to that of an efficient foreign government. However, he recognized no double standards so far as the reaction to an unjust government was concerned. There was only one prescription towards the unjust government – be it a foreign or a native one and that was the moral duty of fearlessly resisting its unjust and oppressive nature. Thus, Tilak's protest, assuming the form of a *dharma*, transcended the parameters of being merely a natural or inalienable right of a citizen, and was, more importantly, conceived as a bounden duty or moral obligation of the subject individuals. Therefore, he said, "Do not be afraid of speaking out things which are plain in themselves. There might be some trouble, but nothing can be had without any trouble."[29]

Tilak recognized the existence of mutual obligation between the ruler and the ruled. Thus, while he enunciated an active loyalty for the subjects towards the benevolent ruler, he entailed upon the ruler to do all the needful for the happiness and well-being of his subjects. A natural corollary of this enunciation was his recognition that if the ruler failed to fulfil his obligations towards the subjects and exploited or oppressed them, then, the ruler committed treason towards the subjects. In all such cases Tilak conceded to the people the right to impose their will on the ruler and even revolt against him.[30]

An oppressive and unjust government, Tilak contended, destroyed the dignified existence of the individual. It not only curtailed his growth and development but also stifled all efforts by the individual to make just assertions in his life. Thus, it annihilated the qualities indispensable for the individual's meaningful personal and social existence. This loss of freedom, for Tilak, lay at the root of the nation's misery, poverty and humiliation.[31] Freedom from such oppressive and unjust regime, therefore, Tilak advocated, was the elan vital (*chaityana*) of a nation and as such essential for the existence of a society.[32] Consequently, Tilak's resistance to the British rule in India assumed the character of an active challenge to the existing nature of things under the colonial rule and sought to motivate it to act in the manner desired by the Indians, rather than being run on the basis of selfish colonial interest or personal whims or fancies of the British. He assailed not only their inherently unjust rule but also denounced the validity of their claim of being reposed with the providential duty to guide India out of the "dark ages".

Tilak's protest continuously endeavoured to serve as a communication medium to the authorities in the society seeking to convey to them the grievances of the oppressed and exploited Indians. He asked the government to respect and identify itself with the sentiments and aspirations of the Indian public and to simultaneously work for the fructification of their hopes. To a government seeking to function on these lines, Tilak asserted that his protest did not seek to overthrow the existing government. Thus, even in his most extreme demand of *swaraj* or self-rule he visualized it as a programme for political achievement within the parameters of British sovereignty.[33] Thus, in his speech at Kanpur Home Rule Conference on January 1, 1917, he said, "Now one aspect of Home Rule is to encourage you to acquire the freedom which you enjoyed in these various departments of life and to that standard by the cooperation of, and under the sovereignty of, the British rule. This result is not to be achieved by any unlawful and unconstitutional means, but I am sure by a desire and interest to raise your status to achieve this goal by means of the sympathy of the British people and by remaining a permanent part of the Empire."[34] Similarly, in his address at Yeotmal in 1917, he said, "The *swaraj* of today is within the Empire and not independent of it."[35]

In order to seek a favourable reaction from a government, Tilak recognized the need for the maximum exploitation of as many means available in a given situation. These, as is evident from his political activism, varied from conciliatory and cooperative ones to those of the confrontationist types. Largely preferring an initial recourse to the constitutionally available means for the redress of grievances, namely, petitioning, passing resolutions, submitting memorandums, etc., Tilak advocated the notion of "responsive cooperation" which, while deciding to accept whatever was conceded by the government, sought to continue to agitate for more and more till the whole of the demands raised initially was conceded. Elaborating its meaning, he said, "We are expected to cooperate, but first there must be something to cooperate over. Let the authorities declare in what way they are prepared to cooperate with us and we will assure them that if they cooperate we will surely reciprocate. Cooperation is not a one-way traffic; it is mutual, what I call responsive."[36]

However, Tilak's own experience of the darker side of the colonial rule in India influenced him to concede the possibility of an existing regime becoming so unsympathetic, unresponsive and oppressive that such means of modest protest like that of prayer, petitioning, etc., failed to realize the cherished demands.

Tilak recognized that any advocacy which emphasized upon all political protest to be carried on within the bounds of a constitution, especially when neither a constitution nor a spirit of constitutionalism existed, was an absurd proposition. He was also emphatic about the essential distinction between the legal and a constitutional provision of a nation. While the latter, he conceded, provided some valid criterion for the evaluation of a political agitation as being within the permissible or acceptable level; the laws, especially when these were unjust and their enactment or amendment was subject to the will, fancy or caprice of those in power, could not serve as the valid criterion for the evaluation of justness or rightness of a political agitation. Such a view influenced him to contend that whatever was legal was not necessarily righteous and just. In such conditions of a given political system, Tilak suggested that the values of justice, morality, historical tradition and progress were capable of serving as the basis for the decision to take recourse to protest.[37] Consequently, Tilak advocated the transcendence of protest from the constitutional type to the extra-constitutional type. In his recognition, when an existing government became unsympathetic and unresponsive, then, militancy, not mendicancy, would become the need of the hour and moderation would transcend into the realm of extremism. Thus, he said, "For the last twelve years we have been shouting hoarse, desiring that the Government should hear us. But our shouting has no more affected the Government than the sound of a gnat. Our rulers disbelieve our statements or profess to do so. Let us now try to force our grievances into their ears by strong constitutional means."[38] Likewise, in his Calcutta speech in 1901, he said, "I say that we should force them (British) to fulfil their promises, but we should not make the application in such a way that it would be rejected. In demanding and begging there is a great difference."[39] Consequently, Tilak advocated the supplementation of constitutional means with those of passive resistance within the fold of which he envisaged the recourse to boycott, *swadeshi* and national education.

So far as the advocacy of boycott was concerned, Tilak defined it in very simple words and said, "Do not help the Government, rule for yourselves. This is called boycott."[40] He recognized it as an alternative means for those who had neither the power nor the inclinations to take up arms against the evil or unjust government. Thus, he said, "If you have not the power of active resistance, have you not the power of self-denial and self-abstinence so as not to assist the foreign (unjust) Government to rule over you? This is boycott and this is what is meant when we say boycott is a political weapon."[41] Tilak also recognized its positive and negative character. As a political weapon, in its negative aspect, he recognized it as implying a refusal to assist the government in such activities like that of collecting revenue, keeping peace, fighting beyond the frontiers of the nation, administration of justice and payment of taxes. On the positive side Tilak recognized its capacity, along with its complementary *swadeshi*, to bring about solidarity among the protesting subjects as well as to build self-reliance and thereby destroy the hypnotic spell which made them accept the omnipotence of the unjust rulers. These were also envisaged as a means for economic salvation and as a powerful lever for liberation. Similarly, through national education, Tilak sought to awaken the consciousness of the subjected people about their exploited condition, make them aware of the important national and international events happening around them, infuse into them courage, moral strength, spirit of social service and patriotism, and make them self-reliant. Through these tools of passive resistance, Tilak sought to realize *swaraj* or self-rule which, in his view, was concomitant with the values of freedom, equality and justice.

When the policy of the government assumed the form of total apathy accompanied by brutal repression of even the moderate course of protest, then, Tilak recognized, constitutional agitation and rebellion became synonymous.[42] Such statements and his applause of some of the revolutionary acts of individuals, both in India and such other places like Russia and Ireland, have influenced a few scholars to opine that Tilak personally believed in, and favoured, the cult of violence so far as the resistance to the unjust and oppressive government was concerned.[43] This controversy is further deepened on account of the differing statements on the issue by Tilak's contemporaries. Tilak's activism too has revealed virtually conflicting views on violence. Thus, Tilak denounced the politics of senseless murder and never in his public activism took personal recourse to it even under the worst provoking times; yet, through his writings on a few occasions, he lauded the courage and patriotic sentiments of those who took to a revolutionary course; he even defended their acts. Through his literary writings, as acknowledged by some revolutionaries, he provided the impetus and incitement to resort to violence for pure or ethical goals like that of *swaraj*. It is also a fact that he had close associations with most of his contemporary revolutionaries and had an important role in the plan to manufacture guns in Nepal with the consent of the king there. Such activities of Tilak have complicated the controversy. However, one thing is certain; he was never an advocate of absolute *ahimsa* nor recognized its extensive implication as conceived by Gandhi so far as the act of resistance to the unjust government was concerned. Another noticeable fact is his comparatively lesser militancy and belief in the futility of violence to settle political issues towards the last four or five years of life, that is, especially after his release from the Mandalay jail.

Notes

1. D.B. Mathur, *Gokhale: A Political Biography, A Study of His Services and Political Ideas*, P.G. Manaktala and Sons Pvt. Ltd., Bombay, 1966, p. 388.
2. Stanely A. Wolpert, *Tilak and Gokhale: Revolution and Reform in the Making of Modern India*, Oxford University Press, Delhi, 1991, p. 299.
3. Ibid., p. 197.
4. Gokhale's speech, The Work Before Us, in *Speeches and Writings of Gopal Krishna Gokhale*, D.G. Karve & D.V. Ambekar (eds.), Vol. II (Political), Asia Publishing House, Bombay, 1966, p. 217.
5. Ibid.
6. See Note 1, p. 395.
7. Gokhale's speech, Students and Politics, in *Speeches and Writings of Gopal Krishna Gokhale*, D.G. Karve & D.V. Ambekar (eds.), Vol. III (Educational), Asia Publishing House, Bombay, 1967, pp.196-97.
8. Ibid.
9. Note 1, p. 461.
10. For details see Gokhale's speech, Indianisation of Public Services, in Gopal Krishna Gokhale, *Political Thinkers of Modern India - 2*, V. Grover (ed.), Deep & Deep Publications, New Delhi, 1991, p. 527.
11. Gokhale's speech, *The Reform Proposal*, Note 4, pp. 298-99.
12. Note 1, p. 219.
13. Ibid., p. 217.
14. As quoted by D.B. Mathur, Note 1, p. 394.
15. Note 1, p. 217.
16. See Note 1, pp. 217-78.
17. Note 2, p. 198.
18. Note 4, p. 218.
19. Note 1, p. 399.
20. Note 4, p. 218.

21. Note, 2, p. 201.
22. T.R. Deogirikar, *Builders of Modern India: Gopal Krishna Gokhale*, Publication Division, Ministry of Information and Broadcasting, Government of India, New Delhi, 1992, p. 5.
23. Gokhale's speech, *Our Political Situation,* Note 10, p. 571.
24. Ibid., p. 577.
25. Note 4,25., p. 218.
26. V.V. Raman Murthy, *Non-violence in Politics: A Study of Gandhian Techniques and Thinking*, Frank Bros. & Co., Delhi, 1958.
27. Gokhale as quoted by D.B. Mathur, Note 1, p. 397.
28. Gokhale's speech, *Indians in the Transvaal*, Note 4, p. 414.
29. Ravindra Kumar (ed.), *Selected Documents of Lokmanya Bal Gangadhar Tilak*, Anmol Publication, New Delhi (to be cited hereafter as *SDLT*), Vol., 3, 1992, p. 51.
30. For a detailed examination of this view see Shanta A. Sathe, Tilak's Connotation of the Concept of Swaraj, in N.R. Inamdar (ed.), *Political Thought and Leadership of Lokmanya Tilak*, Concept Publishing Company, New Delhi, 1983, pp. 41-42.
31. Note 2, p. 297.
32. See Note 30, p. 36.
33. See V.P. Varma, *The Life and Philosophy of Lokmanya Tilak*, Lakshmi Narain Agarwal Educational Publishers, Agra, 1979, p. 446.
34. *SDLT,* Vol. 3, p. 43.
35. Ibid., p. 55.
36. N.G. Jog, *Builders of Modern India: Lokmanya Bal Gangadhar Tilak*, Publications Division, Ministry of Information and Broadcasting, Government of India, New Delhi, 1990, p. 171.
37. For details see Note 30, p. 40.
38. Note 36, p. 55.
39. *SDLT,* Vol. 1, p. 15.
40. Ibid.
41. Note 36, p. 101.
42. See *SDLT,* Vol. 1, p. 41.
43. For a detailed examination of the above view see V.P. Varma, Note 5, pp. 446-50 and also T.V. Parvate, *Bal Gangadhar Tilak: A Narrative and Interpretative Review of his Life, Career and Contemporary Events*, Navjivan Publishing Company, Ahmedabad, 1958, pp. 491-502.

5

Satyagraha: Conceptual Concern

Gandhi, like a political thinker, speculated on several subjects conventionally falling within the domain of politics. However, through a revolutionary interpretation of some of the traditional concepts coming within the scope of political theory, he proffered to the world a distinct vision of politics. This vision was manifested in his enunciation of certain idealized political goals, both structural and procedural, and the means to realize them. An important segment of his political speculation was that of protest, the various facets and nuances of which he enunciated through *satyagraha*.

His notion of protest evolved simultaneous with his political activism. Deeply disquiet of the discriminatory practices of the racist South African local governments, Gandhi had initially taken recourse to pleading, petitioning and appealing to their good sense to undo those laws or policies which sought to perpetuate racial prejudices and the concomitant evils. However, when such efforts failed to produce the desired effect, he decided to resort to protest to seek the redress of the grievances of the Indians. This protest was recognized by him as *satyagraha*. As the protest progressed, and Gandhi delved into the various aspects of it, *satyagraha* gradually acquired the necessary traits of a protest and progressed towards the accrual of a distinct identity of its own. Gandhi, in all humility, admitted in 1939 that he had not yet been able to work out the science of *satyagraha* in its entirety;[1] nevertheless, by this time *satyagraha* came to acquire a very distinct image as a method of protest comparable with, and distinguishable from, hitherto existing theories of protest.

Gandhi enunciated his doctrine of *satyagraha* as a means for a conscientious man to engage in the vindication of truth and freedom against all forms of tyranny and exploitation – be it political, social or economic. Raising truth to the highest pedestal, he subordinated every temporal authority to it. Simultaneously, he recognized that every pursuit of truth and the application of any temporal sanction for any violation of it should conform to the principle of non-violence. Consequently, in his enunciation of the individual-state relationship, he recognized the principles of truth and non-violence as the principal basis. In his idealized vision he cherished a stateless political order in which each individual conducted his life activities in a righteous manner and with a vision of simultaneous well-being of all his fellow individuals. Nevertheless, the ground realities of the phenomenal world and the weakness of mortal man made Gandhi acquiesce in a political order in which the state existed with minimum functions to perform and with the least amount of coercive force at its disposal to discharge these appointed functions. Towards such a state which discharged its functions in a just and largely non-violent way, Gandhi recognized the need of the subject individuals to cultivate a sense of loyalty which, in more concrete terms, demanded a widely diffused sense of moral obligation of the citizens to obey the laws of the state. However, this morality was itself subjected to the twin principles of truth and *ahimsa* and made meaningful by making it more obligatory on the part of citizens to abide by these principles steadfastly. In case the laws of the state stood in contradiction to them, then, conceiving it to be their moral and principal duty, Gandhi emphasized upon the need for the individuals to oppose and find remedy to the untruth sought to be perpetuated by such laws or acts of the state. He recognized that the state, when it became corrupt, or its laws became largely unjust and inhuman, or its agents became capricious and conducted the administration according to their own whims and fancies, resulting in the merciless exploitation of its subject people, then, loyalty in such a state tantamounted to a sin; and in all such cases disloyalty was a virtue.[2] Consequently, one finds in Gandhi's enunciation of the relationship between the individual and the state, Raghavan Iyer says, "a desire to find place for both active loyalty and for the sacred right of disobedience together with the wish to leave it open to the citizen to decide in any given state, inevitably imperfect and unavoidably coercive, whether he felt obliged to show active loyalty or total opposition to that particular state, to resist none or all or a few of its laws."[3] The onus of responsibility, irrespective of the nature of conduct of the citizens vis-à-vis the state, was placed by Gandhi upon the conscience of the citizen who at all costs was required to uphold truth and pure non-violence under all circumstances.

Meaning, Nature and Objectives

Gandhi explained the term "*satyagraha*" from various viewpoints. As a compound word constituting two traditional Indian notions of *satya*, meaning truth and *agraha*, meaning holding fast or steadfast adherence or insistence, *satyagraha* connoted the implication of clinging to truth or a steadfast adherence to truth. Explaining the etymological dimension of the term, Gandhi said, "Truth (*satya*) implies love and firmness (*agraha*) engenders and therefore serves as a synonym for force. I thus began to call the Indian movement *satyagraha*, that is to say, the force which is born of truth and love or non-violence."[4] Recognizing *satyagraha* as a means of active resistance to evil by good, he contended it to be a weapon of the morally vigilant, courageous and the active, rather than being a weapon of the weak or the coward or the unarmed and the helpless.[5] He recognized it to be essentially an attitude of mind and a way of life based on the firm desire to vindicate just causes, correct wrongs and convert the wrong doers by voluntary self-suffering and by patient and active use of means which are non-violent and intrinsically just.[6] Giving a comprehensive description of *satyagraha*, James Luther Adams regards it as a non-violent public violation of a specific law or laws, or of policy of government having the effect of laws, expressing a sense of justice in a civil society and of cooperation among equals, which is generally undertaken in the name of a presumed higher authority than the law in question, and as a last resort for the purpose of changing a law simultaneous with the intention of accepting the penalty which the law imposes.[7]

Gandhi designated his struggle in South Africa as *satyagraha* instead of the earlier term "passive resistance" used to denote his struggle against racism there. By using a different terminology

Gandhi thus wanted to differentiate between *satyagraha* and passive resistance. When he came to realize the narrowness of passive resistance, its use as a means by the morally weak and timid persons and its non-renunciation of hatred and belief in violence, Gandhi thought it appropriate to redesignates his struggle as *satyagraha* and also to contend that *satyagraha* was not a passive but an active struggle which demanded lot of courage, adherence to morality and altruistic values and renunciation of hatred and violence as a matter of principle.

The concept of truth is the most important or deterministic value of Gandhi's thought and activism. For him it is the *raison de'etre* of all existence and is not only therefore the all inclusive deterministic principle but also the most logically preferred principle. It is considered by Gandhi as the indispensable principle for the individual if he is to evolve as a human being. This desire for truth, according to Gandhi's advocacy, extended to the desire to observe truth in thought, speech and action. However, truth for Gandhi is more importantly to be practised as a principle by the individual rather than placing it merely at the ideational or thought level.

The *satyagrahi* envisioned by Gandhi is a person who discovers truth and on the basis of his understanding of truth (relative truths as he called it) acts upon it in a dedicated manner. For the discovery of truth, Gandhi recognized the need for the individual to take recourse to his rational faculty, self-experience and faith. Gandhi's own life and activism is illuminative of the use of all these faculties which have influenced human beings' thought and action since his evolution. Such an effort to discover truth, according to Gandhi, should be a continuous effort so that one can progress towards the realization of the ultimate truth which he equated with God. Thus, according to Gandhi, clinging on to relative truth and efforts to accumulate more and more relative truth to reach the ultimate truth is the ideal goal of every *satyagrahi*. Simultaneously, he also considered it the right of every individual to determine truth for himself.

Since the relative truth is not the final truth, the *satyagrahi*, according to Gandhi, should always be ready to examine the point of view adopted by him from time to time. Such a view also reflects Gandhi's position of viewing truth as a dynamic, multifaceted and evolving in nature. Such being the nature of truth for Gandhi, along with his belief that as mortal beings all individuals have inherent weaknesses, he contended that the final or ultimate truth cannot be realized and therefore it is essential that the value of non-violence has also to be steadfastly adopted by the individual. Thus, for the *satyagrahi*, non-violence is as indispensable as his belief and practice of truth. Therefore, Gandhi concluded that truth without non-violence is not truth but untruth.

According to Gandhi, non-violence and truth are like the twin sides of the same coin, the absence of one denies the absence of the other. Therefore, the idea of non-violence, like truth, is also central to the philosophy of *satyagraha*. Thus, one can also say that a *satyagrahi*, while trying to realize the goal of truth, tries to do so by adopting non-violence as the means.

According to Gandhi, the whole of universe is governed by the principle of non-violence. His conception of non-violence is one of the widest interpretations of the term available in philosophy. He did not limit it to the negative understanding of the concept, namely, absence of or refraining from violence. On the contrary, he included in it the positive notion of love for the opponent and suffering his attacks without retaliation in words, actions or thoughts. Gandhi's belief in this regard was that such an attitude could only be cultivated by an individual who believed in non-violence as a matter of principle or faith rather than as a matter of policy. This, together with such other emphasis like selfless motive, courageousness and active efforts to resolve conflicts, differentiates *satyagraha* from "passive resistance", a term which was mistakenly used by Gandhi to refer to his protects in South Africa and in his book *Hind Swaraj*.

Like truth and non-violence, morality too is an inseparable aspect of *satyagraha*. Elaborating a close relationship between truth and morality, Gandhi contended truth to be the basis of all morality. Observing moral laws, therefore for Gandhi, meant the cultivation of all the values manifested by truth like tolerance, honesty, non-violence, altruism, simple living, self-restrain, sincerity, discipline, etc.

One of the essential manifestations of Gandhi's emphasis on observing moral laws by the *satyagrahi* was his advocacy of the principle of purity of ends and means. This principle emphasized upon the purity or sanctity of not only the goals that are sought to be achieved but also upon the means adopted to realize these goals. Means for Gandhi was the end in the process of making and therefore only pure means could ensure the purity of the end. Thus, he said, "The means may be likened to a seed, the end to a tree, there is just the same inviolable connection between the means and the end as there is between the seed and the tree."[8] This emphasis of Gandhi on purity of ends and means also led him to stress upon the inculcation of discipline and self-restrain by the *satyagrahi*. In this context, he emphasized upon many vows like *astheya, aparigraha, brahmacharya,* etc., to be adhered by a *satyagrahi*.

Gandhi's philosophy of *satyagraha* and his actual socio-political *satyagraha* campaigns were indicative of the wide range of objectives which could be attained without taking recourse to violence. While in South Africa he took recourse to it to fight racial prejudices and the concomitant socio-economic and political evils that largely prevailed in the colonies, in India, he offered it not merely for seeking the redress of particular grievances pertaining to the social, economic and political life of the Indians, but for a more wider goal like that of vindicating the inviolable principles lying at the core of an ordained governmental responsibility and *swaraj*. The wide variety of the application field and the various purposes of use – public cause, social change, self-purification, self-education, etc., revealed that *satyagraha* was a very comprehensive concept and, as a tool to fight injustice or evil, had universal applicability. It possessed both negative and positive implications. While negatively it enjoined upon the individual the duty to check and eradicate evil from the inhabiting cosmic order of which he was a part; on the positive side it reminded the individual of his obligation to serve his community by creating those conditions which would be conducive to its moral and spiritual progress.

Gandhi recognized both specific and generalized objectives of *satyagraha*. He recognized that *satyagraha*, in certain specific form like "civil disobedience", was to be resorted to only infrequently and applied at the level of individual or a few select individuals in the initial stages. However, this was to be the case only in normal and general cases; in abnormal and specific situations wherein the entire body politic seemed to be corroded with violence, injustice and untruth, Gandhi envisaged the need for complete civil or peaceful rebellion in which the subject individuals refused to obey even a single state made laws or orders passed by the government. Generally, *satyagraha* was intended to seek the amelioration of specific grievances or to realize a demand that was consistent with truth. There is no scope for exaggeration or suppression of truth in *satyagraha*. Therefore, the demand, by its very nature, became both the minimum and the maximum. Gandhi regarded it to be a recourse to dishonesty if one took up a position, having seen the opportunity in the course of his *satyagraha* campaign, which was originally not conceived when the campaign was launched. He recognized that the *satyagraha* should conclude when the demands for which it was accepted.[9] However, in his recognition, if the adversary himself created new difficulties for the *satyagraha* while the struggle was in progress, these became automatically included in the objective of the *satyagraha* campaign. Therefore, he said, "A *satyagrahi*, without being false to his faith, cannot disregard new difficulties which confront him while he is pursuing his own course."[10] While recognizing the application of the "Law of Progression" to a genuine *satyagraha*, Gandhi compared *satyagraha* to the mighty River Ganges which absorbed many other streams in the course of its flow. To quote him, "As the Ganga advances other streams flow into it, and hence at the mouth it grows so wide that neither bank is to be seen and a person sailing upon the river cannot make out where the river ends and the sea begins. So also, as a *satyagraha* struggle progresses onward many other elements help to swell its current and there is constant growth in the result to which it leads."[11] Between these two dissimilar views about the objectives of the *satyagraha*, Gandhi seemed to have recognized no dichotomy. He believed that the *satyagrahi*, as he worked towards the short-term determinate objectives suggested to him by his efforts to make his life conformable with his principles, gradually developed more comprehensive ends and became more clearly aware of the relations in which they stood to his chosen means.[12]

Gandhi recognized the importance of the exploited being conscious of their experience of injustice and disprivilege. Therefore, he endeavoured to raise the consciousness of the individuals about their exploited condition and motivate them to actively work toward the amelioration of their grievances rather than being apathetic, despondent and fatalistic. Recognizing the importance of arousing such a consciousness, Gandhi said, "A *satyagrahi,* for instance, must first mobilize public opinion against the evil which he is out to eradicate by means of a wide and intensive agitation."[13] The apathetic or the callousness of the authorities was sought to be confronted by way of creating public opinion against their evil act and in favour of the *satyagrahi*'s objectives. Therefore, he recognized *satyagraha* as a process of conflict resolution by mutual understanding and by educating public opinion through reason, discussion and self-suffering.[14]

Recognizing an awakened and intelligent public opinion as the most potent weapon of a *satyagrahi,*[15] Gandhi was emphatic about the need for the *satyagrahi* to first mobilize public opinion in favour of justice and fairness. He believed that when public opinion was sufficiently roused against a social abuse, "even the tallest will not dare to practice or openly lend support to it".[16] Thus, to realize the set objectives of a *satyagraha* campaign, Gandhi was emphatic about a dependence not merely on the appeal of the *satyagrahi*'s own conscience but also on the awakening of the slumbering conscience of a large number of people and, ultimately, the stifled conscience of those responsible for enacting or administrating unjust laws and social abuses.[17] Through the mobilization of public opinion in favour of the objective of the *satyagraha* campaign, Gandhi sought to meet effectively the problem of "reference public". During the course of his *satyagraha* activity, both in South Africa and in India, he made constant efforts to rope in the support of influential people for his campaigns and appealed to them to make use of their resourcefulness to influence the decisions of those in authoritative positions in the political system.

Gandhi laid down stringent conditions for the application of *satyagraha*. One of the conditions was that *satyagraha* could not be resorted for any unjust cause. Since it implied a steadfast adherence to truth, he recognized that there could not be any acquiescence in untruth for a *satyagrahi*. Consequently, Gandhi recognized that a feeling and experience of specific grievances constituted an indispensable part of a *satyagraha*. This feeling or experience and the consequent reaction, he recognized, ought to be serious and intending to provoke ameliorative action rather than being a trivial and chronic opposition indicative of a casual reaction. He said, "If you dissent you should take care that your opinions voice your innermost convictions and are not intended merely as a convenient party cry."[18] Therefore, Gandhi made the basis of *satyagraha* some ethical considerations or a shared system of values cherished within the particular society of which the *satyagraha* constituted a part. According to Gandhi, honesty or sincerity was an essential quality of a *satyagrahi,*[19] and this sincerity was not just a matter of having an intense position on moral questions but also a matter of accepting the costs that a person was willing to pay in order to see these principles realized.[20]

Gandhi did not accord any element of divinity to the institutional basis of authority. It was his contention that no authority could be absolute because no individual could lay claim to absolute truth. He believed each individual to be a sacrosanct being endowed with a moral personality permeated by the divine spark of the "Supreme Truth" or God. Therefore, he recognized that no temporal institutions, including the state and the government, could lay claim to sanctity more superior than that of the individual or demand blind adulation for it. By accrediting to the individual a logically and morally prior place than the state, Gandhi reposed in the individual the right to review state actions and exercise the power of veto in the form of *satyagraha* campaign whenever the state violated the fundamental principles of truth and non-violence. Thus, in Gandhi's views of politics, says Raghavan N. Iyer, "The derivative authority of any institution, apart from its force of power, presupposes the moral authority of its members, their right to recognize its commands as reasonable or unreasonable, as worthy or unworthy of acceptance, as morally or legally valid or invalid."[21]

Gandhi conceived *satyagraha* as a means which could be adopted only by the spiritually strong person. He recognized it as a weapon of a man possessing steady wisdom and indomitable courage and mental strength. Even, the physically weak could take part in a *satyagraha* provided they were spiritually strong. Thus, he said, "A *satyagraha* is a struggle in which the oldest and the weakest in the body may take part if they have stout hearts."[22] Only a spiritually strong person, Gandhi believed, could transform himself into an impersonal moral force latent with the capacity to remove injustice and transform relationships amongst individuals. For realizing such a transformation of his self, Gandhi emphasized that the individual should purify and discipline his self. He advised the adherence to various vows like that of *satya, ahimsa, aparigraha, astheya* etc. to start with and later on to be supplemented with rigorous training in self-suffering, fearlessness, methodological nuances of *satyagraha* etc. Such being his conception of a *satyagrahi*, Gandhi was optimistic about the *satyagrahi's* capacity to successfully perform the toughest task. Although *satyagraha* was characterized by an element of appeal and rational persuasion of the perpetuator of injustice to renounce his evil intentions and refrain from unjust acts and take positive action for the simultaneous well-being of each and every constituent member of the society, this appeal or persuasion was neither a sign of despondency nor of servitude. The evil and injustice continued unabated, Gandhi contended, on account of the general apathy of the individuals in the evil of the system; or because of their sense of fatalism, inadequate moral awareness, and acquiescence in the perpetuation of the evil or unjust act. He recognized that every citizen silently, but nonetheless certainly, sustained the government of the day in ways of which he had no knowledge and therefore rendered himself responsible for every act of his government.[23] In order to remove these maladies he recognized *satyagraha* as an instrument of self-education and self-perfection.[24] Moreover, the emphasis on adequate training of the individual before becoming a *satyagrahi* and the participation in the "constructive programme", which was considered as a complementary part of *satyagraha*, further indicated the fact that in *satyagraha* there existed no element of weakness or despondency on the part of its adopters.

The *satyagrahi* in a political campaign demands those in authoritative positions to take actions which conformed to truth and non-violence. However, all such communications to those in authoritative positions were not inhibited by the narrow goal of promoting the specific interest of the *satyagrahi* alone. Instead, *satyagraha* seeks to ennoble the opponent and strives for promoting simultaneously the welfare of those against whom it was launched. In effect it tries to remove the animosity of the opponent towards the *satyagrahi* and brings about a change, as Thomas Merton says, in relationships that is evil into others that are good, or at least less bad.[25] To effectively check the evil, Gandhi thought it more important to motivate the perpetuator of the evil to cultivate an aversion to the evil mentally. He believed that when an individual or a group of individuals became transformed internally, their resultant action would be peaceful, there would be a reduction of the volume of violence in the practice of voluntary politics.[26] Envisaging to transcend beyond the immediate objective of merely obstructing particular policies of the authorities, Gandhi recognized the need to bring about positive changes in the prevailing attitudes and values of the individuals in the society. Through *satyagraha* he sought to bring about a moral and spiritual elevation of all individuals living in the society. Thus, unlike other protest activities, *satyagraha* transcended the objective of merely seeking to affect particular government policy or decisions. Instead, by accumulating the forces of moral voluntary power, it seeks to activate positive values of life and alter the normative structure of the society, and take it towards a higher realm of existence characterized by qualitative differences in human life.[27]

Constitutionalism formed an essential part of *satyagraha*. Its exhaustion was deemed by Gandhi as a precondition for launching a direct action of the extra-constitutional type and facing the penalties thereof in a civilized manner. It was conceived by Gandhi as a means to make up for the deficiencies of the existing laws or constitutional provisions rather than for the defiance of the law itself. To this extent *satyagraha* conformed to the notion of protest. Thus, Gandhi held that when people had national power, dissent should pass through legislative channels; if their needs were frustrated, then they could resolve to use non-cooperation and civil disobedience.[28] He said, "Since *satyagraha* is one of the most powerful methods of direct action, a *satyagrahi* exhausts all other means before be resorts to *satyagraha*. He will therefore constantly and continually approach the constituted authority, he will appeal to public opinion, educate public opinion, state his case calmly and coolly before everybody who wants to listen to him, and only after he has exhausted all these avenues will be resort to *satyagraha*."[29] Gandhi advocated a recourse to such constitutional devices like wait and watch, assessment of facts by public enquiry, tours, negotiations, arbitration, political associations, protest meetings and processions, etc. before inaugurating a *satyagraha* struggle.[30]

Gandhi used such concepts like compromise and negotiation in his philosophy of *satyagraha*; nevertheless, the normally understood notion of negotiation and compromise, implicit in other forms of political protest, did not form a part of *satyagraha*. This could be explained by the fact that in *satyagraha*, Gandhi emphasized, the demands ought to be reduced to the barest minimum which was thought to be consistent with truth. It being so the minimum in it was also the maximum and no *satyagrahi* could compromise with the eternal principles implicit in the minimum demand. However, the notion of voluntary self-suffering to be undergone by the *satyagrahi* and the recognition of the weaknesses of the mortal self made Gandhi concede to compromises in regard to the details and personal interest; but even in such possible compromises or negotiations the terms were expected to respect the dignity and honour of the *satyagrahi* apart from its general consonance with the principle of truth and non-violence. The absence of the conventional notion of negotiation or compromise did not imply any stubbornness on the part of the *satyagrahi* to review his original stand from time to time. As an inward-looking process through which it sought a process of self-transformation and self-illumination while proceeding on the course of realization of truth, *satyagraha* initiated in the individual a process of self-questioning, and as the process unfolded in the individual, he deepened and broadened his understanding of the general issues to the extent that his personal transformation confirmed it.[31] Consequently, Gandhi laid it as a fundamental rule for the *satyagrahi* to endeavour in a persistent examination of weaknesses within himself or the campaigning group of which he was a part; to search avenues of cooperation with the opponent on honourable terms; and before accepting any settlement, insist upon a full agreement on fundamentals.[32]

Yet another factor which distinguishes *satyagraha* from other forms of protest is its insistence on the abstention from violence or use of coercive tactics. While *satyagraha* relies on persuasive methods and voluntary suffering to effect a "change of heart" of the opponent and influencing him to act justly and in consonance with truth, other forms of protest rely on a combination of persuasive and coercive tactics for the redress of their grievances. Believing all coercion to be a manifestation of *ahimsa* and therefore contradictory to the principles of truth and non-violence, Gandhi recognized no place for coercive tactics in *satyagraha*. A chief objective of *satyagraha*, he said, was "to neutralize and ultimately entirely to displace violence and enthrone non-violence instead, to replace hatred by love and to replace strife by concord."[33] When rational persuasion seemed to prove ineffective to influence the opponent to desist from evil or doing injustice, Gandhi emphasized upon the need for the *satyagrahi* to voluntarily undergo suffering on his self and thereby influence the opponent to act in a righteous manner. This element of voluntary suffering entirely substituted the coercive tactics or threat of its use which protesters are likely to resort to when their rational persuasion fail to produce the desired effect.

Gandhi contended that violence begot more violence and proved ineffective to wean away the opponent from acting in an unrighteous manner. It was his firm belief that coercive tactics could not resolve conflicts on an effective and permanent basis. Instead, recognizing the potency of self-suffering as means to effect a lasting solution to all conflicts, he said, "But suffering is infinitely more powerful than the law of the jungle for converting the opponent and opening his ears, which are otherwise shut to the voice of reasons. I have come to this fundamental conclusion that if you want something really important to be done, you must not merely satisfy the reason, you must move the heart also. The appeal of reason is more to the head, but the penetration of the heart comes from suffering. It opens the inner understanding of man."[34] Gandhi conceived a wide variety of tools and forms of *satyagraha* – non-violent non-cooperation, civil disobedience, fasting, peaceful picketing, *hartal*, etc. Nevertheless, the mode and tactics to be used were to be decided according to the emergent situation of the *satyagraha* campaign. Therefore, he said, "In a *satyagraha* campaign the mode of fight and the choice of tactics, e.g., whether to advance or retreat, offer civil resistance or organize nonviolent strength through constructive work and purely selfless humanitarian service, are determined according to the exigencies of the situation. A *satyagrahi* must carry out whatever plan is laid out for him with a cool determination giving way to neither excitement nor depression."[35] Every such tactic was to be used with civility, discipline, discrimination and non-violence, otherwise, he recognized, it would result in certain destruction.[36]

The Satyagrahi

In the course of his long series of *satyagraha* experiments Gandhi reflected upon several aspects of a genuine *satyagraha*. The conception of an ideal *satyagrahi* was one amongst them. Enumerating the essential qualifications of a *satyagrahi*, Gandhi recognized him as an individual who

1. had a living faith in god;
2. made a creedal adherence to truth and non-violence;
3. had faith in the inherent goodness of human nature;
4. led a chaste life and abstained from such vices as that of wine, wealth and sex;
5. was ever ready and willing to sacrifice everything including his life, for the sake of a righteous cause;
6. carried out with a willing heart all the rules of discipline that were laid from time to time; and
7. cultivated respect for all such civil rules which acknowledged his dignity and integrity.[37]

In his capacity as an individual, as a prisoner, as a unit and in a communal fight, Gandhi expected the *satyagrahi* to behave in an exceptionally humble and responsible manner so as to carry on the movement in conformity with the ethical principles implicit in a *satyagraha* struggle.[38] Gandhi's objective in describing the ideal *satyagrahi*, it may be pointed out before going into details, was not intended to stake claims of actually possessing all these qualities either by him or by his followers; rather it was symbolic only of an effort that merely set forth the implications of *satyagrahis* as they ought to be.[39]

Since *satyagraha* implied a steadfast adherence to truth, Gandhi emphasized that the ideal *satyagrahi* should subscribe to a life of truth, or in other words, he recognized that the *satyagrahi* in the conduct of his life activities should conform to the doctrine of *sathvika*.[40] However, the absolute truth being unrealizable by any mortal man, Gandhi recognized that the *satyagrahi* should hold on to the relative truth and make it the beacon, the shield and buckle of his endeavour to progress towards the realization of the absolute truth. In the interpretation of relative truth, Gandhi, advocating great care and attention, said, "No matter how insignificant the thing you have to do; do it as well as you can; give it as much of your care and attention as you could give to the thing you regard as most important."[41] Thus, Gandhi recognized a thorough understanding of the prevailing conditions and facts by the *satyagrahi* as an essential part of his steadfast adherence to truth.

Although Gandhi considered the fearlessness of the *satyagrahi* as one of his greatest strengths, this strength, he recognized, ought not to instil in the *satyagrahi* a sense of vanity or haughtiness. Considering anger and hatred as being antithetical to truth and non-violence, Gandhi deemed it as essential for the *satyagrahi* not to retaliate even in the strongest provocative situation. He said, "Victory is impossible under the greatest provocation. Calmness under fire is a soldier's indispensable quality. A non-cooperator is nothing if he cannot remain calm and unperturbed under a fierce fire of provocation."[42] This non-retaliation however did not imply a meek submission or passive acquiescence in the act of evil. Instead, Gandhi visualized the *satyagrahi* as a morally courageous individual who magnanimously upheld the integrity and dignity of his being by refusing to cooperate with the diabolic designs of the evil-doer and pitching his soul-force against the evil that was sought to be perpetuated.

Although, *satyagraha* as an act of defiance of immoral orders or laws had in it an element of disobedience to those giving such orders, this act, Gandhi emphasized, ought to be in a civilized manner and preceded by a conscious rendering of obedience to every moral laws and such laws of administrative nature which were prescribed by those in authoritative positions for the sake of the larger interest of the society. He said, "A *satyagrahi* obeys the laws of society intelligently and of his own free will because he considers it to be his sacred duty to do so. It is only when a person has thus obeyed the laws of a society scrupulously that he is in a position to judge as to which particular rules are good and just and which unjust and iniquitous. Only then does the right accrue to him to the civil disobedience of certain laws in well-defined circumstances."[43] Emphasizing the civil nature of disobedience, he said, "Whether all of us realize or not the method of non-cooperation is a process of touching the heart and appealing to reason, not one of frightening by rowdyism. Rowdyism has no place in a non-violent movement."[44] Gandhi also recognized the humble acceptance of punishments, except when they showed disrespect to the dignity of the *satyagrahi* or his moral convictions, as an essential part of the civility implied in an act of civil disobedience.

The *satyagrahi*, Gandhi observed, should make a clear distinction between the evil and the evil-doer; he should seek to destroy the evil than the evil-doer. Trusting in the inherent goodness of human nature, Gandhi recognized that no man was beyond redemption. He therefore advocated the need for the *satyagrahi* to cultivate such a faith in human nature so as to be able to patiently persuade the opponent and to voluntarily undergo suffering while attempting to resolve conflicts. Simultaneously, Gandhi advocated an unending trust in the opponent no matter how often he betrayed the trust reposed by the *satyagrahi* in him. He said, "A *satyagrahi* bids goodbye to fear. Even if the opponent plays him false twenty times, the *satyagrahi* is ready to trust him for the twenty-first time for an implicit trust in human nature is the very essence of his creed."[45]

Gandhi also recognized the need for the *satyagrahi* to think from the standpoint of the opponent. This, he recognized, was indispensable not only to do justice to the opponent but also for the speedier and effective resolution of the conflict itself. He said, "Total of the miseries and misunderstanding in the world will disappear if we step into the shoes of our adversaries and understand their standpoint. We will then agree with our adversaries quickly or think of them charitably."[46] The *satyagrahi*, he recognized, should refrain from exploiting the weaknesses or difficulties of the opponent and should never resort to secrecy or any kind of deception; instead, he should always desire honestly to utilize every opening for effectively resolving the conflict with the opponent and that too on honourable terms for both the parties involved in the conflict.

Recognizing the importance of quality, rather than quantity, Gandhi was very optimistic about the possibilities of *satyagraha* making limitless achievements. Thus, he said, "Strength of numbers is the delight of the timid. The valiant in spirit glory in fighting alone. Be you one or many, this valour is the only valour, all else is false."[47] He further recognized that "the best and the most solid work is done in the wilderness of minority".[48] To quote him further, "In every great cause it is not the number of fighter list that counts, but it is the quality of which they are made that becomes the deciding factor. The greatest men of the world have always stood alone. Take the great prophets, Zoroaster, Buddha, Jesus, Mohammed – they all stood alone like many others whom I can name."[49] Thus, J. Bandyopadyaya comments, "Time and again Gandhi has explained that the effectiveness of *satyagraha* depends on quality not on the strength of numbers. Active non-violence is powerful, universal and timeless force which, when adopted by an individual and practiced in a pure form, will inevitably produce results far out of proportion to the physical significance of the individual or the numerical value of his actions. Moral power operates on an altogether different dimension, as it were, from physical power, and is devoid of quantitative significance."[50] Gandhi therefore emphasized that the *satyagrahi* ought to be always self-reliant in his campaign against evil, untruth or injustice and said, "Then again, the strength of the spirit within mostly evaporates when a man gets and accepts support from outside. A *satyagrahi* must always be on his guard against such temptations."[51]

However, this did not mean that Gandhi failed to recognize the importance of public opinion and the mass basis of a national struggle. He was quite modern enough to recognize the importance of numbers in a struggle like that of a *satyagraha*.[52] It being so, he recognized the importance for the *satyagrahi* to tap various means such as the press, platform, parades, processions, songs and visuals and verbal propaganda which could help in mobilizing public opinion.[53] While seeking to mobilize the masses in the *satyagraha* struggle, Gandhi recognized the need for expert guidance, supervision and vigilance from an able *satyagrahi* leader on whom he also vested exceptional responsibility of preparing and training the rank and file participants and carrying on the movement with timely assessment and necessary adjustments wherever required. All such participants in the *satyagraha* struggle, Gandhi emphasized, must strictly adhere to the discipline laid out by their leader. Differences of opinion, Gandhi conceded, could be aired, but within the group; however, once the decision had been taken at the group level, it ought to be taken or accepted as binding on all the participants within the group.

Lastly, Gandhi also laid it as complimentary for a *satyagrahi* to participate actively in constructive activities. These, he believed, were effective means of inculcating in the *satyagrahi* such qualities truthfulness, non-violence, patience, self-restraint, self-reliance, etc. Gandhi enumerated a list of 15-point constructive programme, amongst which were listed such activities like strengthening of communal unity, removal of untouchability, prohibition, *khadi*, basic education, adult education, health and hygiene, village industry, promotion of cattle, etc.[54]

Gandhi recognized that the *satyagrahi* should follow certain fundamental and essential principles while launching a *satyagraha.*[55] The fundamental rules which should govern the *satyagraha* campaign according to Gandhi are:

1. There ought to be a grievance and objectives sought should be clear and tangible.
2. There ought to be self-reliance at all times.
3. Initiative should always be with the *satyagrahis.*
4. Propagation of the objectives, strategy and tactics of the campaign.
5. Reduction of demands to a minimum consistent with truth.
6. Non-cooperation in the form of non-payment of taxes, boycott of school or public institutions, ostracism or social boycott and voluntary exile.
7. Civil disobedience or violation of selected laws peacefully.

8. Usurping the function of the government and establishing a parallel government to conduct public functions.

In the course of his *satyagraha* campaigns Gandhi elaborated and employed a wide range of methods. He compared *satyagraha* with a tree and its tools or methods with that of its numerous branches. All these methods had, at their core, a common conformity to the notion of purity and unity of ends and means, adherence to the principle of non-violence and an accordance of importance to such factors like that of time and place. Nevertheless, these varied between the two extreme positions of being the most negative or limited one, to that of the most positive or comprehensive one. For academic purpose, as Raghavan Iyer has done,[56] these could be broadly classified into four categories:

1. purificatory and penitential devices;
2. forms of non-cooperation;
3. methods of civil disobedience; and
4. the constructive programme.

So far as the purificatory and penitential devices were concerned, it could be said that these were strength-giving reagents that enabled the *satyagrahi* to most effectively resolve a conflict situation in the shortest possible time and with the least possible suffering to be undergone in terms of injury to one's body, life and to property. The various purificatory and penitential devices advocated by Gandhi were pledges, prayers and fasts.

Defining a pledge as a vow to do at any cost a thing that one ought to do, Gandhi considered it as a strength[58] inducing element in a *satyagraha* campaign and as being indispensable for character building and self-realization.[59] Through this, he believed, not only did its adopter progress towards self-purification and perfection but also, as a consequence of this evolution, made the *satyagraha* action a very quick, potent and effective campaign. Laying down the discipline required to be observed by every *satyagrahi* volunteer, Gandhi drew up pledges in which such aspects like that of adherence to the principle of truth and non-violence in thought, words and action, promotion of communal amity, adoption of *khadi,* eradication of untouchability, acceptance to courageously undergo any amount of suffering for the sake of one's religion and country, obedience to the orders of the organizing leaders, etc. were variously emphasized upon from time to time. No matter whatever the pledge was, every pledge was viewed by Gandhi as a part of the sincerity of the *satyagrahi* in the cause that he had resolved to pursue, which in turn implied his readiness to face courageously and non-violently all the hardships of the arduous course that he has selected to act upon in his *satyagraha* campaign. Gandhi contended that pledges strengthened the *satyagrahi's* will power and befitted them for the tasks they wished to embark on.[60] Through the pledges Gandhi envisaged the *satyagrahi* to protest injustice; to refrain from violence to the opponent's life, person and property; and to cheerfully suffer the consequences of his act.[61] Gandhi elaborated a code of discipline that the *satyagrahi* was pledged to abide by in his different capacity as an individual, as a prisoner, as a part of the unit and as a promoter of communal amity.[62]

However, Gandhi's theistic leanings influenced him to contend that even the best of human endeavour was of no avail if it had not got God's blessings behind it. He believed that an individual had numerous weaknesses on account of his mortal existence and consequently he sometimes found it difficult to fulfil the pledges or resolves which he had made in his life. In order to free himself from such weaknesses and be capable of fulfilling the pledges made in his life, Gandhi recognized the need for the individual to seek the divine grace of God. This, he believed, could be invoked by humbly offering prayers to the Almighty God. He said, "There is an eternal struggle raging in man's breast between the powers of darkness and of light, and he who has not the sheet-anchor of prayer to rely upon will be a victim to the powers of darkness... Prayer is the only means of bringing about orderliness and peace and repose in our daily acts."[63] A living faith in God, which helped the *satyagrahi* to overcome the difficulties involved in the *satyagraha* struggle, Gandhi recognized, could not be more better cultivated than by a recourse to prayer. Faith, he recognized, could not be developed except through prayer. This prayer, which reflected a longing of the soul, Gandhi emphasized, should not become a mere mechanical contrivance adopted for stage effect.[65] Rather, it should be one where there was a complete exclusion of physical activities to the extent that it possessed the whole of one's being and enabled one to rise superior to, and completely detached from, all physical functions.[66] Only such a prayer, he believed, could help the individual attain supremacy of the spirit over the flesh and bring about clarity of vision. Gandhi also visualized prayer as an important means for bringing about a "change of heart" in the opponent and considered it as being inherent with the capacity to make great achievements.[67]

Like prayer, Gandhi also recognized fasting as a means to overcome one's distress. He said, "My religion teaches me that whenever there is distress which one cannot remove, one must fast and pray."[68] He went to the extent of recognizing fasting as the sincerest form of prayer and said, "Thus all fasting, if it is a spiritual act, is an intense prayer or a preparation for it. It is a yearning of the soul to merge in the divine essence."[69] Since he considered fasting to be a very potent weapon in the armoury of *satyagrahi,* he advised great caution and care while taking recourse to it. He recognized that it could be undertaken either for self-purification or self-restrain, or for appealing to the better nature of the opponent and influencing him to reconsider his original stand which was fallacious. It was also envisaged by Gandhi to check acts of violence, to remove bitterness among people and to even purify political atmosphere.[70] Gandhi simultaneously outlined the characteristics of a genuine fast. He said, "But the mere fast of the body is nothing without the will behind it. It must be a genuine confession of the inner fast, an irrepressible longing to express truth and nothing but truth. Therefore, those only are privileged to fast for the cause of truth who have worked for it and who have love in them even for opponents, who are free from animal passion and who have abjured earthly possessions and ambitions."[71] He emphasized that it should not be a mechanical effort or a mere imitation but should spring from the depth of one's soul. All fasting should be commensurate, Gandhi contended, with the capacity of the individual to do so and should be undertaken only as last resort and after undergoing adequate training. Yet another necessary condition for fasting which Gandhi recognized was the one which laid down that fasting should only be undertaken by that person who was associated with the individual against whom he fasted and the latter should be directly connected with purpose for which the fast was being undertaken.[72] Recognizing the fact that every real fasting should be of the widest possible character, Gandhi's advocacy of fasting transcended beyond the generally recognized limits of food and appetite; was to be accompanied by fasting of all the senses. He said, "It is my firm belief that the strength of the soul grows in proportion as you subdue the flesh."[73]

Gandhi also recognized silence as a spiritual discipline of the *satyagrahi.* He recognized it to be not only an invaluable aid for the *satyagrahi* in his pursuit of truth and spiritual growth but also as very conducive medium for communion with God. He also recognized it as being essential for the seeker to surmount such natural weakness of man like that of one's proneness to exaggerate, to suppress or modify truth consciously or unconsciously.[74] He further said, "Silence is a great help to a seeker after truth... In the attitude of silence the soul finds the path in a clearer light, and what is elusive and deceptive resolve itself into crystal clearness. Our life is a long and arduous quest after truth, and the soul requires inward restfulness to attain its full height."[75]

Coming to the second category of classification, i.e., non-violent non-cooperation, it could be said that Gandhi regarded it as an intensive form of *satyagraha* which predominantly had the political implication of withdrawing cooperation from the state which, in the non-cooperator's view, had become corrupt.[76] Gandhi contended its operational efficacy on the ground that anyone who sought to perpetuate evil or wrong action cannot succeed without the willing consent or the passive acquiescence in the evil act by such individuals against whom all such acts are directed. Thus, when the latter refused to cooperate with the former, the former will be thwarted in this attempt to perpetuate the evil and the evil itself will be effectively checked at the point of origin. Gandhi therefore observed, "No tyrant has ever yet succeeded in his purpose without carrying the victim with him, it may as it often is, by force. Most people choose rather to yield to the will of the tyrant than to suffer for the consequence of resistance. Hence does terrorism form part of the stock-in-trade of the tyrant."[77] The non-cooperator, Gandhi recognized, should possess not only the qualities of self-restraint and patience but also of a resoluteness of will to oppose evil and injustice and to steadfastly hold on to truth at all costs.

Emphasizing upon the essential nature of non-cooperation, Gandhi said, "Non-cooperation in the sense used by me must be non-violent and, therefore, neither punitive nor vindictive nor based on malice, ill-will or hatred. "Rather, after the opponent had been purged off his evil designs, *satyagraha* envisaged an active cooperation.[79] He therefore said, "Although non-cooperation is the main weapon in the armoury of *satyagraha,* it should not be forgotten that it is after all only a means to secure the cooperation of the opponent consistently with truth and justice."[80] Pinning his faith in the doctrine that no man was beyond redemption, Gandhi advocated the non-cooperator to continuously resist the diabolic designs of the evil doer and, while silently undergoing the suffering on account of the offensive acts of the opponent, try to wean him away from the evil through love, self-suffering and rational persuasion. He was very emphatic about the need for the non-cooperator to convince his opponent about the friendliness and the good intentions of the *satyagrahi*. Consequently, Gandhi advocated that the non-cooperator should always try to reach his opponents heart by rendering him humanitarian service whenever possible.[81] It is in the context that Gandhi recognized non-cooperation as a process of touching the heart and appealing to reason, rather than being one of frightening by rowdyism.[82]

Sincerity, Gandhi recognized, was indispensable for the non-cooperator. Recognizing non-cooperation as a test of sincerity, Gandhi said, "Non-cooperation is not a movement of brag, bluster or bluff. It is a test of our sincerity. It requires solid and silent sacrifice. It challenges our honesty and our capacity for national work. It is a movement that aims at translating ideas into action."[83] Gandhi outlined three important disciplines or lessons which he considered to be essential for a non-cooperator. The first lesson was that of indispensability of a reasoned and willing obedience to the laws of the state. The second lesson was that of tolerance which implied tolerance of many laws of the state even when they were inconvenient. The third lesson was that of suffering which implied that any person who had not got the capacity of suffering could not non-cooperate effectively. This was on account of the fact that acts of resistance are accompanied by many hardships in the form of punishment from those who are resisted or disobeyed. So, any person afraid of suffering these hardships could not be brave and strong enough to disobey or defy unjust orders. Gandhi also recognized that the non-cooperator should be humble and self-restrained and should work within the recognized limits of the doctrine of non-cooperation. A conformation to the prescribed limits of non-cooperation, Gandhi recognized, would make non- cooperation a constitutional means; but actions beyond the prescribed limit, would make it criminal.[84] It was Gandhi's firm belief that when non-cooperation remained within such recognized bounds, it would serve as a catalyst for evolving a true order out of an untrue order.[85] The various non-violent non-cooperative tools which Gandhi recognized were *hartal,* boycott, strike and *hijrat.*

Hartal implied a general cessation of business undertaken to indicate its adopter's attitude of disapproval of some unwarranted law or arbitrary order of the ruler or the government.[86] Gandhi recognized it as a means designed to strike the imagination of the people and the government. Since cessation of business for a great length of time would create a difficult situation,[87] Gandhi emphasized upon its short duration – a symbolic period of twenty four hours[88] as well as refraining from its recourse very frequently.[89] Gandhi also recognized the use of it to lodge public protest against the arrest of *satyagraha* volunteers, and to boycott the visit of officials of an unjust government.[90] Abstention from work during the *hartal* period, Gandhi emphasized, should be entirely voluntary. While persuasion for observing *hartal* by means of leaflets and other propaganda work could be resorted to prior to the day of *hartal*; on the particular day, Gandhi emphasized upon the need to desist from all such acts of persuasion. He even considered it criminal if those partaking in the *hartal* tried to jostle with other people or attempted to stop transport facilities.[91] Recognizing hartal also as an occasion for offering public prayers and observing a state of mourning, Gandhi described the purpose of *hartal* thus, "When we are dissatisfied with anything we often resort to *hartal*. In India, we often consider it our duty to do so in order to obtain redress of our grievances, particularly in the native states. The *hartal* only means that we do not approve of certain measure taken by the ruler."[92] Boundurant, in a similar vein, recognized *hartal* as a method of protest, demonstration of extreme dissatisfaction and, at times, as a national mourning.[93]

If *hartal* was a method of protest demonstrating extreme dissatisfaction and national mourning, then boycott, as conceived by Gandhi, was a means adopted by an individual or a group to express strong desire and declaration of not being a party to the perpetuation of injustice or evil. Through such a strong desire and declaration it sought to expedite justice. Gandhi recognized three types of boycott – political, social and economic. Defining a political boycott as a non-violent means of advocating no compromise with truth, no matter whosoever or however strong the perpetuator of the evil might be, Gandhi extended its recognition to the refusal of favours from the morally corrupt government or encouraging it in any manner in its diabolic designs.[94] In the economic and social realms Gandhi recognized boycott's extension to titles, commodities, persons and institutions as sign of non-cooperation with the evil doer.

Whatever be the nature of boycott, Gandhi was particularly emphatic about the moral aspect of its use as a non-violent and non-coercive measure of non-cooperation with the tyrant. He cautioned about making a recourse to it for settling mere difference of opinion. Emphasizing this aspect of a social boycott he said, "Social boycott is applicable and effective when it is not felt as a punishment and accepted by the object of boycott as a measure of discipline. Moreover, social boycott to be admissible in a campaign of non-violence must never savour of inhumanity. It must be civilized. It must cause pain to the party using it, if it causes inconvenience to its object... Surely non-cooperators have acquired no right to use that extreme pressure against those who do not see eye to eye with them. Impatience and intolerance will surely kill this great religious movement.[95]

Yet another means of non-cooperation that Gandhi advocated to redress a wrong was that of a strike. In its applied manifestation it represented a ceasure of participation, on the part of its adopter, from the diabolic designs of the evil-doer, and through such an act make him realize the folly of pursuing such an act.[96] Strike being basically a labourer's instrument for acquisition of a desired standard of treatment and living from the employer,[97] Gandhi recognized its extension to the political arena for seeking those in authoritative positions in the society to desist from indulging in undesirable and unjust act. Whatever be the purpose of the strike, Gandhi recognized that it ought to be civilized and free from all such violence as that of intimidation, incendiarism or otherwise.[98] Gandhi also recognized certain essentials to which the strikers were required to pay special attention. These were: existence of genuine grievance; self-dependence of the striker; and fixation of an unalterable minimum demand and its declaration before resorting to strike.[99] When resorting to strike for political goals, Gandhi cautioned that it should neither become a means for embarrassing or harassing the government nor should cause inconvenience or harassment to the larger public by way of denying them essential public utility services.[100]

A slightly different form of non-violent non-cooperation from the aforementioned ones was that of *hijrat*. Gandhi conceded the recourse to *hijrat* as a last resort for those who were not able to defend themselves against the injustice and oppression of tyrant rulers. Its recourse implied its adopter's unwillingness to participate or acquiesce in the unrighteous acts of the ruler by forsaking the ruler and his territory and moving to a different place. Although it implied its adopters turning away from the scene of injustice, this act, far from being a cowardly act, was reflective of its adopters desire to uphold the honesty and integrity of his self. Given the limitations of his capacity to suffers which becomes unbearable in existing conditions, the *hijrati* sees wisdom in leaving the place instead of staying there and corrupting his quintessential existence. Gandhi therefore remarked, "Tyranny is a kind of plague, and when it is likely to make us angry or weak, it is wisdom to leave the scene of such temptation. History is full of instances of brave people having sought exile in preference to surrender to *zoolum*."[101] However, he recognized that in purest from of *satyagraha* there did not exist even the need of doing *hijrat*.[102] Instead, he preferred the position of the *satyagrahi* pitching his whole moral force in the process of fighting evil. It was probably on this account that he recognized *hijrat* as not really having a place in a true *satyagraha*.

Yet another form of *satyagraha* was that of civil disobedience. Civil disobedience as a branch of *satyagraha* implied a breach of any statutory and unmoral law and signified the resisters outlawry in a civil and non-violent manner.[103] Gandhi recognized it as an active expression of non-violence[104] and as an essential discipline for those who offered disobedience.[105] For him it was also the logical conclusion, the last stage, the most drastic form of non-cooperation.[106] He called it "a complete, effective and bloodless substitute of armed revolt."[107] He recognized it as a sovereign method of transmuting fury into creative energy.[108] Civil disobedience as envisaged by Gandhi presupposed the habit of willing obedience to laws without fear of their sanctions on the part of its adopter and advocated its practice only as a last resort and that too by a select few in the initial stages.[109] Such an advocacy by Gandhi had its basis in the belief that the conditions essential for embarking on the course of civil disobedience were more easily and more frequently found at the individual or a few select individuals' level rather than being found at the mass level in the first instance. Moreover, Gandhi recognized that any possibility of the disobedience leading to violence or bloodshed could be more easily controlled when the disobedience was limited to the level of a single or a few select individuals. On account of the inherent dangers of a of a mass civil disobedience movement, Gandhi preferred a mass non-cooperation movement. Through the training in the less drastic methods of non-cooperation, Gandhi believed that the masses could become better prepared for undertaking civil disobedience.

Gandhi also recognized a few other distinctions between individual and mass civil disobedience. First, while in an individual civil disobedience movement, every individual existed as a complete unit in himself and one individual's fall did not affect the others, in a mass civil disobedience all participants together formed a whole unit and therefore the fall of one generally adversely affected the rest. Secondly, while in a mass civil resistance leadership was essential, in the case of individual civil resistance every individual was his own leader. Thirdly, while in mass civil disobedience there may exist a possibility of failure, in the case of individual civil disobedience failure is impossible. Fourthly, a state could cope up with a mass civil disobedience, but it could not cope up with the determined individual civil resisters.[110] Fifthly, while mass civil disobedience should always be tried in a calm atmosphere, individual civil disobedience could he tried any time, provided its essentials were uncompromisingly followed. Sixthly, mass civil disobedience, Gandhi recognized, was selfish in the sense that participants in it expected personal gains from their acts, whereas in individual civil disobedience there existed no such narrow consideration. Lastly, mass civil disobedience, he recognized, had to be always spontaneous, while individual civil disobedience could be resorted to after proper education and training on the relevant aspects of civil disobedience.

Gandhi also recognized the distinction between limited civil disobedience and complete civil disobedience. Limited civil disobedience implied disobedience to selected laws or orders considered to be immoral while simultaneously obeying other laws which were considered to be consistent with morality and administrative utility. However, Gandhi recognized the possibility of a state degenerating to a level of being predominantly immoral. In such circumstances he recognized it as the principal duty of every conscious and righteous individual to refuse obedience to every single law made by such a state regardless of the possibilities of the disobedience act leading to violent and bloody repression. Thus, in 1921, he remarked, "I can clearly see the time coming to me when I must refuse obedience to every single state-made law, even though there may be a certainty of bloodshed. When neglect of the call means a denial of God, civil disobedience becomes a pre-emptory duty."[111] Such a refusal to obey every single state-made law was recognized by Gandhi as a complete civil disobedience or a state of peaceful rebellion.[112]

Another distinction that Gandhi made was the one between aggressive and defensive civil disobedience. An aggressive civil disobedience, which was synonymous with an assertive or offensive civil disobedience, Gandhi recognized, was a non-violent, willful disobedience of laws of the state whose breach did not involve moral turpitude and was undertaken as a symbol of revolt against the state.[113] Defensive civil disobedience, on the other hand, was an involuntary or reluctant non-violent disobedience of such laws which were in themselves bad and obedience to which would be inconsistent with the individual's self-respect or human dignity.[114]

Whatever be the type of civil disobedience Gandhi was very emphatic about the need for every act of disobedience to be civil, which in turn laid down the condition that it had to be open and non-violent. He said, "We must therefore give its full and therefore greater value to the adjective 'civil' than to 'disobedience', disobedience without civility, discipline, discrimination, non-violence is certain destruction."[115] Civil disobedience, he recognized, should never be followed by anarchy; if at all it became so, then it degenerated into criminal disobedience and was condemnable. In case of actual outbreak of violence, Gandhi recognized that the votary of civil disobedience should make active efforts to contain this violence even if it meant risking his life.[116] Thus, summing up the noble objectives of civil disobedience, he said, "The plan of civil disobedience has been conceived to neutralize and ultimately entirely to displace violence and enthrone non-violence in its stead, to replace hatred by love, to replace strife by concord."[117] Such being the noble goals of civil disobedience, Gandhi recognized it as the birthright of every citizen.[118] A citizen who bartered with a morally corrupt or lawless state, in Gandhi's recognition, partook in its corruption or lawlessness. It was his contention that an individual who renounced this birthright ceased to exist as a man.[119] However, Gandhi conceded, given the weakness of the individual and the exigencies of time and situation, the wisdom of resorting to civil disobedience in respect of a particular act or law could become a debatable issue and be open to pragmatic advice of delay and caution.[120] But, the right in itself, he recognized, could not be questioned.

Every right presupposes a duty; Gandhi too believed in this doctrine. He said, "The true source of right is duty. If we all discharge our duties, rights will not be far to seek. If leaving duties unperformed, we run after rights they will escape us like will-o-the-wisp. The more we pursue them, the farther will they fly."[121] Extending this recognition to the realm of civil disobedience, Gandhi was very emphatic about the need for the individual to cultivate a spirit of tolerance of state laws before embarking on a course of civil disobedience. He therefore said, "...it is only when people have proved their active loyalty by obeying the many laws of the state that they acquire the right of civil disobedience."[122] He also recognized that the civil resister should be prepared to face extreme hardships because only through the humble and innocent suffering of the resister could the wrong doer, who became weary of wrong doing in the absence of any resistance, be weaned away effectively from the acts of evil. Consequently, he emphasized, "Civil disobedience, if it is really civil, must appear so even to the opponent. He must feel that the resistance is not intended to do him any harm."[123] Gandhi also recognized that the act of civil disobedience should not be carried beyond the point of breaking the unmoral laws. He emphasized that the disobeyer should willingly accept and conform to the sanctions provided for the breach of law, except in all such cases where the punishments violated the dignity of the individual and moral code of conduct.[124] Such conditions being implicit in the notion of civil disobedience, Gandhi considered it as the purest type of constitutional agitation, as a synonym of growth, strength and purity,[125] and recognized its adopter, i.e., the civil resister, as a philanthropist and a friend of the state.[126]

Gandhi recognized several modes of civil disobedience. The prominent among them being picketing, holding banned marches and meetings, non-payment of taxes, and the deliberate defiance of specific laws.

Picketing, as a means of defensive civil disobedience, was advocated by Gandhi for putting socio-economic and political pressure on the government along with the simultaneous effort to create public opinion and inculcation of a spirit of self-reliance. A picketer, Gandhi emphasized, should only take recourse to gentle persuasion of the wrong-doers and take care to protect him from every possible chances of physical and verbal assault. Every picketing, he recognized, should be based on a just cause and should be generally resorted to by individuals only under the aegis of a responsible organization.[127] Any course to such means like that of a formation of human chain to prevent or obstruct individuals who were not willing to conform to the picketers request, Gandhi recognized, tantamounted to indulgence in violence. Gandhi also recognized certain rules and manner of picketing.[128]

Yet another mode of civil disobedience advocated and actually made use of by Gandhi was that of a recourse to banned marches and meetings. Recourse to these, Gandhi recognized, implied the lodging of people's protest against unjust prohibitory orders of the governments and mobilizing the public opinion against the wrong or unjust acts of the government.

The non-payment of taxes was yet another mode of civil disobedience that was recognized by Gandhi. It implied the refusal by its adopter to pay to the government the predetermined taxes or government charges which he thought were unjust. It aimed to strike at an important source of existence and strength of the government, namely, finance, and through it to influence the government to mend its ways or repeal its unjust order. Gandhi emphasized upon its recourse only after the personal experience of the defects of such laws or orders. The recourse itself, he recognized, should be a last resort and to be taken after much deliberation because such acts of defiance were likely to be the cause of various forms of hardships by way of retaliatory measures from those who gave such orders. He cautioned that its adopter should be psychologically well-prepared to face these oppressive measures before deciding to embark on the course of non-payment of taxes.

A similar mode of civil disobedience like that of non-payment of taxes, which Gandhi advocated, was that of a deliberate defiance of specific laws. In it, selected laws which failed to take cognizance of the fundamental needs of individuals or those which violated their basic essence, were sorted out for deliberate defiance. Gandhi advocated that this choice of specific law for defiance should be done with great care and discrimination. Only such laws which were harmful to the subject citizens or were neither moral nor immoral should be chosen for defiance. Moreover, the laws so selected, he emphasized, should also help in the participation of largest number of people.

Coming to the last category of classification of *satyagraha* methods, the constructive programme, it may he said that this constituted the more positive facet of the *satyagraha* campaign.[129] Gandhi recognized it as a training for the non-violence of the brave and as a means for attaining *swaraj*.[130] As an integral part of *satyagraha* movement it strove to promote better understanding and unity amongst the *satyagrahis* as well as preparing them for self-sufficiency and self-reliance which Gandhi considered to be indispensable for effectively carrying on the *satyagraha* campaign. As a training process, which turned a raw *satyagrahi* recruit into a disciplined soldier, it sought to prevent any *satyagraha* campaign from degenerating into violent activities like riots. Similarly, at the interaction level between the *satyagrahi* and opponent, it served as a means to convince the opponent about the good intention and concern of the *satyagrahi* for the opponent. At a still larger level of the society it strove to eradicate such social evils like communal distrust, untouchability, illiteracy, unemployment, etc. Thus, it represented an effort to build or reconstruct the existing system while the *satyagraha* campaign was in progress against any unjust socio-political and economic aspect of the given order. In 1941, Gandhi, while expounding his philosophy of constructive programme as a truthful and non-violent means of winning *Poorna Swaraj,*[132] emphasized upon a 15-point constructive programme which included (1) work for communal unity; (2) removal of untouchahility; (3) prohibition; (4) adoption of *khadi;* (5) development of village industries; (6) sanitation of villages; (7) promotion of Basic Education; (8) promotion of adult education; (9) upliftment of women; (10) promotion of health and hygiene; (11) propagation for the adoption of Hindustani language; (12) encouragement to provincial languages; (13) trusteeship; (14) service to aborigines; and (15) organization of students; farmers and labourers. Later on he expanded it to include such other programme like that of *go seva* or improvement of cattle.[133]

In conclusion, it may be said that Gandhi's deliberations on the purificatory and penitential devices, forms of non-cooperation and civil disobedience and constructive programme have the twin objective of individual or self-transformation as well as social or non-self transformation. Both are necessary for the realization of the ideal order or *Ram Rajya*. Gandhi seems to have understood this relationship and therefore insisted on the inseparability of individual self and that of politics and emphasized upon inner change in the individual to be the starting point of outer changes in the society. Thus, while modern social science tends to ignore this principle, Gandhi reinstates it into political philosophy.[134]

Notes

1. Gandhi as quoted by N.K. Bose, *Selections from Gandhi*, Navajivan Publishing House, Ahmedabad, 1972, p.218.
2. See P. Sitaramayya, *The History of Indian National Congress*, Padma Publication, Bombay, Vol. 1, 1946, pp. 238-41.
3. See Raghavan N. Iyer, *The Moral and Political Thought of Mahatma Gandhi*, Oxford University Press, New Delhi, 1973, p. 258.
4. Gandhi as quoted by K.N. Tiwari, *World Religion and Gandhi*, Classical Publishing Company, New Delhi, 1988, p. 99.
5. See Ram Rattan, *Gandhi's Concept of Political Obligation*, The Minerva Associates, Calcutta, 1972, p. 159-60.
6. Ibid.
7. See James Luther Adams, Civil Disobedience: Its Occassions and Limits, in *Political and Legal Obligation*, Nomos XII, J.R. Pennock & J.W. Chapman (eds.), New York, Atherton Press, 1970, p. 294.
8. Gandhi as quoted by Raghavan N. Iyer, Note 3, p. 361.
9. M.K. Gandhi, *Satyagraha in South Africa*, Trans. V.G. Desai, Navajivan Publishing House, Ahmedabad, 1972, p. 191.
10. Ibid., p. 192.
11. Ibid., p. 191.
12. H.J.N. Horsburg, *Non-Violence and Agression: A Study of Gandhi's Moral Equivalent of War*, Oxford University Press, London, 1971, p. 52.
13. M.K. Gandhi, *Satyagraha*, Bharatan Kumarappa (ed.), Navajivan Publication, Ahmedabad, 1958, p. 77.
14. Gandhi as quoted by Ram Rattan, The Anatomy of Gandhi's Satyagraha, in *New Dimensions and Perspectives in Gandhism*, V.T. Patil (ed.), Inter-India Publications, New Delhi, 1989, p. 45.
15. Note 12, p. 77.
16. Ibid.
17. See Raghavan N. Iyer, Note 3, p. 256.
18. Note 1, p. 225.
19. Ibid., p. 224.
20. R.J. Terchek, *Gandhian Politics*, Note 13, p. 132.

21. Note 3, p. 260.
22. Note 5, p. 170.
23. *CWMG*, Vol. 18, p. 93.
24. See Note 11, pp. 36-77.
25. For a detailed examination see Thomas Merton, The Meaning of Satyagraha, in *Gandhi Marg*, April 1966, pp. 110-12.
26. Anthony Parel, *Gandhian Satyagraha and Machiavillian Virtue, in Meanings of Gandhi,* Paul F. Power (ed.) The University Press of Hawaii, Hawaii, 1971, p. 187.
27. T.K.N. Unnithan, *Change without Violence: Gandhian Theory of Social Change*, Gujarat Vidyapeeth, Ahmedabad, 1987, p. 50.
28. Paul F. Power, *Mahatma Gandhi and Civil Disobedience*, Note 25, p. 177.
29. M.K. Gandhi, *Sarvodaya*, Bharattan Kumarappa (ed.) Navajivan Publishing House, Ahmedabad, 1984, p. 91.
30. For a detailed analysis see Note 5, pp. 197-209.
31. Ramashray Roy, *Self and Society: A Study in Gandhian Thought*, Sage Publication, New Delhi, 1984, p. 169.
32. For a detailed discussion see Joan V. Bondurant, *Conquest of Violence: The Gandhian Philosophy of Conflict*, Princeton University Press, New Jersey, 1958, pp. 38-41.
33. *CWMG* Vol. 43, p. 135.
34. See Note 1, p. 153-54.
35. See Note 28, p. 90.
36. *CWMG* Vol. 22, p. 137.
37. *CWMG* Vol. 69, pp. 69-70.
38. For details see Gopinath Dhawan, *The Political Philosophy of Mahatma Gandhi*, Gandhi Peace Foundation, New Delhi, 1990, pp. 211-13.
39. Note 5, p. 169.
40. Note 1, p. 241.
41. Ibid, p. 242.
42. Note 11, p. 56.
43. M.K. Gandhi, *An Autobiography or The Story of My Experiments with Truth*, Trans, Mahadev Desai, Navajivan Publishing House, Ahmedabad, 1966, p. 357.
44. Note 12, p. 64.
45. Note 8, p. 147.
46. Note 12, pp. 193 – 94.
47. Note 1, p. 245.

48. *CWMG*, Vol. 22, p. 500.
49. J. Bandyopadhyaya, *Social and Political Thought of Gandhi,* Allied Publications, Bombay, 1969, p. 236.
50. Ibid., pp. 235-36.
51. Note 1, p. 246.
52. Note 5, p. 172.
53. M.M. Verma, *Gandhi's Technique of Mass Mobilization*, R.K. Gupta & Co., New Delhi, 1990, pp. 117 – 18.
54. For details see M.K. Gandhi, *Constructive Programme: Its Meaning and Place*, Navajivan Publishing House, Ahmedabad, 1989.
55. Note 32, pp. 38-41.
56. Note 3, p. 301.
57. Note 13, p. 37
58. Ibid.
59. Ibid., p. 38.
60. Note 14, p. 207.
61. Ibid., p. 208.
62. Note 3, pp. 319-22.
63. Note 1, p. 12.
64. Ibid., p. 242.
65. Note 38, p. 123.
66. *CWMG*, Vol. 55, p. 257.
67. See Note 14, p. 208.
68. Note 9, p. 248.
69. *CWMG*, Vol. 55, p. 257.
70. Note 14, pp. 239-40.
71. Note 29, p. 319.
72. Ibid., p. 321.
73. Note 1, p. 247.
74. Note 38, p. 123.
75. M.K. Gandhi, *Truth is God*, R.K. Prabhu (Comp.) Navajivan Publishing House, Ahmedabad, 1987, p. 57.
76. *CWMG*, Vol. 19, p. 466.
77. *CWMG*, Vol. 17, p. 483.
78. *CWMG*, Vol. 18, p. 195.
79. Gandhi as quoted by Gopinath Dhawan, Note 11, p. 144.
80. Ibid.
81. Ibid.

82. *CWMG*, Vol. 24, p. 193.
83. *CWMG*, Vol. 19, p. 220.
84. *CWMG*, Vol. 22, p. 109.
85. *CWMG*, Vol. 18, p. 142.
86. *CWMG*, Vol. 16, p. 386.
87. Ibid., p. 384.
88. Note 14, p. 221.
89. Note 38, p. 229.
90. Note 14, p. 221.
91. *CWMG*, Vol. 16, p. 385.
92. Gandhi as quoted by Ram Rattan, Note 14, p. 221.
93. Note 32, p. 119.
94. *CWMG*, Vol. 19, p. 82.
95. *CWMG*, Vol. 19, p. 367.
96. CWMG, Vol. 21, p. 164.
97. Shridharani as quoted by Ram Rattan, Note 14, p. 222.
98. *CWMG*, Vol. 21, p. 164.
99. Ibid.
100. Note 14, p. 223.
101. *CWMG*, Vol. 63, p. 353.
102. Note 29, p. 289.
103. *CWMG*, Vol. 19, p. 466.
104. *CWMG*, Vol. 21, p. 313.
105. *CWMG*, Vol. 16, p. 386.
106. Note 38, p. 238.
107. Ibid.
108. Note 29, p. 238.
109. *CWMG*, Vol. 19, p. 466.
110. Note 38, p. 243.
111. *CWMG*, Vol. 20, p. 464.
112. Ibid., p. 466.
113. *CWMG*, Vol. 22, p. 362.
114. Ibid.
115. Ibid., p. 137.
116. *CWMG*, Vol. 43, p. 136.
117. Ibid., p. 135.
118. *CWMG*, Vol. 22, p. 143.

119. Ibid.
120. Ibid.
121. Note 1, p. 37.
122. *CWMG*, Vol. 25, p. 560.
123. Note 29, p. 306.
124. *CWMG*, Vol. 22, p. 19.
125. Ibid., p. 137.
126. Ibid., p. 19.
127. Note 29, p. 340.
128. Note 29, pp. 334-37.
129. Ibid., p. 101.
130. *CWMG*, Vol. 47, p. 92.
131. Note 38, p. 191.
132. Note 54, p. 3.
133. Ibid., pp. 8-32.
134. See Anthony J. Parel (ed.), *Gandhi: Hind Swaraj and Other Writings*, Cambridge University Press, New Delhi, 2005, p. lxi.

6

Practice of Satyagraha

The South African phase of Gandhi's life (1893-1914) constituted those crucial years of his life in which he developed his idea and method of protest. His protest, to which he assigned the term of *satyagraha,* had widespread ramification not only for the freedom struggle in India but also for other such movements in different parts of the world which strove to assert the individuality and freedom of the exploited and suppressed section of humanity.

When he set sail for South Africa, Gandhi had no idea of the impending handicaps and humiliations that would be volleyed upon him in the new place. The general condition in South Africa at that time was one which was greatly unfavourable for a coloured man. The White man's domination over the coloured man was considered as being natural. Despite being a minority, the Whites were instilled with a racial superiority that grew out of their plundering exploits and unchecked political power. In their behaviour there was an aura of arrogance and abhorrence for the coloured man. This detestation of the coloured men increased as it dawned upon the White men that the coloured population, by virtue of its numerical strength, could challenge their profitable existence in the resourceful South African continent. To avert the possibility of their being uprooted and thrown out from the country, it was systematically planned to reduce the Black to a position of unflinching obedience and servitude to the White minority, and through this, perpetuate their hegemony over the resourceful continent. With such an objective in mind, and ably assisted by the legal authorities of the land, a series of laws were enacted seeking to impose numerous hardships upon the Black. A policy of segregation of human beings on the basis of racial identity in matters of domicile and civic life, law and administration, education, economy, trade, health care, life, liberty and property came to be followed. With a view to totally subject the Black to the will of the White minority stringent punishments were prescribed and often meted out for every violation of the law.

Although these laws were intended for the Black African natives, in their application these came to be extended indiscriminately to all coloured persons living in South Africa, including the Indian community which consisted of indentured and free labourers, a few merchants and their assistants in office and home. The indentured labourers who laboured in the various plantation sites and mines worked in a condition of semi-slavery. Changing employers on the plea of maltreatment was quite a difficult proposition to realize. Those who failed to renew their indenture after the stipulated years of contract were further hemmed by various handicaps. The European traders, envious of the marginal success that a few Indians had managed to achieve in trade and merchandise, began to vociferously demand the repatriation of every Indian who failed to renew his indenture. Efforts were also made to disfranchise the rich Indian merchants who had become entitled to vote. Trading itself was made difficult in practice by adoption of a licence policy which became a tedious and expensive process for the Indians and other non-Europeans. Likewise, by making it compulsory to pass an education test in a European language, a majority of the potential immigrants desiring to come as traders and merchants in South Africa were effectively blocked.

Apart from the legal handicaps, the Indians also suffered many social disabilities. Every Indian was indiscriminately referred as a "coolie". They were described as "Asian dirt", "person belonging to the uncivilized races of Asia", "semi-barbarous", "chokefull of vice", etc. Even simple things like walking on footpath and staying out of house after nine in the evening were forbidden for them. In trains they had to travel in separate compartments, and in the states like The Transvaal they were not issued first – and second-class railway ticket. They could be unceremoniously bundled out of a railway compartment if a

White passenger objected. In the stage coaches, sometimes, they had to travel on the foot-board. European hotels refused lodging and common dining facilities to them. While the White colonists of The Orange Free State hounded out the Indians from their state by forbidding them to trade or do any business whatsoever in the state, in other states like The Transvaal they were allowed to reside and trade only in specific locations called "ghetto" which were provided with little civic amenities.

Nevertheless, the compulsions of a life and vocation in a foreign land where they were an unresourceful minority, made the Indians reconcile to the disgrace and acquiesce in the perpetuated evil by cultivating an attitude of passive indifference to all such handicaps. They pocketed their humiliations as they pocketed their daily earnings.

Gandhi himself was subjected to various insults and indignities in the course of his life in South Africa. In the very first week of his stay in Durban, Gandhi personally experienced some of the humiliations and handicaps that were heaped on the Indians. However, it was the Martizburg incident that transformed him completely. Thrown out with his luggage from the first class coach of the train, despite having a confirmed ticket to travel, Gandhi, sitting in the waiting room and shivering in the bitter cold, decided on that fateful night that he would not remain a mere spectator or a victim of the wrongs and humiliations heaped upon him; but instead protest, defy and agitate not merely to uphold his personal honour and dignity but to realize these goals for his coloured fellow men too. Commenting upon the importance of the Martizburg incident on Gandhi, Hiren Mukherjee says, "The Martizburg experience gave him no doubt a deep spiritual shake-up. It gave him the first release from the bonds of fear *abhaya,* as our ancients called it, not merely physical courage but the positive absence of fear from the mind. This quality of fearlessness.....was Gandhi's greatest contribution to Indian life-fearlessness of state repression and of social obloquy, fearlessness in respect not only of the coercive machinery of the state, but of landlords and moneylenders and vested interest, fearlessness even in face of starvation and sorrow."[1] Gandhi wrote in his autobiography in this regard, "I began to think of my duty. Should I fight for my rights or go back to India, or should I go on to Pretoria without minding the insults, and return to India after finishing the case? It would be cowardice to run back to India without fulfilling my obligation. The hardship to which I was subjected was superficial – only a symptom of the deep disease of colour prejudice. I should try, if possible, to root out the disease and suffer hardship in the process."[2] While the resolve to protest and suffer, rather than submit to evil, was reflective of Gandhi's intention to creatively use these for the emancipation of people other than his self; the incidents like that of his being kicked off the foot path on the President Street, revealed that Gandhi had already cultivated the value of forgiving the evil-doer rather than taking revenge. Thus, within the first few days of Gandhi's arrival in South Africa, some of the quintessential qualities of a *satyagraha* struggle already came to be conceived and put into practice.

Having pledged himself to eradicate the racial stigma under which he and his compatriots lay, Gandhi did not waste time. Side by side the early Christian contacts that he developed in South Africa, he also began to establish contacts with the Indian community. Within a week of his arrival in Pretoria he called a meeting of all the Indian residents of Pretoria to make them conscious of the disabilities they were suffering. In the meeting Gandhi gave the first public speech of his life. Besides emphasizing upon the need to be truthful even in business conduct and the observance of sanitary and hygienic conditions in life Gandhi also stressed upon the need to forget all distinctions of religion, caste, region etc. and unite together in the endeavour to better their conditions of life. He suggested the formation of an association that would enable them to make effective representation to the authorities concerned with respect to the various handicaps and hardships that were faced by the Indian community. It was proposed to hold regular meetings of the association members and Gandhi offered his services to such an association to the maximum possible extent. Through such meetings Gandhi got acquainted with many Indians in Pretoria and through the exchange of views got more facts about the living conditions of the Indian community. Assisted with such wide acquaintance and knowledge of both people and facts, Gandhi then met the British Agent who was sympathetic towards the

Indian community and secured assurance to do whatever little he could do on his behalf.

Gandhi went about tackling the problems faced by the Indian community in many ways. He tried to establish contact with the Indian community, form the Natal Indian Congress, seek support from influential people and made efforts to unify the Indian community living in South Africa. Through the contacts he developed contacts outside the Indian community, he sought to influence the officials to remove the problems faced by the Indian community. Much of his success in developing such close and lasting contacts, it has been argued, came about on account, apart from his personal character, from the lessons given to him by his legal profession. Thus, Pyarelal writes, "Through the practice of his profession Gandhiji came to know the better side of human nature and the art of entering men's hearts. It taught him the meaning and beauty of true compromise and became in his hands a potent means of reconciliation, which he put to its best use in the service of the community. He never used his legal knowledge to snatch a victory but to bring parties together on the basis of equity and justice."[3]

After settling the case, originally for which he had gone to South Africa, Gandhi was making preparation to leave for India, when, on the day of his farewell party, glancing through the pages of the *Natal Mercury,* he noticed the news about the steps being taken by the Natal Legislative Assembly to disfranchise the Indians. This, Gandhi viewed, was the first nail in the coffin of whatever little rights that the Indians were granted until then. He explained the implications of the Bill to the members present and thus made them conscious of the injustice that was being planned to be done to them. Realizing the implication of what the new Bill sought to do, the members urged Gandhi to stay on and lead them in their endeavour to resist the Bill and its malicious intentions.

Having resolved to oppose the Bill, volunteers were enrolled to carry on the work of such a protest. Telegrams requesting to postpone the discussion on the Bill in the Assembly were sent to key men holding the reigns of the government. Petitions were drawn up and signature on them from the Indian community was secured. It was later dispatched to the Assembly and a copy was sent to the press to influence the decision on the Bill. Despite all these efforts, the Bill was passed by the Assembly. Although there was no favourable effect of the initial activities, the agitation infused new life into the community; made them more conscious of their handicaps and the injustice being done to them; and instilled in them a determination to fight in unity for its political rights. Thus, Gandhi wrote, "But, the agitation infused new life into the community and had brought home to them the conviction that the community was one and indivisible, and that it was as much their duty to fight for its political rights as for its trading rights."[4] A monster petition was decided to be submitted to Lord Ripon who was then the Secretary of State for the Colonies. In the petition Gandhi defended the right of franchise of the Indians on grounds of a principled stand and expedience. He argued that the Indians in Natal had a right to franchise just as they had in India, and that since only a small part of Indian population in Natal was capable of using the franchise, it was expedient to retain it. About ten thousand signatures were obtained on the petition for circulation and distribution. It, for the first time, acquainted the Indian public with its condition in Natal. Copies were also sent to the newspapers and publicists in England and India. Through these steps Gandhi sought to create a reference public sympathetic to the grievances of the Indian community and sought to mobilize their influencing capacity to make those in authoritative positions in the Natal to concede to the Indians' demands and ameliorate their specific grievances.

Increasingly it dawned upon Gandhi that it would be virtually impossible for him to leave Natal in the near future and so he made plans to settle down in that place after consultation with his close friends and prominent members of the Indian community. He applied for admission as an advocate of the Supreme Court and secured it with some difficulty.

Gandhi soon realized that a permanent institution was indispensable for carrying on any sustained activity. Thus, he formed the Natal Indian Congress in May 1894 after deliberations with prominent members of the Indian community. Regular meetings were held to plan, discuss and improvise upon the course of resisting the Natal government. Side by side the question of internal improvement was also taken up. Lectures were therefore delivered, debates were held, and suggestions were made in the Congress meetings on subjects such as domestic sanitation, personal hygiene, the necessity of having separate buildings for houses and shops, etc. The Natal Indian Educational Association was formed to impart general information about India to young Indians who knew very little of their motherland. Efforts were made to create a love in them not only for their motherland but also for the various section of Indian community living there. These formed, Gandhi contended, a natural course of preparation for *satyagraha.*[5]

There were numerous attacks on the Congress from the government, nevertheless, it withstood all these and emerged scatheless. Gandhi decried the habit of exaggeration and every criticism was evaluated in an unprejudiced manner. Whenever weaknesses were found to exist, corrections were made. Thus, accepting the fallibility of its conception and functioning, the Natal Indian Congress duly acknowledged whatever force that existed in the arguments of its critics. It was always ready for self-introspection and openness, and believed in its capacity to progress to the utmost limit. Every occasion, where it was possible to cooperate with the Europeans on terms of equality and self respect, was heartily availed by the Indians.

When he came to India in the middle of 1896 to fetch his family, he engaged himself in highlighting the miserable condition of the Indians settled in South African colonies. He met important leaders like Gokhale, Pherozeshah Mehta, Badruddin Tayabji, Ranade, Tilak, etc., and received not only commendation for his work in South Africa but also assurances of whatever little help these leaders could make towards the amelioration of grievances faced by the Indian community.

Gandhi had to leave his work midway in India when he received a cablegram from South Africa informing him that the Natal Parliament was scheduled to meet in January 1897. So he started for South Africa in 1896. Misreporting by the newspapers of Gandhi's indulgence in vilifying attacks on the Natal Whites, and the rumour spread by them that he was coming to Natal with two ships loaded with Indians in order to swamp Natal with his countrymen, increased the existing antagonism and hatred of the Europeans for Gandhi. They left no stones unturned to prevent him from landing at Durban and when such efforts failed to deter

Gandhi, they virtually lynched him to death on his way to Rustomji's house and later on converged in on his place to get hold of him and finish him. However, Gandhi bore no grudge against his assailants and declined to prosecute them. This approach once again reflected his ethical maturity in terms of seeking no vengeance on others for the injury caused by them to his self; and of forgiving the sinners for their ignorance rather than punishing them for their sin.

Meanwhile his experiments in *brahmacharya* and simplicity of life continued; and from these experiments, it may be said, he only stood to gain during his *satyagraha* struggle in South Africa and later on in India.

When the Boer war broke out, one of the most discussed topics was whether the Indian community in South Africa should cooperate in the war efforts of the British. A few adverse comments were made about the Indian community which was initially disinterested to cooperate with British in their war efforts. They were referred as "money grubbers"; "a dead-weight upon the British"; "worms which settle inside wood and eat it up hollow"; "lacking the sense of gratitude for their masters and their host country which has done a great lot to them" and such other comments.[6]

Gandhi favoured the cooperation of the Indian community in the war efforts of the British and was able to convince his colleagues about the aptness of such a stand. In his argument he provided his conception of "loyalty to the state" and the prospects of challenging it when it tread a path that was unethical and, therefore, unacceptable to the non-cooperator. In a few ways it is akin to the Socrates' understanding of loyalty and disobedience to the state. Gandhi argued that the Indian community's existence in South Africa was solely in the capacity of a British subject. Not only had it expressed its pride in being so but also had enjoyed whatever little rights they could claim on account of their claim to British citizenship. He regarded it as unbecoming of one's dignity as a national if one remained apathetic to the dangers threatening the nation, especially in the case of a war. That the British indulged in maltreatment of the Indians, Gandhi contended, could provide no valid basis for an apathetic attitude. Having gained whatever they could on account of their British citizenship,

Gandhi argued, the crisis situation provided the opportunity to reciprocate favourably to the needs of the British Empire. Although he agreed that justice was on the side of the Boers, he said, "....every single subject of a state must not hope to enforce his private opinion in all cases. The authorities may not always be right, but so long as the subject own allegiance to a state, it is their clear duty generally to accommodate themselves and to accord their support to the acts of the state."[7] Moreover, cooperating in the war efforts of the British, Gandhi believed, would not only provide an opportunity to disprove the malicious allegations levelled against them but also act conducively in the Indian community's efforts to enjoy more freedom and welfare.[8]

However, Gandhi did not advocate blind obedience to every dictate of the state. He conceded that any individual who considered the action of his government to be immoral, before he helped or opposed the operation of such orders, should endeavour to dissuade the government from pursuing such a course.[9] The Indian community in South Africa, Gandhi argued, had not contemplated a course of dissuading the British government from participating in the Boer war; nor were they facing a moral confrontation in offering to cooperate in the war efforts of the British Empire. Hence, they were not justified in remaining a mere spectator when their host country was already knee-deep in the war. He said, "Our ordinary duty as subjects therefore is not to enter into the merits of the war, but when war has actually broken out to render such assistance as we possibly can."[10] Non-cooperation merely to escape the wrath of the repercussions following on a future date, Gandhi regarded, was a sign of effeminacy and hypocritical loyalty.[11]

The Indian community subsequently offered its services to the military corps. Gandhi organized an Indian Ambulance Corps for the British Army to attest his loyalty. Though initially the offer of the Indians was not entertained, as the casualties of the war increased and as the offer was continually renewed by the Indians, they were ultimately asked to form an Ambulance Corps to carry the wounded and the dead to the base camp. The Indians did the job well in spite of adverse and risky conditions and were commended for their services. With the hope that the good work done by the Indians in South Africa would not only enhance their reputation but also influence the British to take measures towards the amelioration of the various grievances faced by them in South Africa, Gandhi planned to return home.

He returned to India in 1901 and settled in Bombay and began his practice in the high court. Hardly had he been in Bombay for three to four months, he received an urgent cablegram from his South African counterparts asking him to come to South Africa. Gandhi wound up his Bombay office and set sail for South Africa towards the end of 1902.

When Gandhi reached South Africa he realized that the condition of the Indians settled there, instead of improving, had slumped to a worse situation. Thus, the hope of an improved living condition on account of the cooperation that the Indians lent to the British during the Boer war was dashed to the ground. The authorities, afraid of Indian traders' competition, and because of racial prejudice, became more determined to keep South Africa under the domination of the White minority. So they decided to prevent fresh emigration of the Indians and made the position of those already residing in South African colonies much more uncomfortable than before. These, they hoped, would force many of the Indians to go back to their land, while the remaining few would lead a life of slavery. A separate Asiatic Department was created to deal with the interests of the Asians settled in South Africa. The authorities of this department treated the Indians with utter contempt and insulted them whenever they got the opportunity. To make matters worse it was afflicted with corruption. The new department thus became a dreaded institution of oppression for the Indians.

Lord Chamberlain, in the meanwhile, made plans to visit the South African colonies. When he came to Natal, Gandhi, leading a deputation of the Indian community, met him and communicated to him the various grievances faced by them. Lord Chamberlain gave a courteous hearing and promised to do the needful in consultation with the Natal government. However, given the hostility of the Natal government towards the Indians and Britain's policy of appeasing the governments of South African colonies to protect and promote their colonial interests, Gandhi did not expect the changes to come about soon. Nevertheless, he made every attempt to ventilate the Indian community's grievances and seek their amelioration through every available constitutional means. He subsequently sent a deputation of The Transvaal Indian community to meet Lord Chamberlain. However, The Transvaal government prevented him from meeting Lord Chamberlain and even insulted him. The Indian deputation wanted to return without meeting Chamberlain for the insult done to Gandhi; but Gandhi persuaded them to meet Lord Chamberlain under a different leader and hand him the memorial with which they had come prepared to make him aware of the problems faced by the Indians in The Transvaal. Likewise, deputations of Indian community also waited upon other public dignitaries and government officials to convey them their grievances. Gandhi simultaneously launched his journalistic venture in South Africa in the form of *Indian Opinion*. Through it Gandhi ventilated the grievances of the Indian community and sought to create a reference public sympathetic to the Indian cause.

In the meanwhile an important thing happened. After the establishment of the British rule in The Transvaal and the Orange Free State, a committee was appointed to prepare a list of such existing laws which were prejudicial to the British. Significantly, no reference was made to go into the list of anti-Indian laws. It was very ironical that this committee which prepared the list of Acts that pressed hard upon the British also came out with the list of anti-Indian Acts. These were published in the form of a book which served as a handy manual to be easily used against the Indian community. Hitherto existing laws that were unjust to the Asian community in general, came to be more strictly enforced by the staff manning the Asiatic Department. Gandhi had nothing personal against the corrupt officers; but he disliked their way of official functioning and therefore condemned them. Nevertheless, he lent a patient hearing to whatever these officials had to say in their defence. He therefore wrote, "Such large-mindedness and such patience are essential to the understanding of *satyagraha* and above all its practice. *Satyagraha* is impossible in the absence of these qualities."[12] Similarly, his differentiation of the individual in his private capacity from that of his public capacity also formed an essential principle of *satyagraha*. He wrote, "Man and his deed are two distinct things. Whereas a good deed should call forth approbation and a wicked deed disapprobation, the doer of the deed, whether good or wicked, always deserves respect or pity as the case may be."[13]

Soon The Transvaal government came with a plan to check the immigration of the Asians. An effective re-registration of the Indian residents was envisaged. The new registration card was to contain the signature of the holder resident, or his thumb impression if he was an illiterate. Besides, his photograph was also to be pasted on the registration card. The Indian community had hardly agreed to cooperate with the government in this regard when The Transvaal government introduced in the Assembly in 1906 the notorious bill, known as the Asiatic Bill. The Bill sought to strike at the very root of the Indians' existence in The Transvaal. The Bill was full of contempt and hatred for the Indians and sought to humiliate the Indians through the harsh registration process. Reflecting on the provisions of the Bill, Gandhi commented that it was not only an insult on the Indians if they acquiesced in it but also a humiliation to their motherland.[14] Consequently, he advocated the Indians to resist the Bill and thereby uphold their individual honour and dignity. Moreover, he opined that the Indian community in South Africa had done nothing wrong to receive such a harsh treatment, and since injustice was being done to them, they should resist the Asiatic Bill.

A meeting was held in the old Empire Theatre in which about three thousand delegates from various places in The Transvaal attended. Among the few resolutions passed, the most important one was that by which the Indians solemnly resolved not to submit to the Bill if it became a law and, in the process of resisting it, undergo all the sufferings attached with such non-submission. Inspired by the advocacy of an old member, Sheth Haji Habib, to pledge to resist the Bill in the name of God, Gandhi advocated every member present there to take such a pledge after fully understanding the implications of such a pledge. He therefore explained the members the full implication of the holy pledge and advised them to indulge in a soul-searching endeavour with regard to the implications of protesting the Bill and, if their inner voice assured them of the necessary courage and strength, to take the pledge before God. To the leaders he warned that only if they believed that they had the will and ability to stand firm by the pledge taken should they pledge themselves. He therefore said, "Everyone should fully realize his responsibility, and understand that he himself must be true to his pledge even unto death, no matter what others do."[15] Simultaneous efforts were launched to meet the local authorities, communicate their grievances to them and seek redress of the same. The *Indian Opinion* was used to carry out a series of articles on the various obnoxious provisions of the Asiatic Ordinance; to denounce its inherent unjust, inhuman and unethical basis; and to contend the justification of the protest by the Indian community.

Initially, the movement was referred as "passive resistance"; but later on due to the inappropriateness of the term for the Indians' resistance movement an open competition was announced in the *Indian Opinion* to suggest a suitable name for the movement. Maganlal Gandhi suggested the word *sadagraha,* meaning firmness in a good cause, but Gandhi made a little improvisation upon it and coined the word *satyagraha.*[16]

Despite the resistance of the Indian community, The Transvaal Legislative Council passed the ordinance. Even then Gandhi and his colleagues were optimistic to believe that the British King would withhold his assent to the Bill. With this hope they resolved to send a deputation to England to appraise influential persons in Britain. Gandhi and H.O. Ali were chosen to go to England. Gandhi declared a two-fold objective of his journey:

1. to request Lord Elgin, the Secretary of State for Colonies, to refuse the King's permission to the Registration Act; and
2. to seek the appointment of a commission to inquire into the allegation of a flood of illegal Indian immigration which had served as a pretext for the Registration Act.

A memorial was prepared and submitted to Lord Elgin. Gandhi and Ali also met the Secretary of State for India, Mr. Morley, and also certain prominent British personalities like Sir Lapel Griffin, Sir W.W. Hunter, Redmond, etc. Dadabhai Naoroji too was approached and through him the British Committee of the Indian National Congress was contacted. Cooperation of some impartial and well-known Anglo-Indians was also sought. It was also decided to organize a standing committee in which all those who could cooperate and help the Indian cause were sought to be brought under one fold. Thus, the South African British Indian Committee was established. While in England, a large number of circulars and pamphlets were sent by the deputation to important public personalities.

At this point of time Gandhi was full of praise for the Englishman. Extolling the character of the British he assigned to this character the cause of Britain's success and glory in the domestic and international arena. He considered the British as highly capable and balanced men who contained, like the sea, all within themselves and could excel in whatever manner they chose to lead their life.[17] It was his advice to the Indians to imbibe these virtues of the British. Thus, he said, " ..... we must learn to recognize our rulers' virtues, which alone we should follow.... We should conclude, without looking at their faults or envying them, that they deserved all they have and for the most part of it is necessary to behave as they do."[18] To a great extent he personally tried to abide by this advocacy during his stay and activism in 1906. Thus, J.D. Hunt remarks, "In many ways, this effort in the autumn of 1906 represented the climax of Gandhi's efforts 'to behave' as they do. He intended to adopt the dress and manners of an English lobbyist, to marshal support among the most respected of Englishmen, and to enter the citadel of power with a message delivered in the accepted vocabulary of the British Constitution."[19]

After a stay of about six weeks in England, Gandhi returned to South Africa. On his way back he received the news that Lord Elgin had declared that he would advise the British King not to sign the Asiatic Ordinance in haste. The Indians were jubilant; but their joy was short-lived. When Sir Richard Solomon, a noted lawyer of South Africa and a representative of The Transvaal colony, met Lord Elgin, the latter advised him that until the time when The Transvaal was a Crown colony of Britain, the particular Bill would not be given assent by the King; however, after The Transvaal was conferred a responsible government, if it passed such a Bill then the King would not refuse his assent. Thus, Lord Elgin, while outwardly made a show of friendliness and support for the Indians, in reality supported The Transvaal government and encouraged it to pass the same Bill which he had vetoed earlier on. Gandhi described this act as crooked. He said, "I have characterized this as crooked policy, but I believe it could be given a still harsher name with perfect justice.... This is not the only or the first case of such tortuous policy followed by the British Empire. Even an indifferent student of history will easily recall similar incidents."[20] Despite these disappointments, Gandhi still considered the British rule as essentially just and as one wherein all grievances could be redressed by a recourse to representations. He said, "We have seen that British rule is essentially just and we can find redress of our grievances through representations."[21] Before he left London he wrote a polite letter of thanks in which he said, "The lessons we have drawn from above (championship of South African Indians' cause during the brief stay in London) is that we may rely upon the British sense of fair play and justice...."[22]

Encouraged by Lord Elgin's advice to Sir Richard Solomon, the new legislature of The Transvaal passed the Asiatic Registration Act, which, except for some alteration in dates, had identical provisions of the earlier Bill. The new Bill was rushed through in a single sitting on March 21, 1907, and was proclaimed to take effect from July 1, 1907. The Indians were called upon to apply for registration before July 31, 1907.

The prospects of the *satyagraha* struggle becoming imminent on account of the failure of constitutional means for redressing their grievances, a need was felt for a separate agency through which to carry on the struggle more effectively. Therefore, a new body named Passive Resistance Association was started. When finally the permit offices were opened to the Asians to get themselves registered, it was decided to picket these offices. Volunteers were posted on the roads leading to the permit offices and these volunteers were required to plead the Indians not to register themselves. At the same time, they were emphatically advised to refrain from the use of coercive tactics to prevent those who still intended to register themselves. The picketers were instead required to hand such people pamphlets explaining the injuries implied in submission to the Black Act. Towards every individual they were to behave with due respect and this included even the government officials. They were to suffer peacefully any ill-treatment imposed upon them by the authorities for such acts. Meanwhile, through the *Indian Opinion,* important news regarding the Indian community and its heroic struggle were communicated to the public in South Africa, England and India. It served as an open book for every such person, irrespective of his outlook of the *satyagraha* resistance, who wanted to measure the strength or weakness of the Indian community. Openness was deliberately kept a part and parcel of the movement by Gandhi. He remarked, "The workers had realized at the very outset that secrecy had no place in a movement, where one could do no wrong, where there was no scope for duplicity or cunning, and where strength constituted the single guarantee of victory. The very interest of the community demanded that if the disease of weakness was to he eradicated, it must be first properly diagnosed and given due publicity. When the officers saw that this was the policy of the *Indian Opinion,* the paper became for them a faithful mirror of the current history of Indian community."[23]

As the last date for getting registered drew to a close, court orders were served on those members who had not registered themselves. They were ordered to leave the country within a week's or a fortnight's time. When even these orders were not obeyed the authorities resorted to imprisonment of the defaulters. As the prison cells began to swell with *satyagrahis* who were steadfast in their determination not to submit to the Act, the government stepped down to the process of negotiating and effecting a compromise with the Indian community. Albert Cartwright, the editor of *The Transvaal Leader*, acted as a mediator between the government and the Indian community. Finally, Gandhi and General Smuts met and agreed upon a compromise formula by which Smuts promised that the Black Act would soon be replaced by General Botha as soon as most of the Indians underwent voluntary registration. General Smuts also assured that every such registration would be legalized. Commenting about the nature of compromise Gandhi said, "Compromise means that both the parities make large concessions on all points except where a principle is involved."[24] Simultaneously, Gandhi also emphasized upon the courageous and ever-trusting nature of the *satyagrahi.*[25]

Whether there existed a law or not, the government, Gandhi argued, could not exercise control over the subject without their cooperation. Differentiating a *satyagrahi's* cooperation in rendering obedience to laws, Gandhi argued that such obedience followed as a consequence of not the fear of punishment when disobeyed, but out of the consideration of such cooperation as essential for the common good. The Indians voluntarily registered in good faith and hoped that the Black Act would be soon replaced if they did so. General Smuts' subsequent action, however, shattered their hopes. He not only retained the Black Act in the statute book but also introduced in the legislature a measure which made it compulsory for every new Indian entering The Transvaal and those who had not yet registered, to get themselves registered as per the provisions of the Act.

Once again Gandhi organized a meeting to discuss the new situation with his Indian fellow men; wrote to General Smuts; discussed with a few influential Englishmen; wrote a series of articles in the *Indian Opinion* on the latest development; and presented petitions to the government on behalf of the Indians. When these constitutional means failed to bring about the desired result, an ultimatum was sent to the government in which it was stated that the certificates of registration of all the Indians would be collected and made a bonfire of if the Asiatic Act was not repealed before a specific date as determined by the Indian community. It was also declared that the Indian community would humbly face the consequences following from such an act.

When the issued ultimatum expired, once again a meeting was organized and all the registration certificates that were collected were burnt in a cauldron set up on a platform in one corner of the meeting ground of the Hamidia Mosque at Johannesburg on August 16, 1908. It was also decided to include in the *satyagraha* struggle the protest against The Transvaal Immigrants Restriction Bill which treated as prohibited immigrants all those who could pass the education test but were ineligible for registration under the Asiatic Act. The inclusion of the protest against this act was defended on the basis that it was a fresh attack on the rights of the Indian community and done with the same ulterior motive as that of the Asiatic Act. However, Gandhi did not support the view of a few colleagues who clamoured for the inclusion of the whole mass of anti-Indian legislation in The Transvaal to be given a similar treatment. Neither did he support those who suggested the mobilization of all the Indians in South Africa for a simultaneous *satyagraha* campaign against all anti-Indian legislations prevalent in all the colonies. Gandhi denounced opportunism in a *satyagraha* struggle and insisted that a *satyagraha* struggle, once it had been launched, should stick close to the original demands for which it was launched. Nevertheless, he made room for the inclusion of every such issue developing out of attempts by the adversary to create new difficulties while the struggle was in progress.[26]

To oppose The Transvaal Immigrants' Restriction Bill, it was decided that the Indians would enter individually and in groups into The Transvaal and thereby, defy the new law. The group under Daud Seth, as it tried to enter The Transvaal, was arrested and brought before the magistrate who ordered the members to leave The Transvaal within a week's time. Instead of obeying the orders, the group proceeded to Pretoria where the members were arrested and brought to court which sentenced them either to pay a fine of fifty pounds or undergo three months' imprisonment with hard labour. The group cheerfully elected to go to jail. Indians from The Transvaal joined their compatriots from Natal by either hawking without a licence or by not showing their registration certificates upon entering The Transvaal from Natal. Jails began to be filled and the authorities left no stones unturned in harassing the Indian prisoners. Finding that the threat of arrest did not deter the Indians from crossing into The Transvaal or hawking without licence, the government started deporting the Indians to their homeland. This created a furore in India and the Indian government promulgated a new law which sought to prohibit any further migration of indentured labourers to Natal. The Transvaal government was ultimately forced to stop the practice of deportation of the *satyagrahis*. Although the conditions within the jail became more harsh and difficult, the *satyagrahis* endured these with great courage and determination. However, as the struggle prolonged, both the government and the *satyagrahis* lost some of their initial vigour. While the government realized that it could not dampen the spirit of *satyagrahis* by arrest or deportation; the Indians on their part were not in a position to put up a strong fight for lack of sufficient number of *satyagrahis.* The government lost some cases which it had taken to the courts, while the Indians were weary and had become sagged in spirits.

Meanwhile, the efforts to form the Union of South Africa continued. The Indians did their bit of work by sending a deputation to England to protect and secure the basic rights of the Indians settled in South Africa. Once again Gandhi came to London in July 1909 with the aim of bringing imperial pressure to bear upon The Transvaal legislature. However, he was not beaming with the optimism he had displayed on his earlier visit. Being pessimistic about the possible outcome of the deputation, he relied greatly on the ongoing *satyagraha* struggle in South Africa. In London the deputation sought to work under the guidance of Lord Ampthill's Committee.

Not only did Gandhi have a tough time trying to influence officials in the higher echelons but also faced such allegations like that of the South African movement being fomented and funded by revolutionary and seditious parties operating in India. Called upon to clear his position, Gandhi said, "Will you excuse me for saying that I know of no Indian here, in South Africa or in India, who had so steadily, even defiantly, set his face against sedition – as I understand it – as I have. It is part of my faith not to have anything to do with it, even at the risk of my life. Most people, that is, most Indians and Anglo-Indians, expressed their detestation of bomb throwing and violence in words or in unreasonable action. The movement in The Transvaal, with which I have identified myself is an eloquent and standing protest in action against such methods. The test of passive resistance is self-suffering and not infliction of suffering on others. We have, therefore, not only never received a single farthing from 'the party of sedition' in India or elsewhere, but even if there was any offer, we should, if we were true to our principles, decline to receive it."[27] He regarded the South African Indian movement as a practical demonstration to the party of violence in India that they were entirely on the wrong track and that so long as they pinned their faith on violence for obtaining relief of any kind whatever, so long were they beating the air.[28] Despite all these valiant efforts by Gandhi, he was not successful in putting to rest the doubts raised about his loyalty. Naturally, Gandhi's prediction of making no gainful accomplishment from the deputation to London came true.

Gandhi's prediction of the futility of the Indian deputation was not a freak forecast. His growing disillusionment and bitter experiences in Britain and his own spiritual evolution by that period, culminated into a scathing attack on modern civilization. It was his belief that Britain, which had fallen into the satanic trap of modern civilization, could not renounce its vested colonial interest and think in broader, creative and humanitarian terms. From the political regime of such a representative of modern civilization, Gandhi, therefore, did not hope to make any gainful achievement. His dejection with the negative role of Britain in resolving the South African Indian issue was acute; and he did not hide his frustration. Thus, he said, "The more experience I have of meeting so-called big men or even men who are really great, the more disgusted I feel after such meeting. All such efforts are no better than pounding chaff."[29] To quote him further, "Those who occupy positions of power show little inclination to do justice. Their only concern is to hold on to their positions. We have to spend a whole day in arranging for an interview with one or two persons, write a letter to the person concerned, wait for his reply, acknowledge it and then go to his place. Even after all this fuss, one cannot be very hopeful about the outcome. If considerations of justice had any appeal, we would have got what we want long before now. The only possibility is that some concessions may be granted through fear. It can give no pleasure to a *satyagrahi* to have to work in such conditions."[30]

This scathing attack on modern civilization by Gandhi assumed the form of a powerful book – *Hind Swaraj* or *Indian Home Rule* written aboard the ship while returning from London to South Africa in 1909. He concluded herein that India was being ground down, not under the English heel, but under that of modern civilization. Thus, recognizing modern civilization as the real enemy of India's freedom, Gandhi advocated the renunciation of all things manifested by modern civilization. Merely driving out the British from India, he contended, would not solve the maladies affecting his contemporary India. The cultural threat of modern civilization, Gandhi recognized, could only be effectively dealt with by a personal regeneration of the Indians, which in turn implied the imbibing of the spiritual values inherent in Indian tradition. India, he contended, could regain its splendour and enjoy real freedom only through such a course, rather than taking recourse to violence, or any other means, to push out the British from India. His conclusion being so, he did not much object to the presence of British in India and holding the reigns of the government. Nevertheless, he was emphatic about the British adhering to a value-based political administration and serving the cause of the Indians. Thus, in the concluding part of *Hind Swaraj,* he wrote, "I admit you (the British) are my rulers. It is not necessary to debate the question whether you hold India by the sword or by my consent. I have no objection to your remaining in my country, but although you are the rulers you will have to remain as servants of the people. It is not we who have to do as you wish but it is you who have to do as we wish….."[33]

This critical tone in the *Hind Swaraj* highlighted a progressive deviation from Britain – a great nation which he admired greatly in his initial years of stay in England as a student and his deputation visits to the land as a South African Indian activist. Simultaneously, it also characterized a more positive and forward-looking approach of Gandhi towards India's rich cultural heritage and the path for regaining its lost resplendence, both of which were implicit in *Hind Swaraj.* Thus, J.D. Hunts writes, "This renunciation of London in 1909 marked the intellectual divide between Mr. Gandhi, Barrister-at-Law, and Mahatma Gandhi. The popular title did not appear for many years nor was the transformation completed in an instant, but after *Hind Swaraj* the direction was set."[34]

Meanwhile, the Union of South Africa came into being and a fresh crisis cropped up in 1913 when the Supreme Court of South Africa, in its decision in the Searle case, recognized only the validity of Christian marriages in South Africa. The marriages performed in any other traditional manner were thenceforth to be derecognized in South Africa. Consequently, while the women married in non-Christian traditions were reduced to the status of concubines, the progeny out of such marriages were deprived of their right to inherit parental property. Gandhi wrote to the Government asking whether it adhered to the Searle judgment of the Supreme Court or, if not, whether it intended to amend the law so as to recognize the validity of marriages performed according to religious customs that were recognized as legal in India. Soon, the Indian community held a meeting to discuss whether an appeal against the judgement should be made. It was decided that the idea of appealing should be dropped as the government seemed to be unwilling to side with the aggrieved in such a case of unspeakable insult. The *satyagraha* campaign once again gained its lost vigour. Women joined the ongoing struggle now. They entered The Transvaal without permits. However, when the government purposely desisted from arresting them, they took to hawking; but again the government simply ignored them with the hope that such an approach would weaken the movement. To meet this challenge it was decided that most of the remaining members at the Phoenix, mostly women, would cross over into The Transvaal and get arrested. Simultaneously, the women who had entered The Transvaal but were ignored by the officials were to enter Natal and proceed to Newcastle coal mine if they were not arrested, and there they were to request the indentured Indian labourers to go on strike. When the Phoenix members tried to cross the border and refused to reveal their identity to the police, they were arrested and taken to court which sentenced them to three months' imprisonment with hard labour. Meanwhile, the women party entered Natal and proceeded to Newcastle where they appealed to the labourers to strike work. As the women told the pathetic story of the wrongs heaped upon them by the government, the labourers were moved and decided to go on strike. The arrest and subsequent harassment of women in the jail stirred the hearts of Indians both in South Africa and in India.

The labourers of the Newcastle coal mine left their work and decided to join the *satyagraha* struggle. They faced the hardships imposed by their masters quite bravely. Gandhi reached Newcastle and advised them to shake-off the shackles of bondage and be prepared to participate in the *satyagraha* struggle. It was planned that an army of *satygrahis,* about five thousand in number, would march on to The Transvaal border and cross into it. While preparation for the march was going on, Gandhi received an invitation to meet the coal owners to resolve the issue. Therefore, he left for Durban. He sought their influence to motivate the government to repeal the Three Pound Tax. However, no concrete gains could be made out of this meeting. Finally, the march began. Gandhi made fervent attempts to reach a settlement, but to no avail. He was arrested twice, but given bail. Even such arrest of personalities like Gandhi did not dampen the spirit of the *satyagrahis*. Their non-violence and determination forced the government to take action to stop them rather than face ridicule from the English public for its failure. Gandhi was arrested for the third time on the fourth day of the eight-day-long march of thirty-six miles.

Meanwhile preparation was also made to arrest the marching *satyagrahis*. They were prosecuted and sent to jail. The coal mine compounds were declared as outstations of the jails and the arrested *satyagrahis* were forced to work in these mines. Those who refused to work were given brutal treatment. The news of such brutality spread far and wide through the press to those who remained outside the jail. In India, the South African question became the most important issue. Lord Hardinge, the Viceroy, severely criticized the functioning of the government and defended the *satyagrahis*' cause and action. Other indentured Indian workers, on hearing the facts of inhuman treatment of their brethren, decided to take a plunge in the *satyagraha* struggle. The government now resorted to the policy of "blood and iron" to force the Indians to join work. This further created adverse opinion about the government. Under pressure from all corners, ultimately it was decided to appoint a three-member commission to go into the Indian demands and give suitable recommendations to end the conflict. There were not only no Indians in the committee; worse still, it even included two members who were well known for their anti-Indian stance. So, the Indian committee lodged its protest with the government. Moreover, the majority of the *satyagrahis* were still lodged in the jail and their release too was demanded. However, when the government did not give any consideration to these issues, Gandhi went ahead with his plans.

Gandhi once again made preparations for a *satyagraha* march. Meanwhile, the European employees of the Union Railways planned to go on strike. When called upon to commence the Indian march at the same time as that of the railway strike,

Gandhi declined to agree to the proposal. Instead, he contended that the *satyagraha* movement could neither indulge in or side with a party intending to harass the government. Such chivalrous acts and other acts of humility and nonviolence, together with the pressures underplaying the scene, finally created an atmosphere favourable for a settlement. A series of dialogues between General Smuts and Gandhi continued and finally a provisional agreement was reached whereby it was agreed that the government on its part would drop the cases against the *satyagrahis* lodged in the jails and take necessary actions regarding the suggestions offered by the Commission set up to go into the cause and ameliorative means of the Indian community's grievances; the *satyagrahis* were to suspend their agitation and accept the Commission with its original proposed members and create no hindrances in its working.

The Commission finished its inquiry and, among many other things, recommended the abolition of Three Pound Tax; validation of marriages of Indians performed in any Indian tradition; and a few other concessions. Within a short time of the issue of the report, the Indians' Relief Bill was introduced in the parliament to mitigate the grievances of the Indian community with regard to the Three Pound Tax, marriages, domicile, etc. Administrative matters which did not come under the Indian's Relief Bill were settled by correspondence between General Smuts and Gandhi. Thus, the great *satyagraha* struggle ended after eight years and Gandhi decided to leave South Africa and come to India. He left for London *en route* to India on the July 18, 1914 and reached India on January 9, 1915.

Thus, Gandhi's activism in South Africa highlights the systematic and organized manner in which he went about tackling the problems of the Indians living there. His endeavour to establish contact with the Indian community, formation of Natal Indian Congress and holding its regular meetings not only enabled him to awaken the awareness of the Indian community about the officials' indifference to the basic human values and the needs of the Indian community but also helped him to create a platform for declaration of the Indian community's objection, disapproval and dissent of the unjust policies being pursued by the government in South African colonies. Through these efforts he tried to unify the diverse elements present in the Indian community in South Africa. Likewise, from the contacts he developed outside the Indian community, Gandhi sought to create an influential group of people who had the potential to impress those in authoritative position to take favourable actions to redress the grievances of the Indian community in South Africa. Simultaneously, he tried to gain sympathy for the Indian community's cause and legitimacy for its protest.

Gradually, from a lawyer enjoying good practice being concerned merely with material progress of his self and family, Gandhi started to tread into the realm of public activism to uphold the dignity of the Indians in particular and the individual in general and also into his own conscious moral or spiritual perfection. As Gandhi consciously entered into these realms he also embarked into the course of maturing political philosophy which is implicit with great significance.

The South African phase of Gandhi is significant on many counts. Practically, all the immediate demands of the Indians settled there were satisfied, at least temporarily. As a public figure Gandhi got ample focus not only in South Africa but also in England and India. His shy and timid nature quickly vanished and a brave and innovative public activist was in the process of evolution. It was during this period that one of his most important contributions to the world was made in the form of *satyagraha* or Gandhi's theory and practice of protest. Through his heuristic enterprise in South Africa, and later on in India, Gandhi gradually evolved this theory of *satyagraha*. Gandhi's work in South Africa thus produced a political method that was rich in its associative meanings and marked by an earnest commitment to gentle reconciliation between races, as well as between rulers and the ruled.[35] This activism in South Africa also prepared Gandhi for leadership of the Indian national struggle because through it he got the invaluable experience of leading poor Indian labourers, of seeing their capacity to sacrifice and bear hardship and their morale in the face of suppression.[36]

Gandhi in India (between 1915-1917)

Being away from India for twenty-eight years, and his ideas being formed outside the Indian soil, Gandhi accepted the suggestion from Gokhale – his political *guru* – to study his contemporary Indian conditions thoroughly for a year. In this year of probation from January 1915 to January 1916, Gandhi made an extensive tour of India, met important people, studied the day-to-day life of the common man and showed interest in their problems, observed the working of existing institutions and visualized his embarkation on the course of training young people for the service of their nation. For this purpose he also established the *Satyagraha Ashram* at Ahmedabad in May 1915.

As a probationer getting first-hand knowledge of Indian conditions, and also as promised to Gokhale, Gandhi refrained from speaking on controversial topics on public platform for a year. In his public address and interviews to the newspapers he largely conformed to his promise to Gokhale. He thus thanked for the felicitations offered to him for his work in South Africa; shared his *satyagraha* experiences with the people; talked about social service and the moral, material and economic regeneration of Indians; emphasized the importance of vernaculars; expressed concern for the downtrodden section of the Indian society; and expressed his concern for health, hygiene and sanitation. Although he cherished to perform social service to the nation, during the period he could not manage to conceive any concrete plan except that of the *Satyagraha Ashram* and the training therein.

Circumlocuting his views on the issue of political agitation in India, whenever he did speak, he was more emphatic about the Indians evolving their character and capacity or "reform from within" in order to facilitate the concomitant grant of privileges and rights from the Imperial Government.[37]

Gandhi also clarified his trilateral facet of being a vehement critic of modern civilization, an avowed Indian patriot and a loyalist of the British Empire. Thus, in his speech at the Madras Law Dinner on April 24, 1915, despite his earlier conclusion of Britain having unfortunately fallen into the trap of satanic modern civilization, Gandhi declared that Britain still stood for certain ideals that he cherished. Under its aegis he claimed to find not only the freest scope possible for his energies but also the satiation of his conscientious and anarchist leanings. These aspects of the British Empire, he claimed, were absent from all other governments of his contemporary time. It being so, he felt motivated to be a loyalist of the British Empire and aspired for its prosperity.[38] Moreover, it was his firm belief that Indians, on account of their rich spiritual heritage, could accept the British as their rulers while rejecting the culture represented by modern civilization. Thus, he said, "... I think that we have forces within ourselves to enable us to reject that culture (modern) without having to reject the rulers themselves."[39]

The year of probation and silence came to a conclusion by the end of December 1915. From the beginning of 1916, Gandhi started expressing his views more lucidly and succinctly on subjects which he had hitherto circumspectly avoided or circumlocuted whenever he decided to speak on them. The feeling that the British government in India was failing to satisfy the growing aspirations of the Indians and, therefore, the imminent need for the Indians to be prepared for a struggle against the government to realize these, already seemed to take root in his mind by the end of his probation period. Thus, in his speech on Arya Samaj Annual Celebration at Surat on January 2, 1916, Gandhi said, "In order to make the progress that they (Europe) are making, there are certain rights we must demand and secure from the Government. For that purpose we must get ready for a struggle... May you, therefore, read and think and learn from others in order to give a fight to the Government along the path of truth."[40]

However, more significantly, in a simple chronological sense the beginning of Gandhi's public life in India could be associated with the deliverance of his speech on the opening ceremony of the Banaras Hindu University on February 6, 1916. In his speech he thought so "audibly" about self-government and its realization by Indians, anarchist violence and mistrust of the Indians by the Englishmen, that his speech was interrupted by Mrs. Besant who requested the Chairman, Maharaja of Darbhanga, to stop him from such an objectionable speech. As Gandhi continued his speech, Mrs. Besant, The Maharaja and the Princes left the dais. Despite the controversy that the speech generated, this speech was repeated throughout the country and the echoes were heard from the Himalayas to Cape Comorin.[41] A significant part of his speech was also his statement, "If we are to receive self-government, we shall have to take it. We shall never be granted self-government. Look at the history of the British Empire and the British nation, freedom-loving as it is, it will not be a party to give freedom to people who will not take it themselves. Learn your lessons if you wish to from the Boer war."[42]

A significant conclusion drawn by Gandhi during his year of probation was the one regarding the Indians' aspiration for self-government. He was convinced that this demand was just and consistent with the principle of truth. However, he recognized that though India was vibrating with a passionate spirit of patriotism, its common mass so much feared the power of those in the authoritative positions that they desisted from fearlessly expressing their views on the government's functioning and influencing it to concede to their just aspirations.[43] These conditions, together with the super-arrogation of the British vis-à-vis the average Indians, Gandhi contended, had given rise to an unhappy relationship between the Indians and their ruling British counterparts.[44]

Gandhi visualized the Indians perfecting themselves and becoming fearless so as to generate a catalytic force for the inflow of *swaraj* or self-rule, and often expressed these views in his public speeches. Nevertheless, he seemed nonplussed in giving a pragmatic shape to any plan to realize these objectives. The death of Gokhale, he found, at this point of time, was a great setback for him personally as he was at a loss to know what to do or whether whatever little he did was being done in the right direction.[45] To make matters worse, his unique views, especially those on modern civilization, spiritualized politics, vernaculars, etc., made him unacceptable to the existing institutionalized fold of Indian politics through which he could carry on his political activism.[46] The Champaran discontentment and its amicable resolution provided him with the much needed break from this dilemmatic situation.

Champaran district in Bihar had been seething with agrarian discontentment for some time when Gandhi decided to associate himself with the resolution of the conflict. By the beginning of 19th century quite a few indigo farms and factories were set up by the European planters in Champaran. The recourse to the "tinkathia system" by them forced the farmers to reserve three-twentieth part of their land for indigo cultivation. These crops were assigned a fixed and uneconomic price. The cultivators had been either coaxed or coerced into signing agreement with the planters. They could not free themselves from this exploited situation because of the overbearing force of the structural violence inherent in the colonial set-up.

With the arrival of synthetic indigo, natural indigo was virtually driven away from the market. Consequently, the cultivation of indigo greatly declined. The planters exploited the new situation too. They agreed to release the cultivators from the obligation of growing indigo for a specific amount in return. They claimed this as "compensation" or "damages" from the peasants for not growing indigo. These planters were also responsible for inflating land-rent and a multitude of illegal exactions, in cash or kind, from the peasants. Those who tried to protest and resist the planters' exploitation were subjected to corporal punishment by the planters. The legal expenses and delays made it virtually impossible for the exploited peasants to seek the redress of their grievances.

Rajkumar Shukla, son of a prosperous Brahmin cultivator in Champaran, pleaded and persuaded Gandhi, who was by then known for his championship of the cause of indentured labourers in South Africa, to intervene in the situation and help the cultivators to seek redress of their grievances. Gandhi condescended, to visit Champaran and after having suffered various vicissitudes on the way, reached Patna on April 10, 1917.

Within a few days of his arrival in Bihar, Gandhi learnt enough to become anxious to investigate the facts himself. From Patna he went to Muzaffarpur and from there to Motihari, the district headquarters of Champaran. While at Muzaffarpur, he met L.F. Morshead, Commissioner of the Tirhut Division, within the administrative jurisdiction of which Champaran fell, and explained to him the good intention of his mission and sought the cooperation of local administration in his mission. However, Morshead was not only unconvinced about any conducive role being played by Gandhi but also recognized his intention as being a desire to precipitate an agitation. In his letter to the Champaran District Magistrate, W.B. Heycock, he requested him to serve Gandhi with an order to prevent him from remaining in

Champaran. The District Magistrate condescended to Morshead's request and served Gandhi with an order to leave Champaran by the next available train.[48] Gandhi refused to comply. He informed Heycock of his decision to disobey the orders and also wrote to the Viceroy's Private Secretary about the Champaran problem; his activism in this direction so far; and the response of those in authoritative positions.[49] Having decided to resort to *satyagraha* he, apprehending his arrest or removal from the scene, gave out detailed instructions for investigation to his workers. He appeared in the District Magistrate's Court, Motihari, and read out a statement explaining his defiance of the order. The case being outside the normal routine of such a court, the Magistrate postponed judgement, pending consultation with the local government.

The Bihar government in the meanwhile opined that the District Administration had committed serious mistakes in dealing with Gandhi. It issued orders to abandon proceedings against Gandhi and provide him with every reasonable facility during the course of his investigation. Simultaneously, it cautioned Gandhi about the excitable condition of the peasants and cautioned about any disturbance being caused to public peace.

Gandhi started his investigation. He carefully sifted evidences that were brought before him. He cross-examined each witness searchingly and discouraged exaggeration. He was convinced that the situation in Champaran was far worse than in Fiji and Natal. He described the condition of Champaran peasants as no better than that of slaves.[50] Though Gandhi originally intended to reach some sort of private agreement with the planters in resolving the vexed issue of Champaran, as his inquiries progressed he became convinced that such a compromise was virtually impossible on account of the planters' adamant stand not to condescend to the essential demands of the peasants. When Gandhi realized that the planters were too powerful for any private agreement to be feasible, he demanded Government intervention in the form of setting up a committee of inquiry for Champaran and take effective steps to prevent the prevailing abuses. Gandhi had a series of parleys with the local, district and state level officials. He also communicated the grievances to the Government of India.

As the situation worsened and the possibilities of a *satyagraha* struggle became imminent; the Government of India decided to intervene. The Viceroy soon wrote to the Governor of Bihar suggesting the appointment of a Commission of Inquiry on which a seat was to be offered to Gandhi. Initially the Governor resisted the suggestion, but on the instance of the Government of India, appointed the Champaran Agrarian Committee.

By now Gandhi, through his investigation had learnt all aspects of the agrarian problem in Champaran. Being knowledgeable, persuasive and firm, he was able to make out an irresistible case for the peasants in the course of the inquiry by the Champaran Agrarian Committee. Subsequently, the committee recommended the abolition of the oppressive "tinkathia" system and the illegal exactions under which the peasants were groaning in agony. As for the illegal recoveries, the Committee recommended a 25 per cent refund; legislations were also passed embodying the recommendations of the Committee.

The Champaran *satyagraha* was of immense significance to Gandhi's career. Before 1917 his reaction to Indian problem had largely been theoretical; the Champaran *satyagraha* provided him with a personal experience of the typical unresponsive functioning of the British government in India so far as the needs and aspirations of the Indians were concerned.

His activism in Champaran gave him an all-India public reputation. A very large number of Indians came to know about him and his way of working. He came to be regarded as a "patriot of the first order", as a "courageous man ready to brave jail and the displeasure of authorities in the cause of suffering humanity"; as a "self-abnegating and suffering patriot"; and many other such adulations were expressed in the press. Applause greeted him at the podium of the Congress. Consequently, much of criticism, levelled prior to 1917 against his idiosyncratic mannerism, ceased from being aired openly now; instead, adulation and laurel for his self and his work poured in great numbers.

A significant achievement of Gandhi was the fact that he, for the first time in India could practice politics in his own cherished way. The launch of the Champaran *satyagraha* singly, without any aid from the institutionalized fold available in his contemporary Indian political arena, greatly added to his confidence. That he could act in such a novel way and could actualize some of the ideals of his idiosyncratic mannerism served as an encouragement for him in the course of his future political activism. This was evident from the fact that he increasingly resorted to, or threatened to use, this technique of *satyagraha* for correcting unjust situations or "wrongs". On the political plane it served him as a means for realization of India's *swaraj* or self-rule.

Gandhi's Champaran *satyagraha* also left its mark on some of the members of the existing institutional fold of Indian politics. The actual implementation and the reasonable degree of success of the *satyagraha* technique made a few in the existing Congress fold to nurse some amount of optimism regarding the relevance and efficacy of this novel technique of protest. In its form it provided with an alternative mode of protest hitherto untried in Indian politics, and also as an alternative to the "unproductive" techniques of moderation and extremism so far as the realization of the aspirations of Indians were concerned.

The Champaran *satyagraha* also shaped the British government's dealing with Gandhi. His increased popularity and commendation made them very cautious and hesitant to take adverse action against him. No doubt several factors went into their consideration before they dealt with Gandhi as they did in the Champaran *satyagraha* and in future. Increasingly, as autocratic power was being tempered by schemes of constitutional reform and public opinion in England not willing to tolerate repression where conciliation was possible, the British government had to weigh the advantages and disadvantages of having Gandhi with or against them. This decision of the British depended primarily on their assessment of Gandhi's following. As a result Gandhi's public image became a pawn in politics.[51]

Through the Champaran *satyagraha* Gandhi was also able to create an inner coterie of his followers on account of whose dedication and untiring efforts Gandhi was able to stand in good stead in several of the future *satyagraha* campaigns against the British government in India and also in his dealings with the established or leading personalities within the institutionalized fold of Indian politics.

Kheda Satyagraha

Central to the Kheda *satyagraha* was the issue of the condition of the crops during 1917-18 harvesting season. Excessive rains had destroyed much of the *khariff* crops in the Gujarat region. Although the *rabi* yield was comparatively better, in the Kheda district of Gujarat, much of the cultivated land having been given over to *khariff* cultivation, the farmers could not get the advantage of *rabi* yield. The spread of plague, cholera and the inflationary and adverse conditions created by World War further added to the plight of the Kheda farmers. Confounded by these problems, the farmers requested the local authorities for remission in land revenue.

Gandhi maintained that the officials had overvalued the yield. He also contended that the suspension of land revenue, whenever adversely affected by natural calamities was, as a matter of principle, one of legal right of the peasants[52] rather than being a concession by grace of the authorities in charge. He demanded the setting up of an impartial inquiry committee to look into the issue. Being confronted with a negative and adamant attitude of the government, Gandhi advised the Kheda farmers not to pay their land revenue. This, when done in a civil manner, he contended, was not an unlawful act.[53]

On the February 4, 1918, in a public meeting at Bombay, he hinted at launching a *satyagraha* in Kheda.[54] He approached authorities both at the provincial and district level to sort out the issue; but did not achieve much success. He also personally verified facts and, on being convinced of the genuineness of the farmers' grievances, made a request for postponement of revenue collection and establishment of an independent inquiry if the government was not willing to accept his findings. When this request too was turned down, Gandhi announced the decision to launch *satyagraha* from March 22, 1918.[55] Thus, it may he pointed out that before the launch of the *satyagraha,* a brief period of petitioning and pleading was carried out. This period, around mid-December 1917, thus, continued up to March 22, 1918.

The launch of the *satyagraha* was marked by a pledge by the *satyagrahis* to refrain from paying their land revenue and suffer the consequences of such an act of defiance.[56] Gandhi not only tried to mobilize public sympathy for the Kheda *satyagrahis*' cause through mass media facilities, personal tours, etc. but also worked hard to give strength and solidarity to the campaign from within.

However, towards the end of April 1918, the crisis generated by World War influenced the British government to refrain from embarking on a collision course with the Kheda *satyagrahis* who were led by Gandhi. Craving for the native Indians' support in their war efforts, the Government of India asked the Provincial Government to make concessions consistent with preservation of the essential rights of the state. This order percolated down to the local administrative level too and the Collector of Kheda announced a few concessions and asked the local officials to deal with the defaulting farmers in a sympathetic manner. Gandhi consequently terminated the *satyagraha* on June 6, 1918.

Kheda *satyagraha* had immense significance in Gandhi's development as a leader. Not only was he able to once again successfully articulate the interests of an important segment that constituted the mass of the Indian society and to mobilize them for an effective participation in the vortex of politics in the years to come, but also was able to give a further boost to his public image.

It also brought him a step closer towards real political activism. By delving into such significant political issues like that of "government by consent,"[57] "principles of true *swaraj*,[58] "fearless resistance to abused authority,"[59] etc. during the course of the *satyagraha* struggle, Gandhi seemed to shrug off his veil of political isolationism. The following that he was able to muster, as well as adulations for his work, greatly boosted his confidence and stood him in good stead in creating a place for himself amongst the ranks of the politicians in India. Like a conventional politician he used the techniques of petitioning, organizing mass meetings, making public speeches, using the press, etc. to the best of his ability for mobilizing opinion in favour of the *satyagraha* goals and influencing the reluctant government officials to step down from their negative and adamant stand with regard to some of the cherished aspirations and just demands of the Indians. His leadership filled enthusiasm and courage in them.

This confrontation posture of Gandhi definitely told upon his relationship vis-à-vis the British rule in India. Although his integrity and concern for the Indian masses remained unquestioned by many in the authoritative positions, nevertheless, his activism was causing growing inconvenience to the authorities. Thus, for instance, in his speech at Aklacha, he said, "The Government says that authority must be respected. Authority is blind and unjust. A Government that says that such authority must he respected cannot last. Under This British rule, we are taught from our childhood that there is a rule of justice. This is their ideal. It seems to me that in place of this ideal, we have these days the rule of despotism. That is why we should rise against this Government."[60] Similarly, he said, "A Government that will not yield to such public opinion (of the Kheda peasants) deserves to he destroyed. Indeed it courts destruction. I am endeavouring to show both the government and the people that all force is utterly useless before the force of the public opinion which disdains to use violence and is based only on truth as it is apprehended by the people who are prepared to suffer to the utmost."[61] The government finding itself in an uncomfortable position was not willing to condescend to shower the same amount of favour to Gandhi as before. It was only the public force behind Gandhi and the crisis situation of war on the international scene which influenced them to concede whatever minimum they wanted to give by way of discretion. Even in granting these concessions the authorities endeavoured not to sacrifice the essential rights of the state, which under the British rule had so far been virtually synonymous with their colonial interest. The strain in the relationship between Gandhi and the British rule also became evident by the fact that not only did the authorities exercise secret vigilance on Gandhi but also, within a section of those in authoritative positions, Gandhi came to recognized as a "Bolshevik", "very dangerous person", lier, etc.[62] Thus, Judith Brown states, "It is almost unnecessary to add that Gandhi was far expanding what credit he had with the raj. The shine of the Kaiser-i-Hind Gold Medal which he had received in 1915 was tarnished by Champaran, Kaira virtually obliterated it."[63]

Although Kheda *satyagraha* helped Gandhi to carve out a place for himself in the ranks of the politicians, Gandhi, by virtue of his inclination to remain outside the realm of any particular political party or being subordinated to any of the recognized politicians of the time, was able to not only create his own coterie of able assistants but also put into practice the theory or ever growing science of *satyagraha* and thereby, testify to the public its efficacy in a variety of conflict milieu. The growing trust reposed in his leadership and the efficacy of *satyagraha* helped Gandhi immensely in his future *satyagraha* campaigns against the British rule.

The Ahmedabad Mill-Labour Satyagraha

The dispute over the amount of dearness allowance to be paid to the textile workers began with the withdrawal of a special bonus which had been granted to the workers in August 1917, to persuade them to continue work during the plague epidemic which had spread there. When, in January 1918, the mill-owners made known their intention to withdraw the bonus, the mill-workers appealed to them for granting at least 50 per cent increase on the July salaries as a continuing cost of living allowance. The basis of their claim was the contention that the cost of essential goods had actually risen more than two fold times the old prices.

Gandhi, who had by then become a public figure not only in Gujarat but also in India, was requested by Ambalal Sarabhai to intervene in the dispute and resolve it amicably in the interest of both the workers and the mill-owners. Gandhi agreed and started his investigation. He held talks with representatives of Ahmedabad mill-owners and mill-workers. Both sides subsequently agreed to submit the dispute to an arbitration board to consist of three representatives from each side and the Collector as the chairman. While Gandhi, Shankarlal Banker and Vallabhbhai Patel represented the workers; Ambalal Sarabhai, Jagabhai Dalpatbhai and Chandulal represented the mill-owners.[64]

The arbitration had scarcely got underway when the mill-workers in some of the mills, acting upon the fear of a threatened lockout, struck work. Thereupon the arbitration endeavour broke down. The mill-owners, angered by the workers action in striking before the award was given by the arbitrators, declared that they would not abide by the arbitration now. They resorted to a lock out on February 22, 1918. They also resolved to dismiss all those workers who were not willing to come to work accepting 20 per cent increase as their living allowance. On March 12, 1918, when the mill-owners ended the lock-out, the mill-workers, not satisfied with the offer made by their employers, struck work from the same day.

Gandhi's investigation led him to conclude that a 35 per cent increase was a just demand of the workers, and thereupon advised the workers to demand no more and no less that a 35 per cent increase. The goal to realize the minimum became a part of the sacred pledge undertaken by the workers at Gandhi's instance. When the mill-owners rejected this demand, Gandhi, who had entered the situation as a conciliator, became the leader of the workers and advised the resort to *satyagraha* as a means through which a constructive solution could be achieved.

Gandhi visited the workers' houses and spoke at public meetings to educate the workers about the struggle. He wrote several leaflets "with a view to fixing firmly in their (workers) minds the principles and significance of the struggle, and to supply them with simple but elevating literature which would conduce to their mental and intellectual development and enable them to leave for posterity a heritage of the means for its progress."[65] Daily parades were taken through the streets of Ahmedabad with banners reading united resolve. The *satyagraha* pledge was repeated daily at meetings.[66] Daily information bulletins were issued and every emerging problem was tackled in the daily meetings. Abiding by the principle of self-sufficiency, Gandhi advised the workers to earn a living by undertaking other forms of labour during the strike period. He also instructed the labourers on health and hygiene observances.

When some workers found it difficult to continue the strike, they decided to accept the 20 per cent increase in dearness allowance announced by the mill-owners and to resume work. Gandhi, disturbed by such actions and other weaknesses emerging from within, intensified his appeal to the labourers to remain firm in insisting the demand for a 35 per cent increase and to continue the strike until this just demand was conceded. When such appeals fell on deaf ears, Gandhi announced his resolve on

March 5, 1918 to undertake fast till all the workers desisted from going to work in the mills. On March 18, the evening of the third day of fast, Ambalal Sarabhai, the leader of the mill-owners, offered to concede 35 per cent increase to the workers. He also brought to Gandhi's knowledge the mill-owners pledge and the confounding difficulties in resolving the conflict.[67] He requested for a compromise formula to settle the issue.

Gandhi agreed to settle the dispute by arbitration and to compromise on the details of the settlement.[68] Prof. Anandshankar Dhruva, Vice-Principal of Gujarat College, was made the arbitrator and requested to submit his decision within three month's time. Gandhi ended his fast upon the announcement of the settlement. Leaders from different sections of the labourers made speeches in which they expressed their gratitude to Gandhi; sweets were distributed to express their joy.

The Ahmedabad *satyagraha* helped Gandhi to build up an even firmer base for himself in Gujarat. Thus, while the Kheda *satyagraha* provided him with an effective rural base so far as his leadership was concerned, the Ahmedabad *satyagraha* served as a catalyst in his building an urban base in Gujarat. The Ahmedabad *satyagraha* ensured him the support base of industrial workers – an important constituent of Indian mass. At the same time, the alliance between Gandhi and the Ahmedabad industrialists too was not strained because in Gandhi's friendship the industrialists' interests seemed to be more effectively served.

Although Gandhi secured the position of a very powerful leader in Gujarat's public life, he secured this position by delving into issues which did not conventionally come within the scope of political activism prevailing in India. Nevertheless, it may be said that the *satyagraha* techniques used in these cases helped Gandhi to influence public events. Thus for instance, his fast in the Ahmedabad *satyagraha* was a forerunner of his hunger-strikes in all-India politics.[69] Some of the essential principles of *satyagraha* like demanding a minimum consistent with truth, steadfast adherence to this minimum truth, compromising on details without compromising on principles, recognizing the importance of a pledge, striving to realize self sufficiency or self-reliance, working for the mental and intellectual development of the protesting *satyagrahis*, etc. were advocated or emphasised by Gandhi during the conduct of this *satyagraha*.

Gandhi in Indian Politics

Pre-Rowlatt Satyagraha Period

The pressures of the First World War on Britain and the consequent British policy towards India played a significant role in Gandhi's transformation into a political leader of national stature. Embroiled in the World War, Britain sought to secure their hold over India as it was one of its most resourceful colonies and, therefore, indispensable for Britain if it wanted to win the war. In order to secure their position, they followed a "conciliation-repression" policy. Thus, while on the one hand, they planned a further devolution of power to contain the growing discontent of the Indians and attract their Indian sympathizers who would provide a stable foundation to their rule, on the other hand, they sought to pursue a repressive policy against those Indians who sought to threaten their authoritative position in India.

The devolution of power, one of the most significant aspects of Britain's conciliatory approach towards the Indians, came on August 20, 1917 by way of Montague's announcement, as the Secretary of State for India, that Britain would like to seek an increasing association of Indians in every branch of administration and the gradual development of self-governing institutions with a view to the progressive realization of responsible government in India as an integral part of the British Empire. This announcement produced a mixed reaction amongst the Indians. Thus, on the one hand, there was a section of Indians who welcomed the announcement and tried to influence the touring Montague and Chelmsford to protect and promote their specific interests, on the other hand, there was a section which criticized the reform as inadequate when it was finally passed as an Act in 1919.

In the acceptors of the Reform proposals, Britain found its Indian collaborators who would participate in the actual implementation of the Reform and also help it to continue its colonial rule without conceding to the Indians anything substantial that would adversely affect their vested colonial interest. Towards the discontented challengers, Britain sought to pursue a policy of repression. Thus, it sought to restrain through internment some prominent leaders like Annie Besant, Ali Brothers, etc., who had become a constant source of embarrassment to the British rule in India.

Gandhi, having acquired a public image, could not withdraw himself from expressing his opinion on the Montague-Chelmsford Reform. He declared that he cherished the goal of self-rule for Indians, but before that could be realized the Indians should become capable of exercising self-rule. Although not anti to the Montague-Chelmsford Reform, he had his reservations. The proposal, he commented, "deserved a sympathetic handling rather than a summary rejection".[70] Its shortcomings, he opined, could be removed through an agitation.[71] He was also emphatic about the British interest being subservient to the Indian interest, and for that reason, the rejection of the provision of diarchy in the proposal and a simultaneous increase in Indians' participation in the administration.[72] By condescending to express his opinion on such an important event happening in the Indian political scene, Gandhi departed from his hitherto adopted position of refraining from taking an all-absorbing interest in controversial politics. However, this was not only inevitable for him because he had come to acquire a public image but also could not have been postponed for long keeping in view the course of events occurring on the Indian political scene. As a public man, his fame being given a boost by his Champaran, Kheda and Ahmedabad *satyagrahas,* his comments on the Reform proposals carried considerable weight and several Indian politicians valued his approval and angled for his support on the reform question.

Yet another all-India issue with which Gandhi made his presence felt in the Indian political scene was that of helping Britain in its war efforts by way of military recruitment from the Indian soil. Defending the British participation in the war on account of its stated objective of preserving and promoting the freedom of humanity in general, Gandhi actively participated in the recruitment drive. He argued that Indians had the moral responsibility of helping Britain in the war because under the British aegis Indians had drawn quite a few benefits and must, therefore, reciprocate their gratefulness by way of helping Britain in its time of difficulty.[73] Participation in the war, he contended, would be a training for the Indians in courageously and self-reliantly defending themselves, which in turn, was indispensable for realizing and enjoying *swaraj* or self-rule.[74]

Two incidents which were symbolic of the repressive facet of British policy in India: (i) Annie Besant's internment, and (ii) Shaukat and Mahomed Ali Brothers' internment also marked Gandhi's embarkment in controversial issues in Indian Politics and protest against the established rule to seek the amelioration of grievances flowing from such repressive measures. Perceiving Annie Besant's internment to be a grave injustice or "wrong", Gandhi made a nation-wide appeal to protest this action and get the injustice undone. He criticized the government for having committed a big blunder and demanded the revocation of the internment order. He even advocated to the Congressmen to adopt passive resistance to seek the revocation of the internment order. Similarly, Gandhi considered the internment of Ali brothers as a great act of injustice and made an all-out political effort to champion their release.

These two incidents, and Gandhi's reaction to them, immensely contributed to Gandhi's stature as a politician. Sensing the mood and aspirations of the Indian masses, he now seemed to shrug off the veil of cautious aloofness from controversial issues in Indian politics and seemed more forthcoming in his criticism of British government and activism in protesting their unjust acts. These incidents prepared him for the national role he was to play in the future as an ardent champion of the rights of the Indians. Thus, he entered the political arena of India as a serious political protagonist. Moreover, as a consequence of his championship of Ali brothers' cause, Gandhi not only came to be recognized as a non-Muslim leader having considerable backing of the Muslim community and as its spokesman, but also as a leader who could effectively mobilize them for a definite cause. One also finds a few strains of Gandhi's thought regarding state's duties towards its citizens and the citizen's reciprocal loyalty and duty towards such a state. Gandhi also aired his views on such subjects like the importance and need to protest a state which attempts to commit injustice or "wrongs" and the manner in which to go about protesting such actions of the state.

Rowlatt Satyagraha

The recourse to the Rowlatt Act marked a step further in the direction of consolidation of British regime in India through repressive measures. Through the Rowlatt Bill the hands of the government to control crime and sedition were sought to be strengthened. The government defended the Act by claiming that it was only a preventive measure to be brought into operation only when the Governor General was satisfied about revolutionary activities threatening the administration in any part of India. It was also contended by the British that the existence of an investigating authority to examine the proofs upon which such orders were served against persons further prevented the misuse of the Act. Nevertheless, the Indians conceived it as opposed to the principle of liberty, justice and elementary rights of the citizens. It was also perceived as not only a fall back on the promise made by British statement before war but also an indication of the British being least interested in granting genuine self-rule to the Indians.

The contemporary politicians unanimously decried this action of the government. However, given the limitations of their conventional protesting methods, they were at a loss to devise a strategy that would help them to effectively counter such repressive action of the British government. Gandhi, through his advocacy of resorting to *satyagraha* on the issue, provided a way out of this political impasse.[75]

Gandhi was deeply stirred by the proceedings of the government with regard to the Rowlatt Bill. He recognized the Bill as not merely a stray example of lapse of righteousness and justice but as an evidence of a determined policy of repression by the British Administration.[76] Resisting such an autocratic or tyrannical rule, he exclaimed, was an open challenge to the Indians and warned the government about a massive agitation if it was adamant in carrying forward such a devilish legislation.[77]

A *satyagraha* pledge was drawn on February 24, 1919. It stated that the Rowlatt Bill, being unjust and subversive to the principle of liberty and justice, and destructive of the elementary rights of individuals on which the safety of the community as a whole and the state itself was based, would be civilly disobeyed in the event of it becoming a law, and continued to be done so until it was withdrawn. It further stated that the protesters would abide by truth and non-violence.[78] Gandhi also communicated his intention to offer *satyagraha* and commit civil disobedience in the event of the bill becoming an Act.

He appealed to the government to reconsider its decision on the Rowlatt Bill. During the entire month of March, wide-scale publicity was given through press, meetings, pamphlets, etc. to the Rowlatt Bill and its unjust aspects. A *Satyagraha Sabha* was also established with Bombay as the headquarters for the movement and a committee was constituted to select laws which were to be civilly disobeyed. A call for *hartal,* on March 30, 1919, was given. Later on, the date was postponed to April 6, 1919. Gandhi appealed to the people to observe the day as one of "humiliation and prayer" and every *satyagrahi* was required to observe a 24-hour fast as a discipline to fit him to offer civil disobedience. Those who did not undertake the pledge or fast were also permitted to participate provided they pledged to follow "truth" and refrain from violence under all circumstances.

Unfortunately, in some areas like Delhi, the *hartal* was observed on 30th March on account of communication gap. Demonstrations were taken through the streets and shops were closed. However, there were incidents of violence and scenes of rioting. The police resorted to firing and a few people lost their lives. Gandhi condemned the government action and emphasized about the responsibility of the *satyagrahis* to uphold "truth" and non-violence and maintain peace and order. In other parts of country, April 6, 1919 was observed as a day of *hartal.* At Bombay Gandhi addressed a huge gathering and emphasized upon several aspects of the struggle against the Rowlatt Bill.[79] In a series of leaflets, public addresses and press statements, Gandhi issued several instructions and guidelines for the *satyagrahis*.

The *Satyagraha Sabha* at Bombay issued instructions for defiance of laws governing prohibited literature and registration of newspapers. Gandhi's *Hind Swaraj, Sarvodaya* and *Story of a Satyagrahi,* along with the *Life and Address of Mustafa Kamal Pasha,* were the selected literature for dissemination.[80] The first issue of Gandhi's *Satyagraha,* came out without registration. Gandhi communicated to the people through a series of leaflets through which he explained the concept of *swadeshi,* emphasized upon communal amity and educated as to how to civilly, courageously and nonviolently defy selected laws.[81]

Gandhi decided to visit Delhi to pacify the people there over the incidents that occurred on March 30, 1919 and to express sympathies to the victims. On way to Delhi, however, he was served with orders on April 9, 1919, restricting his entry into Punjab and Delhi. When Gandhi decided to disobey the order he was put under arrest and sent to Bombay where he was set free.

The news of Gandhi's arrest spread like fire. An all-India *hartal* was planned to protest his arrest on April 10, 1919. However, this *hartal* was marked with incidents of incendiarism, riot and mob violence in certain places like Ahmedabad, Amritsar, etc. Some Europeans were killed and public property destroyed. Some Indians lost life when the police opened fire. In Punjab Gandhi's arrest coincided with the arrest and deportation of two prominent Punjab leaders – Dr. Satyapal and Dr. Kitchlew – by the Punjab government. To protest these arrests and the repressive measures of the martial regime under Michael O'Dwyer, the public organized demonstrations and processions. There were also incidents of mob rising, police firing and killing of several Europeans. At Jallianwalla Bagh, in Amritsar, a gathering of about ten thousand in strength had assembled to protest against the arrest of their leaders and the tyrannical rule of O'Dwyer. Brigadier General Dyer, under whose command the military troops had succeeded in quelling mob violence, decided to break-up the meeting. He marched up to the garden with his troops and fired at the gathering without warning. The appalling casualties that followed terribly shook the Indians. There were also scenes of disturbances in Bombay, Viramgam and Nadiad. In Calcutta riots and bloodshed occurred. There were also instances of stone throwing, burning of public buildings and cutting of telegraph lines.

Deeply disturbed by the turn of violent incidents in the course of the *satyagraha,* Gandhi suspended the *satyagraha* on April 18, 1919.[82] He described this *satyagraha* endeavour as a "Himalayan blunder" and announced a three days penitential fast. He also advised the *satyagrahis* to fast and confess their guilt. He realized that the people had not been properly prepared for offering *satyagraha* and decided that before any such movement was launched in future by him, he would create a band of well-tried, pure-hearted volunteers who understood the essence of *satyagraha*. Gandhi, therefore, raised a corps of volunteers and commenced the work of educating the public regarding the meaning and practice of *satyagraha*.

The Rowlatt *satyagraha,* being suspended before it reached its natural conclusions, was not able to realize the objectives that it had set forth. However, the strong reaction of the public expressed through the *satyagraha* influenced the government to drop the second Rowlatt Bill which sought to bring a permanent change in the ordinary Criminal Law of the land. The Rowlatt *satyagraha* deviated greatly from the idealized principles of a *satyagraha* campaign as conceived by Gandhi. The course of the events greatly disturbed Gandhi and he acknowledged his mistake in launching the Rowlatt *satyagraha*.

Nevertheless, the Rowlatt *satyagraha* played an important role in Gandhi's political advancement in India. He established himself as an all-India leader with immense potential. Through his method of *satyagraha,* he offered a way out of the existing impasse in the political scene so far as the aspirations of the Indians and the adamant attitude or resistance of the British government to concede these were concerned. As a technique of resistance to abused authority and tyrannical rule, *satyagraha,* under Gandhi's guidance, became the articulating force of multifarious local grievances and enabled their alignment with the national cause to get a decent treatment from the Imperial Government.[83]

The unfortunate course of events in the *satyagraha* demonstrated certain weakness of Gandhi's all-India leadership. Conscious of his strengths and weaknesses, Gandhi subsequently decided to play a more direct, active and larger part in Indian politics in order to lead India towards his vision of certain idealized goals and in conformation with certain idealized pathways. His participation in the Congress at Amritsar was reflective of this mood of Gandhi. He himself acknowledged, "I must regard my participation in Congress proceedings at Amritsar as my real entrance into the Congress politics. My attendance at the previous Congress was nothing more perhaps than a renewal of allegiance to the Congress. I never felt on these occasions that I had any other work cut out for me except that of a mere private, nor did I desire more."[84] He, thus, became a serious contender of leadership not only in the forum of Congress but also for India.

Non-Cooperation Movement

One motivating factor for Gandhi in the termination of Rowlatt *satyagraha* was also the event of announcement of the Royal Proclamation of December 1919 which accompanied the Reform Act and called for a new era of cooperation between the rulers and the ruled. It raised in Gandhi a flicker of hope and he believed that the British rulers in India would be true to those ideals which were an inherent part of their system in Britain. This hope, which lay at the core of his loyalty to the British rule, influenced him to recognize the proclamation and the reforms as an earnest intention of the British to conform to these ideals and, in the Indian context, to do justice to the Indians. He advocated the Indians to cooperate with the British to make the reforms successful and to simultaneously work hard to realize those just hopes and aspirations which remained to be fulfilled.[85]

However, these fond hopes of Gandhi were once again belied by the British. Their failure to keep up their promise to the Muslims with regard to the Turkish Empire and the ruler who was recognized as the Khalipha or the religious leader of the Muslims; the report of the Hunter Commission which acquitted those officials guilty of crimes in Punjab; and the general failure of petitioning, prayers and protest to make the British concede *swaraj* to the Indians or becoming a more responsive and responsible government in tune with the Indians aspirations, dashed the hopes of Gandhi. These events exposed the facade of Britain's claim of a faith in democratic ideals and reflected the flagrant violation of the principles of fair play, justice and respect for individual freedom and dignity. In their essence they sought the perpetuation of the vested colonial interest of the British and maintenance of their enviable position as rulers of India – a position which had become indispensable for protecting and promoting their colonial interests.

The genesis of the Khilaphat trouble in India could be traced to the backing out from the promise that the British made to the Muslims of India with regard to the treatment to the Muslim religious head or the Khalipha, who was the ruler of Turkey, in return for their participation on the side of Britain in World War I. As a result of the terms of the armistice signed after the end of the war, the power of the Khalipha was curtailed to a great extent and Turkey was deprived of some of her erstwhile homelands.

Such a handling of the Turkish issue was not only regarded by the Muslim community as a clear denial of the just claims that they had made to Britain as a precondition of their participation in the war on the side of Britain, but also as an open betrayal of the pledges publicly given by some of the responsible British statesmen like Lord Asquith and Lloyd George. As a fellow countrymen, Gandhi too thought on the same lines as the Muslims.[86] He conceived the British handling of the Khilaphat issue as being unjust and asked the government to secure a proper solution to the grievances of the Muslims with regard to the Khilaphat.[87] He advocated the need to make a common cause for Hindus and Muslims over the Khilaphat issue and recognized that a resort to *satyagraha* should he made if the government failed to make efforts towards the amelioration of the Khilaphat grievances. A *satyagraha* in support of Khilaphat, with a majority of Hindu participation, Gandhi viewed, would go a long way in realizing Hindu-Muslim unity, which in turn would go a long way in the realization of *swaraj* for India.

Efforts towards the redress of grievances with regard to the Khilaphat issue got institutionalized in the form of a Central Khilaphat Committee with Bombay as its headquarters. In its initial phase of working it was characterized by a calculated moderation. There were sporadic meetings to voice Muslim aspirations and fears. On March 19, 1919, the Bombay Khilaphat Committee passed a resolution to pursue a concentrated plan of action. It began to organize an intensive agitation throughout India, entering into close cooperation with the more extreme pan-Islamists in northern India for the purpose. An All-India Khilaphat Conference was organized at Lucknow on September 21, 1919. The most important decision in the conference was that of observing October 17, 1919, as a Khilaphat Day.

Gandhi, in the meanwhile, made efforts for mobilizing both the Hindus and Muslims for the Khilaphat cause. He tried to establish close alliance with some of the Muslim and Hindu leaders; addressed a Khilaphat meeting at Bombay, and welcomed the suggestion of Lucknow Conference to observe October 17, 1919 as a Khilaphat Day. He widened the suggestion by urging both Hindus and Muslims to observe the day as one of prayer, fasting and *hartal.*[88] In the Central Provinces and the presidencies of Bombay, Madras and Bengal there was considerable mobilization of the Hindus and Muslims towards making the observance day a success. In certain places like Delhi there were extraordinary scenes of fraternization between the Hindus and Muslims.

The Khilaphat movement received a boost with the All-India Khilaphat Conference at Delhi in November, 1919. In the Conference the militant Khilaphatists held their sway. One of the important resolutions adopted in this Conference was that of resorting to non-cooperation if the government continued to disregard their views on the Khilaphat issue. A sub-committee was appointed to look into the question of non-cooperation. Gandhi in his speech supported the idea.[89]

Towards the end of December 1919, Ali brothers were released and so was Maulana Abul Kalam Azad. Their militant views on the Khilaphat issue brought them closer to the militant Khilaphat activities like those from United Province and the Bengal. The moderates gradually lost their sway over the Khilaphat movement. The militant delegates, ulemas and journalists now ascended the driving seat. With this change, the movement penetrated beyond provincial centres into small towns and villages.

Another Khilaphat Conference was convened in Amritsar towards the end of December 1919. Both the Congress and the Muslim League participated in it. It was resolved herein to send a deputation to put before the Viceroy the three-fold Khilaphat claim.[90] The Viceroy conveyed his sympathies for the Muslim feelings. Though he assured his best efforts for their cause, he hinted that the Peace Conference would not be able to concede all the demands of the Khilaphat agitators. Gandhi denounced such vague assurances. Mere promises of best efforts, he contended, was not what the Indians wanted from their rulers; instead, they wanted their rulers to identify themselves with their sentiments and make an all-out effort to ameliorate their grievances and fulfil their aspiration.[91]

The next all-India conference on Khilaphat was held from February 15 to 17, 1920, in Bombay. There was great pressure from the militant section to recourse to boycott of British goods and withdrawal of cooperation from the government. Some of the militants had become so frustrated with moderate protest and its inefficacy to resolve the Khilaphat problem in a satisfactory way that they demanded very stringent measures against the British government. Thus, the Bengal Khilaphat Committee passed a resolution to observe yet another Khilaphat Day; while some urged Muslims to abandon their loyalty to the British, others advocated a *jihad* or a holy war against the British. On March 7, 1920, Gandhi came out with his own plan for the amelioration of the Khilaphat grievance. He suggested that March 19, 1920 be observed as a Khilaphat Day and advocated the recourse to *hartal* on the day. He was emphatic about the need to abstain from violence on the day. He also recognized the need to desist from a recourse to boycott or mixing other questions like Egypt with the Khilaphat issue.[92] Most significantly, he advocated that if the demands were not met even after the second Khilaphat Day, then they should resort to non-cooperation.[93] Being the principal member of the committee to decide the plan of non-cooperation. Gandhi suggested a phased manner of non-cooperation. It was suggested that initially the Indians should relinquish their titles and honours and subsequently resign from council membership, withdraw from government services, and finally refuse to pay taxes.

The publication of the Peace Treaty on May 14, 1920 proved true the fears of the militant Khilaphat agitators about the inefficacy of moderate protest on the Khilaphat issue. The need to adopt a stronger means to seek the redress of the Khilaphat grievance, thus, became imminent. Gandhi described the peace terms as "a staggering blow to the Indian Musalmans" and advocated non-cooperation as a way to secure justice.[94] The Viceroy was sent another representation from the Central Khilaphat Committee requesting him to champion the Khilaphat cause of the Indian Muslims. The representation conveyed the message to him that the peace terms were unacceptable to the

Indian Muslims and warned him that the Muslims, along with the Hindus, would resort to non-cooperation from August 1, 1920, if the Peace terms were not revised.

Gandhi sent a letter to the Viceroy in which he said that he was advising the Muslims to adopt non-cooperation because it was the only form of non-violent direct action now remaining with them to seek the redress of their grievances. He declared that though he was advocating non-cooperation to the Muslims, he himself had not lost faith in the British Constitution. By combatting the "wrong" done to the Muslims with regard to the Khilaphat, Gandhi contended, he was trying to correct the "wrong" done and thereby, retain his loyalty.[95] Appealing to the Muslims and Hindus to prepare for non-cooperation from August 1, 1920, Gandhi said, "Let us hope that the Viceroy will have wisdom enough to take up the people's fight. The British Empire, however, is not so fortunate as to see such a glorious day. Hence, we have no choice but to prepare for non-cooperation from August 1. The non-cooperation about which there has been so much talking and which has consumed so much paper and ink is near at hand."[96]

In June, 1920, the Imperial Government published the report of the official inquiry into the cause of general discontentment in Punjab and the events that led to the Jallianwala Bagh massacre. Gandhi had until then not only desisted personally to align the Punjab issue with the Khilaphat issue to mobilize Hindus along with the Muslims but also prevented other leaders' efforts to mix such issues with the Khilaphat question.[97] Like other Indian leaders Gandhi too was pained to note the repressive martial regime under Michael O'Dwyer and the course of violent events happening in Punjab. However, unlike other national leaders, he refrained himself from making comments on the actions taken under the martial law. Rather than criticizing the government actions without evidence in his hands, Gandhi made repeated campaigns for an official inquiry into the unfortunate chain of events in Punjab. When the government announced the appointment of the Hunter Committee to inquire into the Punjab happenings, Gandhi was sanguine and conciliatory. To the dissatisfied Indians, especially those who were critical of the persons appointed to the committee, and those unhappy about it not being a Royal Commission, Gandhi advised to trust it and to bring evidence before it so that it could undo the "wrong" or the injustice that had already been done.[98]

Through the Congress sub-committee, of which Gandhi was a member, appointed to inquire into the events that took place in Punjab, Gandhi got first-hand knowledge of the whole issue. When, ultimately, the Imperial Government published the Hunter Commission Report, Gandhi was so rudely shaken by the efforts of the committee to whitewash the events in Punjab and acquittal of officials who indulged in brutal crimes, that his belief in the British sense of fair play and justice started crumbling. He termed it as a "political freemasonry" and declared that a scandal of such magnitude could not he tolerated by the Indians.[99] He said, "In my opinion the time has arrived when we must cease to rely upon mere petitions to Parliament for effective action. Appeal to the Parliament by all means if necessary, but if the Parliament fails us and if we are worthy to call ourselves a nation, we must refuse to uphold the government by withdrawing cooperation from it."[100] Thus, Gandhi, sensing the British attempt to condone official lawlessness and whitewash the ghastly massacre of the people assembled at Jallianwalla Bagh and their imperviousness to the Indians' aspirations, linked the Punjab and Khilaphat issue in June 1920, and made them the chief issues for embarking upon a course of non-cooperation with the British government. In the special session of the All-India Congress in September, 1920, at Calcutta, these two issues of Khilaphat and Punjab wrongs along with the reluctance of British government to concede the demand for *swaraj* were recognized as the core reasons for non-cooperating with the British government, and a resolution to this effect was passed. The resolutions adopted at the Calcutta special session of the Congress were later confirmed at its annual session at Nagpur in December 1920.

A detailed programme of non-cooperation was conceived and efforts were made to educate the public about it. The Non-Cooperation Movement had within it certain negative and positive programmes besides the warning of civil disobedience as a last resort. The Indian National Congress under the leadership of Gandhi envisaged a seven-point Non-Cooperation Programme, which can be labelled as the negative programme of non-cooperation. These were:

1. Surrender of titles and honorary offices given by the government and resigning from government jobs.
2. Boycott of schools and colleges run or aided by the government.
3. Boycott of elections proposed by the Act of 1919.
4. Boycott of courts established by the British in India.
5. Boycott of foreign goods and trade.
6. Boycott of functions organized by the government.
7. Non-cooperation with Britain's international activities like the one in Mesopotamia.

On a more positive note the non-cooperation had the following programmes:

1. Spinning and propagation of *khadi*.
2. Removal of untouchability.
3. Setting up of arbitration board of traditional *Panch* institutions to resolve interpersonal conflicts.
4. Setting up of national schools and colleges.

If these programmes failed to realize the objectives of the Non-Cooperation Movement then, as a last resort, a warning to adopt civil disobedience was conveyed by Gandhi in his letter to the new Viceroy, Lord Reading.

Gandhi made efforts to reorganize the Indian National Congress on a more representative basis. Not only was Congress membership thrown open to the poor masses of big and small towns and villages but also it was organized in such a way that it continuously functioned efficiently between its annual sessions.

Gandhi promised to the Indian masses "*swaraj* within a year" if they participated actively in the Non-Cooperation Movement and showed courage and readiness to make great sacrifices while adopting peaceful and legitimate means.

Gandhi toured the whole of India with several other nationalistic leaders and informed and motivated the public to participate in the Non-Cooperation Movement. Gandhi himself returned to the Viceroy his South African war medals and his Kaiser-i-Hind gold medal and claimed that he could no longer continue to respect or show affection to the British government which committed wrongs one after the other to defend its immorality. Following Gandhi, many leaders and individuals among the Indian public renounced their British titles and other decorations and enthusiastically participated in the various programmes of non-violent non-cooperation.

The failure of the government's reaction in this regard – be it the initial recourse to a policy of non-interference or the subsequent recourse to appeasement of the prominent leaders on efforts to dissuade them from the continuation of the movement – ultimately compelled it to use its brutal force in the form of arrest of and violent acts against the non-violent non-cooperators. Volunteer organizations were declared illegal; public meetings and processions were forcibly dispersed, mass arrests were made and those arrested were often violently maltreated.

As one whole year (from the Nagpur session of Congress in December 1920 to Ahmedabad session in December, 1921) drew to a close, there appeared to be no signs of achieving "*swaraj* within a year" as Gandhi had promised. There was dissention in Congress ranks; unrest in the public and criticism of Gandhi. Some nationalists yearned for rebellion. However, Gandhi did not support such violent means for realizing *swaraj*. He stuck to his original position (while starting the Non-Cooperation Movement) that violence cannot be the means to realize *swaraj*. He had repeatedly drawn the attention of the participators to the self-purification aspect of a *satyagraha* struggle. At the same time he dispelled criticism of showing cowardice by sticking on to nonviolence in the midst of violence and repression of the government. He made it clear that in the event of the Non-Cooperation Movement becoming violent, he would take all steps to end the same and prevent it from engulfing the nation. He condemned the violence when assaults were made on Europeans, Parsis and others who participated earlier that day on November 17, 1921, in the official ceremony organized when the Prince of Wales arrived at the Gateway of India, Bombay. Gandhi made personal appeals to Indians to refrain from such violent acts and undertook fast until when these disturbances stopped.

Although this burst of violence influenced Gandhi to postpone civil disobedience action, the widespread arrest and prosecution of Congress workers and volunteers in December

1921 and January 1922, made Gandhi review his stand on civil disobedience. However, instead of a nation-wide civil disobedience he preferred a limited civil disobedience at Bardoli in Gujarat where he could personally supervise the activities of the participants. On February 1, 1922, Gandhi informed the Viceroy Lord Reading through a letter about this and gave him seven day's time to suspend all the repressive actions being taken by government against the Indians.

Unfortunately, on February 5, 1922, a violent clash occurred between the non-cooperators and the police at Chauri Chaura, a small village in Gorakhpur district in United Province. The news of this violent incident reached Gandhi three days later and he was greatly disturbed. He exclaimed that India was not yet ready to undertake civil disobedience and revoked the plans of civil disobedience in Bardoli. On February 24, 1922, in the All India Congress Committee meeting at Delhi, at Gandhi's instance a resolution was passed which deplored the Chauri Chaura incident, suspended mass civil disobedience anywhere in India and shifted emphasis to constructive programme. Thus, the Non-Cooperation Movement finally came to a formal end on February 24, 1922.

Despite the fact that the Non-Cooperation Movement was not able to realize the objectives which it had set forth to realize, the movement was of great significance for both Gandhi and India. Under Gandhi's leadership Congress transformed into a truly national and mass movement. To quote M. Mukherjee, "It certainly demonstrated that it commended the support and sympathy of vast sections of the Indian public. After non-cooperation, the charge of representing a microscopic minority, made by Viceroy Dufferin, in 1888, could never again be hurled at the Indian National Congress. Its reach among many sections of Indian peasants, workers, artisans, shopkeepers, traders, professionals white collar employees, had been demonstrated. The spatial spread of the movement was also nationwide."[101] Similarly, Bhikhu Parekh says, "The Non-Cooperation Movement served notice on the Raj and made political independence a widely shared national goal. It radicalized a large number of Indians, drew them into political life and extended the organizational reach and social basis of the Congress."[102] Gandhi's sway on the Congress and the freedom movement was overarching. Gandhi was able to create among the masses a more awakened nationalistic feeling. They believed that Gandhi's promise of *swaraj* was realizable and enthusiastically participated in the national movement according to Gandhi's call. While *swadeshi* and boycott worked detrimentally to British commercial interest, they worked favourably for the poor Indians. The fear of government repression for any act of criticizing or defying the government orders or law virtually vanished from the Indians' mind. Even, the ordinary and the poor mass exhibited great courage and readiness for great sacrifices. By their active courageous and voluntary participation these poor and ordinary people demonstrated that they too have a role to play in the nation's struggle for freedom. It is said that the nation could not capitalize on the fraternization of Hindus and Muslims witnessed during the movement; however this in itself was a great achievement of the movement. The movement once again exhibited the fact that *satyagraha* as a means for realizing various goals is inherent with great potentials or force and that the traditional manner of government's dealing with opposition is unable to slacken the spirit and activism of the *satyagraha*. This was evident from the fact that the British government in India had no appropriate answer to the non-violent *satyagraha* movement launched by Gandhi for realizing *swaraj*. In a nutshell, the apparent failure of the movement to realize its designated goals becomes unimportant when compared with the achievements that it could make. Through this movement Gandhi has also reiterated a basic concern of political philosophy, namely, the essence of public vigilance and value consciousness for good governance. As the people desire so the government exists seems to be his warning when he claimed that every citizen silently but nonetheless certainly sustain the government of the day and that if the citizens withdraw their participation in the governance of the country through various expressions of non-cooperation, then the prevailing government is bound to cease from existence, thus parting way for good governance. Submission to evil governance is therefore unwarranted according to Gandhi and he considered it to be the moral duty of the citizen to actively resist and change it.

Bardoli Satyagraha

The colonial interest of the British rule in India influenced the government to primarily focus its attention on revenue and pay scant attention to the needs of the Indian mass. This was true even in the case of agrarian interests of the Indian peasants. Consequently, agrarian discontent was brewing in several parts of India. A significant place where such a discontent was fearlessly expressed by the peasants and sought to be resolved through the Gandhian technique of *satyagraha* was Bardoli taluka in Surat district in Gujarat.

The principal and initial cause of the agrarian discontent in Bardoli was the government's decision to enhance the revenue assessment in Bardoli Taluka by 22 per cent in the year 1927. The Bardoli peasants contended that such an enhancement was unjust because the tax officials did not make proper investigation and prepared inaccurate report which influenced the government to increase the tax. The peasants submitted that they could not sustain the enhanced taxes. They demanded the setting up of an impartial enquiry committee to judge their real conditions and paying capacity and on that basis decide a more rational and just rate of tax. The refusal of the government to concede this demand finally resulted in the launch of the *satyagraha* movement.

During the Non-Cooperation Movement of 1920-22, Gandhi had selected Bardoli as a model place where civil disobedience would be undertaken in the first instance and thereafter such actions were to be taken in other parts of India to realize the objectives of Non-Cooperation Movement. However, the Chauri Chaura violent incident influenced him to revoke such a decision in February 1922 and suspend the Non-Cooperation Movement itself. The agrarian discontent in Bardoli in 1927 brought Gandhi to the scene who, on February 12, 1928, gave the signal for launch of *satyagraha* in Bardoli. On this day under the leadership of Vallabh Bhai Patel, a resolution was passed advising all the peasants in Bardoli taluka to refuse to pay the hiked revenue assessment until the government appointed an independent tribunal or accepted the existing rate of revenue assessment. An oath in the name of God not to pay the land revenue was administered to the peasants. Extracts from sacred texts like *Gita* and *Koran* were read out and songs of Kabir were sung by the people to mark the beginning of the *satyagraha*. Though he did not directly lead the Bardoli *satyagrahis*, he expressed his views and supported the campaign through his writings in *Young India*. He kept himself informed about the campaign. Although Gandhi supplied the general directions and inspiration to the campaign, the direct leadership was provided by Vallabh Bhai Patel who was assisted by many, including Abbas Tayebji who had worked with Gandhi in South Africa. Natives within the Bardoli Taluka and adjoining area enthusiastically participated in the movement. Not only men but also women participated and led the movement at many places. Many village headmen and officials joined the campaign after relinquishing their government positions. *Satyagraha* camps were established, news bulletins were issued daily, spinning and constructive activities were launched, mass meetings were held, songs were composed and sung and prayers were recited, selected passages from Gandhi's autobiography were read at meetings. The village elders and officials were persuaded to join the *satyagrahis*; officials like the revenue collector were and persuaded not is collect the taxes; the villagers dismantled their casts and equipment's and hid them at places and refrained from violence when officials/police tried to confiscate their property or household articles and tried to sell them at ridiculous price. Together with persuasion methods social boycott was also adopted to motivate the opponents to be a part of the cause of the *satyagraha*.

Gandhi supported the cause of the Bardoli peasants and claimed that their demands were justified.[103] He said, "Every man has the right, nay, it is his duty to resist an arbitrary unjust levy as the Bardoli assessment is claimed to be by its ryots."[104] To support this he pointed out to the Bardoli enquiry conducted by Kunzru, Vaze and Amritlal Thakkar. He forewarned the *satyagrahis* to be ever vigilant and be true to the noble cause of Bardoli *satyagraha*. He tried to instill confidence of the peasants in *satyagraha* by extolling the strength or potency of the *satyagraha* technique and also emphasized on the peasants' steadfast adherence to the basic moral values inherent in *satyagraha*.[105] He appealed the public to support the Bardoli people's cause and also lauded the efforts of people outside Bardoli and India who came forward to support the *satyagraha* movement. He tried to expel any malicious rumour being spread about the movement and challenged that anyone could ascertain for himself and clear his doubts or misgivings about the movement from the audited and published accounts of the Bardoli *satyagraha* movement.

Against the government's thereat of action against the protesting *satyagrahis*, Gandhi said that it had failed to realize that such threats or acts could have no impact when hundreds of thousands of people become *satyagrahis* especially when these *satyagrahis* become a do-or-die class, i.e., class of people who have given up the fear of death and the infatuation for possession and value their self respect above everything else. At the same time he emphasized that the *satyagrahi* should not be angry at the wrath of the Government and never swerves from the path of truth. He emphasised upon the Bardoli peasants to remain true to the pledge taken by them at the beginning of the movement,[106] He supported the movement and said that the *satyagrahis* need an independent and impartial committee to hear their complaints and give justice and also implementation of certain conditions like the release of those who have been imprisoned in connection with this struggle; confiscated land during the struggle be released and restoration of the direct losses suffered by the people and by other individuals for the sake of the people of Bardoli. He said that once the government accepts the above demands then the people should dutifully pay the revenue arrears. He said that the government should draw the lesson from the movement that it cannot go against the people who have truth on their side and who adopt nonviolence to vindicate it; rather it should strengthen its public base by cooperating with the public cause and in return get its goodwill. Similarly, he said the people of Bardoli should draw the lesson from the movement that so long as they remain united in nonviolence they have nothing to fear, not even unwilling officials. Such unity and adherence to nonviolence, he argued, can be cultivated by engaging in constructive programme requiring combined effort and promoting common good. He went at length in his speech at Bardoli explaining the various constructive work which the people of Bardoli should continue.[107]

As the *satyagraha* movement under Sardar Patel refused to budge from its original demand of an enquiry committee and subsequent demands of release of confiscated land and property and of prisoners held for participating in the *satyagraha*, the government made plans to use its brutal force further. Posting of tough officials in Surat, arrest of prominent leaders like Patel, seizure of *satyagraha* camps and request for army support were contemplated by the government. The satyagrahis, however, remained firm in their original demand and submitted to the government's repression nonviolently.

Under such circumstances, and especially when there was much apprehension of Sardar Patel being arrested, Gandhi shifted to Bardoli on August 2, 1928 to assume leadership of the movement in case Sardar Patel was arrested. Sentiments in support of the *satyagraha* movement were echoed in the Bombay Legislative Council, Central Assembly and the British Parliament. Though Viceroy Irwin and Governor Wilson were not willing to favour the idea of holding an inquiry and going back to the old rate of taxes, ultimately on August 6, 1928 the government capitulated. It issued a communiqué in which it stated that an enquiry would be instituted to look into the issue of raised taxes. This enquiry committee was known as the Broomfield Committee. The government also agreed to restore forfeited lands, release the *satyagrahi* prisoners and reinstate subordinate revenue officials who had resigned during Bardoli *satyagraha*. Sardar Patel in return promised that the peasants would pay the old assessed taxes. Thus the Bardoli *satyagraha* movement came to an end. While the peasants started paying land revenue according to the old rates, the Broomfield Committee of R.S. Broomfield and R.M. Maxell acceded to most of the demands of the Bardoli peasants and suggested a new land revenue rate with which the peasants, Sardar Patel and Gandhi felt satisfied.

The Bardoli *satyagraha* was a great success. J. Bandhyopadhyaya says, "The Bardoli *satyagraha* was thus highly successful in so far as the eighty six thousand peasants of the taluka successfully resisted the enhancement of the land tax by the government through nonviolent civil disobedience".[108] The success of the *satyagraha* aroused great enthusiasm in the people of India. For the first time *satyagraha* was tried on such an extensive scale. The whole taluka of Bardoli participated directly in the movement with support coming from other parts of India and even from South Africa. Its success proved that if the people stood firm and refrained from violence or rioting, the British government would ultimately yield to the wishes of the Indians. It instilled hope and strength and a sense of victory in the minds of the peasants not only of Bardoli but of the whole of India. It was a movement which proceeded virtually completely on the steps and fundamental rules of *satyagraha* outlined by Gandhi. J. Bandyopadhyaya therefore comments, "Instead, very few *satyagrahas* would seem to have been as successful and logically consistent with the theory of *satyagraha* as the Bardoli *satyagraha.*"[109] Gandhi recognized such *satyagraha* like that of Bardoli as stepping stones for the attainment of *swaraj* for India. He said, "The struggle has also an indirect bearing on *swaraj*. Whatever awakens people to a sense of their wrongs and whatever gives them strength for disciplined and peaceful resistance and habituates them for corporate suffering brings us nearer *swaraj*."[110] To quote him further, "That every such awakening, every such effort as that of Bardoli brings *swaraj* nearer and may bring it nearer even than any direct effort is undoubtedly true."[111] The movement reinforced the fact that Gandhi was very correct in selecting Bardoli for *satyagraha* at the time of Non-Cooperation Movement in 1922. It also influenced Gandhi to believe that the victory of Bardoli would revive Indians' faith in peaceful methods to actualize their national aspirations.[112] Bardoli campaign came up to his expectation and its success must have surely influenced Gandhi and the Congress to try civil disobedience on a national level because it was soon afterwards that Gandhi launched the Civil Disobedience Movement in 1930.

Civil Disobedience Movement

Gandhi launched Civil Disobedience Movement in 1930 to protest the salt laws which was one of the many evils of British rule in India. The launch of the movement formally started with the beginning of salt *satyagraha* by Gandhi on March, 12, 1930.

In pursuance of their exploitative colonial interests, the British government in India continued with its policy of negation, oppression and repression of the Indians. Discontentment, therefore, was widespread in India when the 1920s decade was drawing to a close. No political party of the day could substantially contribute to effectively check such a government or remove the simmering discontentment prevalent in the Indian masses. There was widespread resentment against the Simon Commission appointed by the government to study and report about the progress of reform of 1919 and make suggestions for further constitutional reforms. The demand of dominion status for India as presented by the Nehru Report of 1928 was not favoured by the British. Within the Congress the youth demanded more effective and radical tactics to pressurize the government to bow to the Indian needs. They favoured complete independence for India instead of dominion status. The Lahore Congress of 1929 authorized its working committee to launch a programme of civil disobedience for realization of this goal of complete independence. The British government did not positively respond to Gandhi's effort to convince them to grant the eleven-point minimum demands mentioned in his letter to Lord Irwin so that the Congress may prevent the launch of civil disobedience for achieving the larger goal of complete independence. In mid-February (14-16) 1930, the working committee of the Congress met at Sabarmati Ashram in Ahmedabad and invested Gandhi with full powers to decide about the launch of Civil Disobedience Movement.

The immediate goal of the salt *satyagraha* was to disobey the Salt Act and thereby protest and seek the removal of such a law which created hardship to the Indians, especially the poor.[113]

The Salt Act passed by the government aimed to levy tax on the salt prepared in India. It sought to establish the government's complete control and monopoly over the manufacture of salt in India. It prohibited the people from manufacturing salt without prior licence to do so. Any violation of this law was punishable with confiscation of the manufactured salt and an imprisonment term of six months.

Gandhi said that such an act by the government adversely affected each and every Indian; it hit the poor very hard. He contended that because of these laws villages have been ruined and the joblessness that it has created has enhanced the misery of the poor. It was according to him one of the most inhuman taxes that could be conceived[114] and asserted that the people had every right to oppose the Act and get justice.[115]

Regarding the long range objective of the movement, it may be said that Gandhi, by a simultaneous scathing attack on the evils of British rule in India, emphasized upon the urgent need to remove these evils. He pointed out that Indians were greatly impoverished because of the exploitation of the colonial rule; it had reduced them to a status of political serfdom and had not only struck at the roots of Indian culture but also degraded Indians spiritually.[116] He said that it would be sinful to wait any longer and be a mere spectator of the government continuing its evil designs. Through a non-violent course of action contemplating civil disobedience, Gandhi hoped to check the government and at the same time wean away the British from pursuing such an evil course. He expressed the hope that the government would respond positively to his appeal, failing which, he cautioned, he would have no other choice but launch the Civil Disobedience Movement in the form of breaking the Salt Act. The proposed date and plan of action violating the Salt Act was conveyed to the government. In his letter to Lord Irwin, Gandhi communicated the above views and requested him to find a way out to avoid the discomfort of the impending events.[117]

The government did not positively respond to Gandhi's initiative. Instead, it expressed its regret claiming that such an action would clearly lead to the violation of law and threaten public peace. Consequently, Gandhi decided to go ahead with his plans. He decided that the Sabarmati Ashram at Ahmedabad would be the starting point from where he could march on to Dandi sea coast located around 240 miles away. There, along with his selected band of *satyagrahis*, he would manufacture salt and thus violate the Salt Act. To the selected *satyagrahis* he gave directions for the future course of action. To the people he explained the various ways by which the salt laws could be violated. Along with such an action, Gandhi said that people could also take up such actions like picketing of liquor and foreign cloth shops, refusal to pay taxes, boycott of courts and refraining from litigation and lastly, resignation from government posts.[118] He was emphatic about a firm adherence to truth and non-violence and cautioned the people about doing any wrong out of anger. He pointed out that such acts of violation would surely bring about government's repressive actions, but the people should neither fear nor retaliate such actions. He argued that the potent force generated by truthful and nonviolent action would not only perplex and puzzle the government about its course of action but also will ultimately influence it to give up its evil acts.[119] He said that in the event of his arrest by the government, the public could look up to the Congress Working Committee for guidance. He wanted the public to actively resist the government with the most active form of non-violence.[120]

To the selected band of *satyagrahi* volunteers, Gandhi gave instructions as to what they ought to do or what they ought not to do during the *satyagraha* march.[121] He also instructed them about food intake. He selected only those volunteers whom he thought were fit for physical exertion and mental endurance. In his speech at the prayer meeting he explained in detail what he expected the Indians to do during this struggle.[122]

Meanwhile, the Congress Working Committee on its part urged all Congressmen and public to fully cooperate in all possible ways with the *satyagraha* struggle. It also emphasized upon the need to strictly abide by the principle of non-violence. After Gandhi violated the Salt Act it recommended the Congressmen and the public to follow Gandhi's steps. Arrangements for alternative leadership at national, provincial and local levels were devised. Vallabh Bhai Patel was chosen to go ahead of the marching *satyagraha*. He educated the public he met about the goal of the movement. He urged them to abstain from liquor, renounce untouchability and take up constructive work.

At around 6.30 a.m. on March 12, 1930, Gandhi started his famous Dandi March. With *'Ramdhun'* echoing all around, the march began with Gandhi leading and his band of *satyagraha* following him. As he progressed from one village to another along the route to Dandi, he spoke to and motivated hundreds and thousands of people to courageously and non-violently participate in India's struggle for *swaraj*. No section of the society remained untouched by Gandhi during this march.

On April 5, 1930 Gandhi reached Dandi. Next day on April 6, 1930, at 6:30 a.m. Gandhi reached the seashore of Dandi, stooped down and picked up a handful of salt to symbolically defy the Salt Act. Shortly afterwards other volunteers were instructed to follow Gandhi's lead. Having received the signal, the whole of

India participated in breaching the Salt Act at various places in the country.

Initially, the government did not adopt a repressive policy but favoured non-interference. It hoped that Gandhi's plan of mobilizing the masses would not succeed. It did not arrest Gandhi as soon as he violated the Salt Act. The Government of India advised the subordinate authorities to refrain from making mass arrests; it suggested minimum use of force if at all any arrests were to be made. It preferred the arrest of leaders in order to discourage or disorganize the movement. However, nothing went the way the government thought it would go. Finally, it adopted the conventional tactics of arrests and brutal force of repression. Not only leaders but ordinary participants were arrested and brutally assaulted.

Gandhi declared that he would continue to defy the salt laws by leading a raid on the Dharasana Salt Works. The rapid spread of the movement and the pressures from officials, Governors and military establishments finally influenced Viceroy Irwin to order Gandhi's arrest on May 4, 1930. At 12:45 a.m. of the intervening night of May 4-5, 1930, a group of armed policemen along with the British District Magistrate of Surat arrested Gandhi and he was sent to the Yeravada Central Jail in Bombay.

Alternate leaders led the non-violent march to the Dharasana Salt Works and the government did not refrain this time from using brutal force and making arrests. Gandhi was approached in jail by the government's representative to reach a compromise. Such a compromise was finally reached when the Gandhi-Irwin Pact was concluded on March 5, 1931. Amongst many other things, the Pact also saw Gandhi's agreement to suspend the Civil Disobedience Movement.

As far as the achievements of the Civil Disobedience Movement are concerned, it may be said that the salt *satyagraha* launched within it realized the immediate goals to a large extent. Though the government did not repeal the salt laws, it gave such an interpretation of the law in order to give relief to the poor Indians. The residents residing in areas near such places where salt could be collected or manufactured were allowed to make salt for their domestic use and for other people within the village, i.e., sell it within the village market and not outside the village.

Certain other concessions like amnesty to the non-violent campaigners, liberal restoration of confiscated properties and withdrawal of the special restraining ordinances were made by the government. It was also agreed upon by the government that in any further discussions on constitutional reforms in India, the representatives of the Congress would be invited.

The Civil Disobedience Movement marked a progressive step in many directions. The anti-imperialist and nationalistic struggle was carried on a much larger scale than before. Effective leadership was not limited to a few or to the national level alone; instead, there were many examples of provincial and local effective leadership and in good numbers too. The government's stepping down to negotiate with the campaigners instilled in the latter a confidence level and strength unseen before. The mobilization for the campaign permeated a wide variety of social strata or section – poor, illiterate, men and women, religious minorities, rural and urban folks, high and the low, students, tribal people, merchants and shopkeepers, etc.[123] Not only in India, but even internationally the movement secured public support especially due to the press reporting done by some foreign journalists.

The opening campaign led by Gandhi and the Dharasana salt campaign was reflective of the strict adherence to the basic principles of a *satyagraha* struggle. The immediate objective of the movement was to realize a just cause, i.e., removal of hardship imposed on the masses, especially the poor, by the Salt Act. These laws were symbolic of the injustice and evils of the British rule and as true *satyagraha* it became the duty of the campaigning Indians to disobey these and assert their right to realize justice and truth. The *satyagraha* abided rigorously to the principle of non-violence. Self-reliance characterized the conduct of the *satyagraha* as they refused material help for themselves or their family while observing civil disobedience. Propaganda through distribution of leaflets and press reporting was done to secure public support. All efforts were made to negotiate and reach an amicable settlement with the government right from the start to the end. The government was kept informed of the various plans of the campaign.

The Civil Disobedience Movement also revealed that the brute force of the state can be effectively checked by adopting *satyagraha*. It showed to the world that organized violence and evils of the state need not be necessarily retaliated in the same way by the sufferers; alternatively a nonviolent course of action exists and this has the potency to check these violence and evils more effectively.

Revival and End of Civil Disobedience

As per the Gandhi-Irwin Pact of 1931, Gandhi agreed to attend the Second Round Table Conference held in England to discuss about the prospects of future constitutional reforms in India. Before sailing for London he said that there were all chances of his returning empty handed from the Round Table Conference. He had sensed that the political mood of leaders in England was averse to the expectations of Indians about the constitutional reforms. The proceedings of the Round Table Conference proved Gandhi correct. Gandhi, thus, returned from England greatly dissatisfied.

Meanwhile, in India, Lord Wellington replaced Lord Irwin as the new Viceroy. Under Viceroy Wellington's leadership the government recoursed to a complete reversal of the policies towards the Congress, its leaders and the nationalistic aspirations and activities of the people. There was open and gross violation of the Gandhi-Irwin Pact. The government unleashed a reign of terror and violent repression.

After nearly four months absence, Gandhi reached India from England on December 28, 1931. The Congress Working Committee met on December 29, 1931. Gandhi requested a meeting with Viceroy Wellington and offered to postpone the resumption of the Civil Disobedience Movement till such a meeting. The Viceroy refused and warned Gandhi that he and the Congress would be held responsible for all the consequences which may follow if the movement is resumed. On January 3, 1932 Gandhi appealed to the nation and asked them to be prepared for another long and more arduous struggle. The government made a pre-emptive strike by arresting Gandhi on January 4, 1932. It also promulgated ordinances which gave it unlimited powers to deal with emergent situation of civil disobedience. Though unprepared, the popular response was massive, they participated in picketing of liquor and foreign cloth shops, celebration of various national days, demonstrations and banned meetings and defying selected government ordinances. They submitted to the arrests made by the government.

The government reacted by sparing no efforts to deal with the Indians. They used severe and relentless repressive force to curb the civil disobedience. Organizations like the Congress were declared illegal and their funds were seized. The participants in the movement were violently dealt with. Rigorous imprisonment and heavy fines were meted out to them. In the jail they were treated inhumanly. Fines and taxes were realized by selling the 'convicted' participants' property at throwaway prices or by confiscating them. Even the women were not spared from maltreatment. The press was severely curtailed.

Such an action by the government severely affected the resumed Civil Disobedience Movement. Gradually, the participation decreased and the enthusiasm shown earlier also declined. There were also some instances where the essential principles of a non-violent struggle were not followed by the participants. Ultimately, on May 19, 1933, Gandhi postponed the civil disobedience for twelve weeks. On July 14, 1933, he gave a call to end all mass civil disobedience activities and supported individual *satyagraha* campaign. This continued for almost one year and finally on April 7, 1934, he decided to end civil disobedience completely.

Vykom Satyagraha

Vykom, a big village in the erstwhile Travancore state during the British rule but now a part of the state of Kerala in India, is a prominent place of worship for Hindus, especially for the devotees of Lord Shiva. During the British rule in India, although the roads around the temple of Lord Shiva were public, the orthodox priests and Brahmins engaged in temple services and living in houses built along these roads, did not allow the so-called untouchables to use these roads or enter the temple on the pretext that if they did so then the temple or the Brahmins themselves would get polluted. Some of the progressive and enthusiastic reformers wanted these roads around the temple to be thrown open to the public irrespective of their caste, creed or other such considerations. So, they thought about adopting *satyagraha*. It was initiated by a Syrian Christian named George Joseph. Initially, it had around fifty volunteers, gradually it increased to hundred and swelled to many thousands which included not only the so-called lower caste people but also the upper caste people.

Initiation of Vykom *satyagraha* was thus not a direct product of Gandhi's thought and activism. Nevertheless, it had his blessings and he offered his guidance and consultation whenever these were sought by the *satyagraha*. Gandhi wrote profusely about untouchability, religion and *satyagraha* in *Young India* while the movement was carried on by the *satyagraha* from 1924-25. He directly participated in *satyagraha* from April 1925.

The immediate goal of the Vykom *satyagraha* was the opening of the public roads around to temple to all the people. However, in essence, it was a movement to realize a basic human right that would recognize the dignity of and doing justice to all the individuals including the so-called untouchables within the Hindu religion. Thus, it aimed at certain fundamental reforms within the fold of Hindu religion. The state of Travancore and many members of Legislative Assembly were not willing to support such reforms but oppose and support use of police force against the campaigning *satyagraha*. All of them, i.e., the state, the Legislative Assembly and the police also became the opponents of the *satyagraha*.

A *satyagraha* ashram was established. Hand spinning and constructive works like building school and keeping the environment clean were taken up. Meetings were held to understand the viewpoint of the orthodox Brahmins and persuade them to renounce their discriminatory practices.

Initially appeals were made and petitions sent to the Regent of the Maharaja of Travancore and to the Brahmins and priests of the temple. When this failed to produce the desired result a *'Savarna Jatha'* or procession of high caste and so-called untouchables was carried along the forbidden road. When the Brahmins attacked and beat those participating in the campaign, the participants refused to retaliate. When one set of leaders of the campaign was arrested, a new set of alternative leaders assumed charge to conduct the movement calmly and non-violently. When the police erected barricades to prevent the *satyagrahis* from entering the roads and temple, the *satyagrahis* started their nonviolent action by prayers and spinning and weaving on daily basis. When the monsoon rains flooded the roads, while the police shifted to boats, the *satyagrahis* turn by turn stood there, sometimes in water up to their shoulders, continuing their campaign by offering prayers; they desisted from removing the barricades or climbing over it.

Gandhi directly participated in the *satyagraha* when he went to the state of Travancore in April 1925. He met the state authorities and tried to persuade them in favour of the protesting *satyagrahis*. However, from the start of the movement Gandhi lent his support.[124] Gandhi wrote profusely in his column in *Young India* on various issues related to the Vykom *satyagraha* and the philosophy in general. He described it as one that sought elementary human rights for the unapproachables and untouchables.[125]

He said that the Vykom *satyagraha* was justified and as far as it kept itself within the proper limits and conducted with strict adherence to nonviolence and truth, it deserved full public sympathy. He expressed his satisfaction on the manner in which the Vykom campaign was being conducted[126] and said that it could serve as a model for future workers following similar path.[127] He advised the *satyagrahis* to continue the campaign and at the same time seek the support of the state and public opinion. At the same time, he advised them to be self-reliant.[128] He recognized the noble cause for which *satyagrahis* were protesting and boosted their morale by telling then that they must have faith in their cause and means and believe that success would surely be achieved by them in the end.

He vehemently criticized the practice of untouchability by the caste Hindus. He recognized the *satyagraha* against untouchability as battle of no less consequence than that of *swaraj*. Regarding untouchability as a hindrance to *swaraj,* he was emphatic about its eradication for hastening realization of swaraj.[129] He recognized it as a fight against an age-long wrong and prejudice. Such practices, he contended, are supported by orthodoxy, superstition, custom and authority. These were, he said, irreligion masquerading as religion and ignorance appearing in the guise of learning.[130] Untouchability, he said, is a sin, which the Hindus were practising and they and must make sincere efforts to remove this practice from their life.[131] This, according to Gandhi, was a shame for the Hindus and they could feel a sense of glory only if they purge themselves of it.[132] For this, he said, they must purify themselves and suffer if needed and thereby pay the debt they owe to their suppressed brothers and sisters. He also said, "To remove untouchability is a penance that caste Hindus owe to Hinduism and to themselves. The purification required is not of untouchables but of the so-called superior castes."[133]

Gandhi also emphasized upon the need to abide by the essentials of a *satyagraha* campaign. He was insistent on the fact that the Vykom campaigners should always stick to truth and non-violence. He said that the *satyagrahis* should try to rationally persuade the opponents to give up such discriminatory practices. He cautioned them to refrain from any retaliation if the opponent inflicted any punishment for their act of opposition or protest. He desired that the Vykom *satyagrahis* should silently suffer all such punishments without bearing a grudge against the opponents. Such goals of reform as envisaged by the Vykom *satyagraha*, he observed, should not be sought by using coercion. The propriety of action, he contended, should be of prime concern to the *satyagrahi* rather than the effect that it may produce. He said that he was sure about the *satyagrahis* success if they retain their patience and spirit of suffering.[134] He advised the *satyagrahis* that if they did so then there would be a voluntary renunciation of the discriminatory practices by the orthodox Brahmins (the "change of heart" as he described it). He was also emphatic about the *satyagrahis* remaining self-reliant and therefore seek no help from outside their fold except for the public support.[135] Towards the opponent, he was also emphatic about showing love and removing all the fear the opponent had about the *satyagrahi*'s goals and activities.

True to Gandhi's prediction, the *satyagraha* succeeded. When Gandhi visited the state of Travancore and persuade the state authorities to remove the barricades, they complied. However, when the barricades were removed by the police, the *satyagrahis* announced that they would not take any undue advantage and would enter the road only when the Brahmins were fully persuaded and willingly consented to their use of the public road around the temple. At last in the autumn of 1925, the Brahmins declared that they were ready to receive the untouchables. Thus, the roads were allowed to be used by the so-called untouchables. In 1937 the Maharaja of Travancore, by a Royal Proclamation, threw open the doors of all state temples to all Hindu citizens irrespective of their caste, colour or creed. Such an opening of temples was followed by opening to all many other public institutions not only in the state of Travancore but also in other parts of India.

Thus, the Vykom *satyagraha* was able to realize its immediate objective of getting the road around the Shiva temple thrown open to the public irrespective of their caste, colour or creed. The Vykom *satyagraha* is also significant on account of the fact that it was symbolic of an urgent need to combat religious redundancies and ignorance. This movement also served as a catalyst for the removal of many other disabilities faced by the untouchables.[136] It influenced many high caste individuals to reconsider their moral duty towards the weaker sections of their society. It showed the path to the so-called untouchables to regain their dignity and get justice. Gandhi's assertion that such a *satyagraha* was no less significant than that of *swaraj* was indicative of Gandhi's assertion that political freedom movement launched against the British Raj cannot simply ignore such fight against socio-economic evils prevailing in India. Thus, Anima Bose says, "He had the insight to see that one could not fight for one kind of freedom and human right, namely, political, and allow the other freedoms and human rights to go by default."[137] Last but not least, it showed that a campaign carried on along the essential guidelines of *satyagraha* as enunciated by Gandhi has great potential to resolve various types of conflicts emerging in a society.

Quit India Movement

The Quit India Movement of 1942 was the last mass movement for Indian independence planned by the Indian National Congress under the leadership of Gandhi. Through his 'Quit India' call to the British, Gandhi asked them to pack up and go back to England after declaring India a free nation.[138] India's independence became the immediate and minimum demand of the nationalistic movement as Gandhi said that there would be no compromise or bargaining so far as this demand was concerned. The mass participated in it with great courage and enthusiasm. The colonial aspirations and the World War situation made the government take brutal measures to suppress the movement.

As the 1930s decade was coming to an end discontentment ran high amongst the Indians. Cripps Mission failed to make any substantial progress with regard to constitutional reform in India. This revealed that Britain was not willing to act as per the aspirations of Indians. Apart from this, it also exerted pressure on India to join its side in World War II. Many nationalistic leaders in India were not willing to meekly submit to such authoritarian attitude of the British. They wanted Britain to first clear its intention with regard to the grant of independence to India. However, the government made no such declaration; instead it made preparations to check and crush any protest and meet the exigencies created by the World War II.

Apart from Britain's unwillingness to transfer real power to the Indians, popular discontentment was also rising due to World War generated conditions of steep increase in prices and shortage of essential commodities. In Bengal and Orissa the government's decision to take into custody the boats of fishermen to prevent any possibility of the invading Japanese using them also angered the public. The Indians also had completely lost their faith in the government's capacity to provide basic security to life and property in case of the Japanese invading India. They thought that Britain would soon collapse from its present status of a colonial nation. Therefore, like the leaders, the masses also desired that India should free itself from the colonial rule as early as possible.

Gandhi understood the mood of the Indians. To reinforce his understanding he sent some of his trusted lieutenants across the nation to study the mood of the mass. When he was sure about the readiness of the Indians to participate in yet another movement to realize their independence, Gandhi visualized a non-violent non-cooperation movement against the government and paralyzing it by an open mass rebellion. This however did not mean, as he emphasized, the contemplation of overthrowing the British government in India or seizure of power. Rather, it was, as he claimed, a programme of transformation of relations ending in peaceful transfer of power.

Gandhi played an important role in formulating the programme of the movement. He drew a 12-point programme while emphasising upon the adherence to the principle of non-violence. In the programme Gandhi envisaged the following:

1. A 24-hour *hartal* throughout the country.
2. Holding public meetings in villages to explain the aim of the Congress in launching the movement.
3. Holding protest marches to convey India's non-cooperation in the recruitment campaign for Britain's war efforts.
4. Resignation from government services.
5. Breaching of salt laws.
6. Students withdrawing from schools and colleges.
7. Picketing foreign cloth and liquor shops.
8. Disruption of rail road communication.
9. Motivating the urban industrial workers to go on strike.
10. Motivating the armed force personnel to revolt.
11. Refusing to pay taxes.
12. Setting up of parallel government.

He said that the programme of action could include all such actions that may come under the ambit of an unadulterated non-violent non-cooperation movement.[139]

Gandhi took on active part in the planning of the Quit India Movement. Through his articles in the *Harijan* and speeches from the platform provided by various associations and the Congress, Gandhi tried to create a public opinion in favour of the movement. Raising such public awareness and support, both within and outside India, Gandhi exclaimed, would be one of his primary tasks.[140] He said that India should assert its claim for complete freedom and compromise with nothing less than that. He gave the famous call of "do or die" to the masses to realize this goal.[141] This call meant that the Indians should show great courage and be prepared to make great sacrifices while trying to free India from the British rule. He said that the Congress and the masses were making legitimate claim while demanding complete freedom from the British rule. He expressed his hope that the international community would support India's cause. Within the Congress, he held a series of discussions with prominent leaders for seeking their views and support for the movement. He travelled extensively to convince and motivate the rural and urban masses for participation in the movement. He went to the extent of saying that he was so much convinced about the appropriateness of this goal of complete independence for India that whosoever might oppose him in this matter, he would not withdraw but move ahead resolutely.

He appealed to the press to freely and courageously discharge this duty.[142] He also appealed to the native rulers to support this demand of complete independence.[143] To the students and teachers he said that they should keep the spark of freedom alight in their heart and courageously support the Congress and be prepared to sacrifice their career for the cause of Indian independence. He made similar appeal to the government employees also.[144]

The Congress Working Committee met at Wardha and on July 14, 1942 and it accepted the idea of a mass struggle as suggested by Gandhi. To ratify this an All India Congress Committee meeting at Bombay was proposed. Many Congress members assembled for the meeting at Bombay on August 7, 1942. Shortly after midnight on August 8, 1942, Gandhi addressed the members and people who had gathered at Gowalia Tank in Bombay. In his mesmerising speech,[145] he said that complete independence for India would be the minimum and immediate goal of the movement and the people should be prepared to "do or die" for realizing this goal. He said that before starting the movement an appeal to the Viceroy, would be made to concede to the Congress's demand. In the meanwhile, he instructed the Congressmen and the mass to involve themselves in constructive programme[146] and, more importantly, to consider themselves and behave as free men or women from that very moment.

A few hours later when the delegates dispersed, the government arrested Gandhi and other prominent leaders of the Congress and sent them to jail. The news of arrest of Gandhi and other prominent leaders sparked the commencement of the Quit India Movement without the leadership of Gandhi and many prominent leaders. The government on its part resolved to suppress the movement with brutal force. With regard to Gandhi, after arresting and sending him to jail, the government did not allow him to communicate with nationalistic leaders. All news of the progress of the movement was barred from reaching him. Thus, Gandhi could not play any role in the actual operation of the movement. The brutal repression by the government enabled it to overcome the mass participation in the movement in a short period of time.

Though the Quit India Movement could not achieve Gandhi's stated objective of "nothing less than freedom" for India, it was significant in many respects. The goal of "nothing less then freedom" for India meant that from thenceforth the minimum demand that the British rule had to concede to the Indians was their freedom from the colonial rule. Simultaneously, it was asserted that this goal could not be perpetually delayed. Popular participation was again marked with great enthusiasm and courage. The establishment of parallel government in some parts of India, although for a short time only, was also a remarkable feature of this movement.

Gandhi still reigned supreme on the national scene. Whenever mass movement was contemplated he became the choice for leadership of majority of the contemporary politicians, activists and the masses. Gandhi on his part played on important role in deciding the programme of action and in the planning of the movement. His belief that a non-violent movement strictly adhering to the *satyagraha* principles could realize even such goals like a nation's independence still remained unshakeable. Similar was his belief that India's independence should come immediately and without any compromise. To realize this he was willing to go all alone if need be; this shows his grit, determination and dedication towards the goal he set forth. The real nature of the colonial rule; its baneful effect on India; the need to protest such a government; the non-violent manner in which to carry on such a protest effectively; resisting armed invasion non-violently; etc. were also some of the theoretical issues that were dealt at length by Gandhi while launching the Quit India Movement. Unfortunately, he could not play any role in the actual implementation of the Quit India Movement because of his arrest and restrictions imposed upon him by the government after sending him to jail.

Notes

1. Hiren Mukherjee, *Gandhiji: A Study*, National Book Agency Pvt. Ltd., Calcutta, 1958, pp. 18-19.
2. M.K. Gandhi, *An Autobiography* or *Story of My Experiments with Truth*, Trans. Mahadev Desai, Navajivan Publishing House, Ahmedabad, 1966, p. 82.
3. Pyarelal, *Mahatma Gandhi: The Early Phase*, Vo1.1, Navajivan Publishing House, Ahmedabad, 1965, p. 314.
4. Note 2, p. 106.
5. M.K. Gandhi, *Satyagraha in South Africa*, Trans. V.G. Desai, Navajivan Publishing House, Ahmedabad, 1972, p. 43.
6. Ibid., p. 65.
7. Ibid., p. 67.
8. Ibid.
9. For details see Ibid., pp. 67-68.
10. Ibid., p. 67.
11. Ibid.
12. Note 5, p. 86.
13. Note 2, p. 206.
14. Ibid., p. 94.
15. Ibid., p. 100.
16. For a detailed discussion on the distinction between passive resistance and satyagraha, see Ibid., pp. 101-07 and CWMG, Vol. 13, 1979, pp. 517-26.
17. *CWMG*, Vol. 6, p. 469.
18. Ibid., p. 472.
19. J.D. Hunt, *Gandhi in London*, Promilla and Co. Publishers, New. Delhi 1978, p. 60.
20. Note 5, pp. 116-17.
21. *CWMG*, Vol. 6, p. 264.
22. Ibid., p. 251.
23. Ibid., p. 134.
24. Ibid., p. 146.
25. Ibid., p. 147.
26. Ibid., pp. 191-92.
27. *CWMG*, Vol. 9, p. 320.
28. Ibid., p. 330.
29. Ibid., p. 313.

30. Ibid.
31. M.K. Gandhi, *Hind Swaraj* or *Indian Home Rule*, Navajivan Publishing House, Ahmedabad, 1990, p. 38.
32. For Gandhi's criticism of modern civilization see Naresh Dadhich and B. Arun Kumar, Gandhi's Critique of Modern Civilization, *Indian Journal of Politics*, Vol. 25, No.4, 1991, pp. 76-85. Some of the latest works on Gandhi's criticism of modern civilization are:
    (i) R.P. Mishra, *Hind Swaraj: Gandhi's Challenge to Modern Civilization*, Concept Publishing Company, New Delhi, 2007.
    (ii) Rudolph L.I. and S.H. Rudolph, *Postmodern Gandhi and Other Essays: Gandhi in the World and at Home*, Oxford University Press, New Delhi, 2006.
    (iii) Anthony J. Parel (ed.), *Hind Swaraj and Other Writings*, Cambridge University Press, New Delhi, 2005.
33. Note 31, p. 87.
34. Note 9, p. 165.
35. See Mridula Mukherjee in Bipin Chandra (ed.), *India's Struggle for Freedom 1857-1947*, Penguin Books India (Pvt.) Ltd., New Delhi, 1991.
36. See V. Geetha (ed.), *Soul Force: Gandhi's Writings on Peace*, Tara Publishing, Chennai, 2004, p. 85.
37. See for instance *CWMG*, Vol. 13, p.55, 66 and 189.
38. Ibid., pp. 59-60.
39. Ibid., p. 65.
40. Ibid., p. 189.
41. See Vincent Sheean, *Mahatma Gandhi: A Great Life in Brief*, Publications Division, Ministry of Information & Broadcasting, Government of India, New Delhi, 1968, p. 85.
42. *CWMG*, Vol. 13, p. 216.
43. See Ibid., pp. 244-45 & pp. 260-61.
44. Ibid., p. 249.
45. See Ibid., p. 245.
46. For a detailed discussion on this aspect see J.M. Brown, *Gandhi's Rise to Power: Indian Politics 1915-1922*, Cambridge University Press, Cambridge, 1972, pp. 40-51.
47. See for detail *CWMG*, Vol. 13, pp. 362-63.
48. See Ibid., pp. 570-71.
49. Ibid., pp. 368-69.
50. Ibid., pp. 418-19.
51. Note 10, p. 80.

52. See *CWMG*, Vol. 14, p. 216.
53. Ibid., p. 217.
54. See Ibid., pp. 182-84.
55. See Ibid., pp. 275-79.
56. See Ibid., p. 279.
57. Ibid., p. 339.
58. See Ibid., p. 311 and p. 344.
59. Ibid., pp. 323-24.
60. *CWMG*, Vol. 14, pp. 323-24.
61. *CWMG*, Supplementary Vol. 1, p. 147.
62. As quoted by J.M. Brown, Note 10, p.111.
63. Ibid., p. 110.
64. See *CWMG*, Vol. 14, p. 214.
65. Ibid., p. 214.
66. See Ibid., p. 215.
67. See Ibid., p. 267.
68. For details see Ibid., p. 267 and pp. 269-70.
69. J. M. Brown, Note 10, p. 119.
70. *CWMG*, Vol. 14, p. 487.
71. Ibid., p. 498.
72. For details see CWMG, Vol. 14, pp. 486-89.
73. See Ibid., p. 378.
74. See Ibid., p. 439, 441, 496 & 498.
75. See *CWMG*, Vol. 15, pp.106-07 & 126.
76. Ibid., p. 87.
77. Ibid., pp. 87-8.
78. Ibid., p. 101.
79. For details see *CWMG*, Vol. I5, pp. 183-89.
80. Ibid., p. 192.
81. See Ibid., pp. 195-203.
82. See Ibid., pp. 243-44.
83. For an analysis of how the local grievances and consequent political action got aligned with the national movement, See R. Kumar's case study of Lahore in his article, The Rowlatt Satyagraha in Lahore, in R. Kumar (ed.), *Essays on Gandhian Politics: The Rowlatt Satyagraha of* 1919, Oxford University Press, London, 1971, pp. 236-97.
84. As quoted by J.M. Brown, Note 10, p. 188.
85. See *CWMG*, Vol. 16, pp. 341-42.

86. For details see *CWMG*, Vol. 15, pp. 295-99, Vol. 17, p. 2.
87. *CWMG*, Vol. 16, pp. 517-18, 525, & Vol. 17, p. 2.
88. See *CWMG*, Vol. 16, pp. 227-31.
89. See Ibid., pp. 309-10.
90. See for details CWMG, Vol. 17, p. 59.
91. See for instance his comment on the Viceroy's speech. *CWMG*, Vol. 16, pp. 135-38.
92. See *CWMG*, Vol. 17, pp. 73-6.
93. Ibid., p. 75.
94. Ibid., pp. 426-27.
95. See Ibid., pp. 502-04.
96. Ibid., p. 514.
97. See his speech at Delhi Khilaphat Conference, CWMG, Vol.16, p. 310.
98. See Ibid., pp. 113-14.
99. See Ibid., pp. 480-82.
100. Ibid., pp. 482-83.
101. M. Mukherjee in Bipin Chandra (ed.), *India's Struggle for Freedom 1857-1947*, Penguin Books 1991 India (P) Ltd., New Delhi, 1991.
102. Bhikhu Parekh, *Gandhi: A Very Short Introduction*, Oxford University Press, New York, 2001. p. 18.
103. *CWMG*, 36, p. 22.
104. Ibid., p. 89.
105. See *CWMG*, Vol. 37, p. 250.
106. *CWMG*, Vol. 36, p. 460.
107. *CWMG*, Vol. 37, pp. 162-69.
108. J. Bandhyopadhyaya, *Social and Political Thought of Gandhi*, Allied Publishers, Bombay, 1969, p. 288.
109. Ibid.
110. *CWMG*, Vol. 36, p. 90.
111. *CWMG*, Vol. 37, p. 73.
112. Ibid., p. 250.
113. See *CWMG*, Vol. 42, pp. 499-500.
114. Ibid., p. 499.
115. Ibid., p. 501.
116. *CWMG*, Vol. 43, p. 3.
117. Ibid., pp. 2-8.
118. Ibid., pp. 46-7.
119. Ibid., p. 37.

120. *CWMG*, Vol. 42, p. 497.
121. Ibid., p. 491-93.
122. *CWMG*, Vol. 43, pp. 46-8.
123. Note 65, p. 282.
124. *CWMG*, Vol. 26, pp. 73-4.
125. *CWMG*, Vol. 25, p. 115.
126. *CWMG*, Vol. 26, p. 73.
127. *CWMG*, Vol. 25, p. 164.
128. See *CWMG*, Vol. 26, p. 297.
129. See *CWMG*, Vol. 25, p. 515.
130. Gandhi as quoted by Anima Bose in Gandhi's Stand on Human Rights in the Vykom Satyagraha in Subrata Mukherjee and Susheela Ramaswamy (eds.), *Facets of Mahatma Gandhi: Non-violence and Satyagraha*, Deep & Deep Publication New Delhi, 1994 p. 180.
131. See *CWMG*, Vol. 25, p. 514.
132. Ibid., p. 479.
133. Ibid.
134. See Ibid., pp. 163-64.
135. See *CWMG*, Vol. 26, p. 297.
136. Anima Bose, Note 94.
137. Ibid., p. 180.
138. See *CWMG*, Vol. 76, p. 105.
139. Ibid., p. 112.
140. Ibid., p. 163.
141. Ibid., p. 392.
142. Ibid., p, 393.
143. See Ibid., p. 184 & pp. 335-36.
144. Ibid., p. 366.
145. For detail see Ibid., pp. 384-401.
146. Ibid., p. 391.

7

Conclusion

Gandhi's theory of protest is a heuristic theory which influenced the nature of his loyalty to the British rule in India. Through his distinct speculation on the various aspects of a justified protest and the concomitant activism, Gandhi has played a significant role in not only helping India to gain its independence from the colonial rule of the British, but also has shown the path for other subjected nations and people to gain freedom, uphold their dignity and realize those cherished quintessential values which they presume to be concomitant with their existence.

As an ardent seeker of truth in its absolute form, Gandhi advocated a steadfast adherence to the principle of non-violence to realize all righteous goals in life. Recognizing the concentration or institutionalization of power as being antithetical to truth and non-violence, Gandhi opined that the state, which represented the highest concentration of power, would wither away in an ideal society. However, the ideal being the more remote or far scene, Gandhi condescended to the retention of the state provided it existed for realizing specific objectives and conformed to certain inviolable principles while functioning to realize these objectives. Through his theory of political obligation he provided a theoretical paradigm which sought to explain the various aspects of the citizens' obligation to the state and its reciprocal obligations towards its subjects. This theory of political obligation was firmly rooted in Gandhi's moral moorings and it visualized politics, like all other human activities, to be governed by certain moral principles.

When the state flouted these principles or did not fulfil the objectives for which it was retained, then, Gandhi believed, it committed a serious fallacy and threatened not only the righteous existence of the subject citizens but also hindered their fundamental progress. However, the moral and metaphysical dimensions of his overall philosophy made Gandhi recognize that the state is not solely responsible for its immoral acts; the citizens were also responsible for this to a certain extent. Therefore, Gandhi advocated the citizens' self-purification through the adoption of such means like fasting, prayer and vows. He even went to the extent of recognizing his protest as a method of securing rights by personal suffering. Through these means, Gandhi believed, the citizens would not only acquire a moral stature to defy the orders of the unjust state but also positively affect the authorities by bringing about a "change of heart" in them to voluntarily renounce their unrighteous acts. This method of resistance to the usurped authority or an immoral action perpetuated by the state constituted an important part of Gandhi's philosophy of *satyagraha* and became the essence of his theory of protest.

Gandhi's prominent and enduring place in the history of thought has been not only the account of his formulation of a strategy of political action which largely determined the form of natural protest and struggle against the British, and culminated in the independence of India in 1947, but also on account of the fact that he created an ideal of national struggle which transcended class divisions and helped to achieve the ideal in the minimum possible time.[1] Believing that any philosophy, in order to be useful, ought to be relevant to the various aspects of day-to-day life, Gandhi's basic concepts did not remain confined to mere formulations in some ivory-tower philosophical detachment; he was much more interested in the practical aspect of his philosophical concepts.[2] Thus, as a *satyagrahi*, Gandhi strove to steadfastly conform to high ideals throughout his life and, more significantly, in his incessant struggle against the exploitative colonial regime of the British in India, very often in the most trying and adverse conditions.

Gandhi's philosophy of *satyagraha*, which could be recognized as a moral and non-violent theory of protest, advocated a ceaseless activism by the aggrieved individuals, who *in foro conscientiae* were convinced about the fact that those manning the authoritative positions in the political system violated certain fundamental principles of just governance and acted in an unrighteous manner when they perpetuated exploitation and injustice. Through their activism, the protesting *satyagrahis* sought to express their objection, disapproval or dissent of the undesirable actions of such an authority and sought to not merely communicate their deeply felt aggrieved feelings to the authorities but, more importantly, to take recourse to an appropriate non-violent and ethical means to vindicate the essential principles lying at the core of their grievances.

Through their protest the *satyagrahis* sought to not only assert their duty but also their right to uphold those quintessential values which they believed to be a part of human nature. For this, they were prepared to make any sacrifice. Concomitant with this understanding was the cognition that the realization of these values presupposed the indispensability of conformity to ethical means. Thus, *satyagraha* as a means to realize these values, which Gandhi himself surmised under the broad notion of truth, was a protest that ultimately sought to vindicate truth and the concomitant values, and in the process to secure the amelioration of the specific grievances of the *satyagrahi*. Significantly, through the protest, the *satyagrahi* strove to help the human agents of the governing institutions to transcend form a baser existence to a more noble existence. The knowledge acquired through the truths revealed during the process of conflict resolution was recognized as a beacon star for making further progress towards the ultimate ideal of a stateless political order in which all individuals acted in such a righteous manner that made all external controls over them unnecessary and, therefore, avoidable.

Satyagraha, as a means of protest, was also viewed by Gandhi as possessing great possibilities of effectively realizing a wide range of objectives without taking recourse to any unfair or unethical and violent means. He recognized it as a weapon of the morally vigilant and courageous persons. Being more an activism than mere verbosity, *satyagraha* has at its core a firm desire to vindicate all just causes consistent with the principle of truth. As a means of protest it was conceived by Gandhi as a means to prevent the usurpation of authority, correct the wrongs already committed, and to create those positive conditions which would not only inhibit such excrescences on the fundamental principles of governance in future but also pave the way for a much better or exalted, moral and humane governance of the subjects.

In order to be able to pursue such noble goals while taking recourse to protest, Gandhi emphasized upon the votary of *satyagraha* to lead a very disciplined and altruistic life. He, therefore, recognized it as inevitable for the *satyagrahi* to undertake such vows of *satya, ahimsa, aparigraha, astheya, brahmacharya, swadeshi*, bread-labour and trusteeship. Gandhi recognized the need for these vows to be supplemented by a steadfast faith in God. The simple and austere life of the *satyagrahi* was to be further characterized by constant efforts towards self-purification by way of fasting and prayer.

Regarding the procedural modalities through which the *satyagraha* campaign was to be pursued, Gandhi advocated numerous steps and tactics, the use and intensity of which was to be prudently determined in accordance with the prevailing conditions of political life. It presupposed the recourse and exhaustion of all available constitutional means to resolve political conflicts. In this capacity it advocated humble requests, petitioning and rational persuasion of the opposing authorities. Public opinion against the unjust act of the authorities was also sought to be activated. Through these methods the grievances of the *satyagrahi* were sought to be communicated to the authorities. The authorities were thereby made conscious of their mistakes and were requested to correct their follies and take steps to mitigate the grievances caused by their actions. When such constitutional means fail to procure the desired actions from the authorities, Gandhi advocated the recourse to such means like that of non-cooperation and civil disobedience with the authorities so as to influence them to cease from doing injustice and becoming unrighteous. An essential part of this recourse to non-cooperation and civil disobedience was the recognition of self-suffering by way of submitting civilly to the punishments meted out to the *satyagrahis* for their acts of defiance of authoritative dictates. Through this voluntary suffering, the *satyagrahi* sought to bring about a change in the officials' outlook and thereby to influence them to voluntarily renounce their diabolic designs and subsequently, to act in a righteous manner.

Juxtaposed in a historical context characterized by certain destructive tendencies inherent in colonialism, modern culture and obscurantist aspects of native tradition, Gandhi evolved his own method of protest to confront and change the undesirable aspects of these forces. The protest, which got crystallized in the form of *satyagraha*, was resorted by him to assert his freedom to pursue and uphold certain well defined principles and the concomitant values and rights which he held dear to his heart and recognized as inviolable by any temporal authority. Primarily a man committed to *praxis* with his distinctive ideas and ways of implementing them, Gandhi recognized that politics bereft of *dharma* was not only antagonistic but also fatal to the spiritual essence of human existence. Through his protest he asserted that the conduct of life in all its domains should be guided by, and subservient to, *dharma* or the religion of moral conduct. Whenever Gandhi found violations of this principles, he launched a *satyagraha* campaign with the optimism to vindicate the essential moral principles lying at the core of such political conflicts and thereby to seek redress of the grievances that arose on account of such excrescences on principled governance. However, this philosophy of protest was neither an instantaneous growth, nor contrived by Gandhi in the conventional mould of a theoretical enterprise. It witnessed a gradual evolution. Although it was conceived by him in South Africa, it finally matured into a philosophy during the course of his struggle against the colonial rule of the British in India.

Gandhi's apprenticeship in the craft of protest began in South Africa. The South African phase of his life played a crucial role in his development from a shy, timid and unsuccessful lawyer to that of an active, courageous, public and saintly man who defied the might of the native South African governments while protesting against all such unjust policies or legislations which smacked of racial prejudice and denied the basic rights and dignity of the Indians living there. As a consequence of his phenomenological enterprises, "creative experiences" and literary pursuits, Gandhi became a unique public activist, queer in approach to life but indulging in a far greater range of activities with greater authority and efficacy than most of his contemporaries.

When Gandhi set sail to South Africa he had no knowledge of the impending indignities that would befall him in the new land. His "creative experiences" instilled in him a determination not to remain a mere spectator or victim of wrongs and humiliations done to him. Instead, he recognized it to be his moral duty to try and root out the disease of racial prejudice and the accompanying evils that largely characterized the prevailing political system in the South African colonies. It became a protracted struggle and Gandhi became inextricably entangled in it. He gradually became a public activist fighting in a principled way for the espousal of the Indian community's cause and influencing the government to function on the basis of certain well-recognized principles.

One of the first references in his protest to those principles which should characterize a just government was made by Gandhi in the context of according due respect to the rights and dignity of the Indians as citizens of British Empire. Another reference was to the fundamental values or principles of justice, fair play and concern for the well-being of subject citizens, which, Gandhi believed, were the inherent spirit of British Constitution and largely reflected in its operational aspect at home in Britain. To a government adhering to these values while discharging its functions, Gandhi professed an active loyalty. Similarly, in his recognition of the British rule as a providential ordainment to creatively vitalize and release the subject Indian citizens from their moribund status caused by certain obscurantist aspects of the native tradition, there was present the reflection of Gandhi's perception of all governance as a moral responsibility on the shoulders of those who held the reigns of such a power. In his recognition this responsibility reposed in the authority the duty to create those positive conditions which would help the subject individuals to progress spiritually. Significantly, Gandhi recognized that this responsibility was accompanied by accountability. Negligence or wanton refrain for discharging this responsibility, he opined, was condemnable as it implied the contradiction of one of the essential ground for justifying the continuation of a government.

Temporary deviance or excrescence committed by individuals at the local level, Gandhi viewed, should be checked. He professed loyalty to a rule conducted largely on the recognized principles of a just administration. Nevertheless, this notion of loyalty did not imply any blind or uncritical adulation of the rulers. Instead, his notion of loyalty evolved and matured to the extent that it recognized the need to be critical about the local or individual excrescences and to protest them to get the consequent grievances redressed. The technical modalities of carrying on such a protest were gradually perfected by him in the course of his public activism. From the importance of an institutionalized protest to that of organizing and mobilizing the aggrieved individuals, creation of reference-public, petitioning, financing and other aspects were given a detailed consideration by Gandhi.

Significantly, in South Africa, Gandhi's spiritual and moral questioning bore fruit in a singular philosophy of life and an overwhelming vision of a man as a spiritual being created to find fulfilment in a life long pursuit of truth.[3] This love of truth, Gandhi acknowledged, lay at the core of his notion of loyalty and method of protest. Simultaneously, some aspects of an ethical protest like that of not nursing hatred for the opponent, renouncing the use of violence, ever-trusting the opponent, cooperating with the opponent when he is in distress, etc., got increasingly manifested in the method of his protest.

Gandhi was thoroughly convinced about the need for some drastic changes in South Africa so as to make it a better living place for the Black and Asian communities. He petitioned, prayed and pleaded for more positive and active role by Britain to resolve these problems. In reaction to the prolonged apathetic attitude of the British government, Gandhi asserted that mere theoretical pronouncements of adherence to values of justice, fair play and concern for the welfare of the subject citizens was not enough; these ought to be reinforced by practical observances.

As the disquiet feeling increased an account of the native governments' zealous pursuit of racial policies and Britain's failure to check and reprimand these governments or initiating steps for the amelioration of the grievances of the Indians, the conviction grew firmer in his mind that the Indian community, if it wanted to safeguard its basic rights and uphold its members' dignity, had to transcend the realm of mere praying, petitioning and pleading to Britain or the native governments to desist from their anti-Indian tirades. Therefore, he asserted that he could not condescend to blindly accept a rule that was devoid of basic humane considerations and righteousness. This feeling of disquiet culminated ultimately in the birth of *satyagraha* as the means of protesting the unjust and unresponsive governments and for securing the redress of the specific grievances of the Indians in South Africa. So far as Britain was concerned, Gandhi hoped that it would try to correct its hitherto committed mistakes and live up to the professed ideals of its Constitution and, as responsible rulers of India, guide it towards the ultimate destiny of *swaraj* or self-rule. With this hope Gandhi continued to maintain his loyalty to the British Empire until he returned to India in 1915.

Following Gokhale's advice, Gandhi decided to get acclimatized with the prevalent conditions. In his year of probation he cautiously avoided getting himself actively involved in controversial political issues of the day. He cherished the goal of *swaraj*, but denounced the recourse to violent agitation to realize it. He was more emphatic about the Indians evolving their character and capacity or "reform from within" to facilitate the corresponding flow of privileges and rights for the Indians from the British government. Recognizing the aegis of the British as that which not only provided the freest scope for his energies and efforts but also as one that facilitated him to think and act as per the voice of his consciences, Gandhi continued to profess his loyalty to the British government. While continuing to assail and reject the culture represented by modern civilization, subservience to which, he contended, characterized the British rule, Gandhi firmly believed that the Indians on account of their rich spiritual heritage could accept the British as their rulers while rejecting the culture which they represented. Thus, he did not think it as an immediate necessity to reject the British as rulers of India and continued to hope that it would be more benevolent while helping to guide Indian towards the goal of *swaraj*.

As the year of his probation drew to a close, it increasingly dawned upon Gandhi that the British government in India was failing to satisfy the growing and just aspirations of the Indians. The unresponsiveness, coupled with the arrogance of the British officials, Gandhi exclaimed, had resulted in the violation of the basic objectives for which they remained as rulers of India. To remove the existing bitterness between the rulers and the ruled, Gandhi requested the authorities to be more responsive and responsible towards the subject Indians' aspirations. Simultaneously, he embarked on a public consciousness raising effort against these maladies and emphasized upon the Indians perfecting themselves so as to not only justify their demands but also to be capable of ruling themselves when power was ultimately devolved unto them.

Gandhi emphasized that there were certain basic rights which were inevitable for realizing the individuals' essential progress. As subject citizens of the British Empire, he emphasized, it was just on the part of Indians to demand and secure form the government these rights. The demand for self-government was for Gandhi only a corollary of this recognition and, therefore also consistent with the principle of truth. It being so, Gandhi recognized that the government had to concede the just demands not merely by way of using their discretion but, as responsible rulers of India, imperatively guide the Indians to effectively realize *swaraj* at the earliest. Increasingly aware of the reluctance of Britain to accede to this, Gandhi wanted the Indians to shed down their fear of British authority and mobilize themselves and acquire a moral stature by self-purification to realize these demands. However, on account of his novitiate position in the political milieu, Gandhi was nonplussed in giving a pragmatic shape to any plan to realize these objectives. The death of Gokhale and the existing institutionalized folds' disinclination to accept Gandhi within their fold, put Gandhi into a dilemmatic situation. His initial *satyagraha* campaigns in Champaran, Kheda and Ahmedabad helped him to transcend this dilemma.

In his relationship vis-à-vis the British government in India during this period, a varied response from Gandhi was evident. This response alternated respectively from confrontation to cooperation in accordance with the government's adoption of unresponsive and repressive policy or a policy of concession to satisfy some aspects of the Indians' aspirations. Thus, while he desired to cooperate with the British government in its war efforts and 1919 Reform proposal, he strongly criticized the government for its unjustifiable action of interning such national leaders like Annie Besant and Ali brothers.

The Rowlatt *satyagraha* marked Gandhi's full-fledged political launch in India. The Rowlatt Bill was vehemently criticized by Gandhi. He was not only critical about its superfluity but also recognized it as a flagrant violation of a principled governance in so far as it represented a lack of trust in the governed subjects; violated the subjects' dignity and basic freedom; and belied the hopes of the subjects who visualized a more benevolent and responsive administration in return for their cooperation with the government in its hour of crisis during the First World War. He recognized the Bill not as a mere stray incident of lapse of righteousness and justice but as an evidence of a determined policy of repression by the government. Resistance to such an autocratic or tyrannical rule which violated the principle of liberty and denied the elementary rights of the individual was recognized by Gandhi as an open challenge which ought to be courageously accepted by the Indians. Emphasizing upon civilly protesting these acts of government, Gandhi dealt in detail the various facets of the *satyagraha* campaign. However, the actual course of events belied Gandhi's hopes of a non-violent and ethical protest against the government. Consequently, he decided to take a more direct and active part in the political agitation for *swaraj*.

When Gandhi realized that the British government was not only unwilling to respond favourably to the Indians' demands but also took recourse to fraud and caprice, coupled with repression, to hide their diabolic designs and persist with it to satisfy their narrow colonial goals, he declared it to be a moral duty of the Indian citizens to be disloyal to such a regime and non-cooperate with it to vindicate truth and the concomitant values and rights. This recognition saw its logical culmination in the launch of the Non-Cooperation Movement in 1920 and Gandhi's complete transformation from a loyalist to a non-cooperator with the British rule.

Gandhi's philosophy of protest and the corresponding activism, although located in the historical context of the racist regime in South Africa and the colonial rule of the British in India, has had a transcending relevance beyond the parameters of a subjected Indian community or nationals protesting to realize some of its cherished and just aspirations under the British Empire. His theory of protest ventured into the vista of speculating on the principles that ought to form the basis of any just political governance and the principles that should form the basis of any resistance movement against the established authority when it failed to conform to the principles that gave legitimacy to it.

There is no dearth of literature on such a speculation in political theory. William Godwin, Henry David Thoreau, Albert Camus and Georges Sorel are only but a few names which may be mentioned in this regard. Although Gandhi's theory of protest has a few shareable commonalties with these theories of protest, it has certain distinct features.

An anarchist leaning could be discerned both in Godwin and Gandhi. Both of them visualized endless possibilities of perfectibility of the individuals and contended that all external controls from institutions like the state and the government would become redundant once perfection was realized by the individuals. However, until such an evolved state was realized, both condescended to the rule of a state or government run according to certain principles so as to help the subject individuals to realize those virtues that were implicit in the *telos* and essential nature of their existence.

Whenever, the state failed to work for the realization of the ordained objectives or violated the essential principles while discharging its functions, both Godwin and Gandhi emphasized upon the need for the subject citizens to effectively protest such excrescences. In this regard while Godwin advocated the individuals to imbibe a critical obedience based upon the test of utility and private judgement, Gandhi recognized it as a moral obligation of the citizens to protest the flagrant violation by applying the test of truth or individual conscience. A virtuous living, being considered as an essential part of an ideal citizenship, both Godwin and Gandhi emphasized upon the purity of the means to be adopted while taking recourse to protest. Consequently, both assailed any recourse to unfair and violent means. They were also emphatic about the need to distinguish between the evil-doer and the evil and, while seeking to end the latter, envisaging to bring about a transformation of the evil-doer so much so that he renounced his diabolic designs and acted in a righteous manner. For this, both Godwin and Gandhi recognized the appropriateness of rational persuasion of the opponent.

However, unlike Godwin who advocated the protester to prudentially submit to or acquiesce in the will of the opponent while seeking to persuade him to renounce his diabolic designs, Gandhi refrained from doing so. Instead, he advocated the individual to be prepared to bear any amount of suffering and thereby, bring about a "change of heart" of the opponent. Moreover, Gandhi, being juxtaposed in a historical context where protest against the narrow designs of a colonial regime became inevitable, was more comprehensive than Godwin while dealing with the procedural modalities, tools and techniques of protest.

Like many other thinkers who have denounced and decried the coercive tendencies of the state, Thoreau too opined that the state subjected the individuals to render obedience to a wide variety of coercive decrees which violated the integrity, dignity and the essence of individual existence. The sacrosanct nature of the individual constituting the core of Thoreau's political philosophy, he became an ardent champion of individual liberty. Recognizing certain quintessential values as being concomitant with human existence, he contended that any authority that violated these essentials should be effectively resisted.

Thoreau wanted the conscientious individual to be brave and unmindful of the consequences of protesting an unjust authority. Neither did he advocate passivity on the part of individuals when such violations occurred, nor did he think it necessary for the conscientious individual to wait for the majority support for his views in order to effectively protest the usurpation of authority. What was important for Thoreau was not the grandiose of the beginning of protest against an act perpetuating untruth or injustice; rather, it was the principled purpose and the beginning of the protest which was more important for him. Making a distinction between the evil state and its human agents, Thoreau was also emphatic about the need for renouncing any feeling of ill-will towards the latter and desired that the protester should make sincere efforts to awaken the slumbering conscience of such human agents of the state and thereby, influence them to act in consonance with the principles of truth, justice and righteousness.

Gandhi, who acknowledged his indebtedness to Thoreau, conformed to his views on protest to some extent. He too viewed with suspect the state and its overwhelming power. Like Thoreau, he placed the individual at a higher pedestal than the state and emphasized upon the state conforming to the quintessential values which were presumed to be given with the individual's existence. Recognizing it as a moral duty of the individual to protest the unjust state, Gandhi advocated the conscientious individual to be courageous while doing so and accorded primacy to the quality, rather than quantity, of protest.

However, unlike Thoreau, Gandhi was more explicit and comprehensive while dealing with his theory of protest. His means of protest or *satyagraha* was to be adopted by the individual while being a part of the society. While protesting injustice or untruth, the non-violent, self-suffering, self-purification and mass mobilization aspects along with the techniques, tools, rules, etc. were more explicitly and comprehensively dealt by Gandhi. The specific historical context of Gandhi's protest together with the various influences upon him greatly shaped his overall thinking which in turn had a bearing upon his philosophy of protest. Consequently, Gandhi accepted Thoreau's advocacies to the extent that these conformed to the essentials that had already taken firm root in his personality. By making creative additions or improvements, Gandhi made his protest more relevant to correct the maladies that characterized his historical juxtaposition.

Similarly, when compared to the theory of Camus, Gandhi transcended beyond Camus' concern. Like Camus, Gandhi, through his theory of protest, provided with a means that would enable the conscientious protester to refuse to obey any such authoritative dictates which was considered by him to be intrinsically wrong and, thereby, to affirm his faith in something which was sacred and inviolable for him. Through the protest, the conscientious protester made an endeavour to uphold certain moral values and, as a man of principle, bore witness to the reality and indispensability of these moral values. Thus, the nature of *satyagraha* and *La revolte* and the character of the *satyagrahi* and the *L' Homme revolte* conform greatly. Similarly, both Camus and Gandhi agree on the futility of violence while taking recourse to protest the unjust or oppressive authority.

However, unlike Camus, Gandhi's staunch advocacy of adopting non-violence as a faith in preference to its adoption as a policy, transcended Camus' recognition of absolute non-violence as being as impossible as absolute freedom. Gandhi also deviated from Camus' line of thinking in so far as he was not willing to acquiesce in force for limiting violence. The metaphysical concerns of Gandhi's protest also distinguished it from Camus' protest, the concern of which was human happiness conceived in more temporal terms.

Gandhi and Sorel have certain common features in their exposition of protest: commitment to and an active and determined pursuit of the goal of an order free from various forms of oppression and exploitation; preference of violence to cowardice; condemnation of unethical compromises, need for making a distinction between the evil and the evil-doer; recognition of the importance of training, discipline and unity while embarking on a course of protest; etc. Nevertheless, the emphases of *satyagraha* were in sharp contrast to the rigours of Sorelian protest. While Sorel's theory of protest had at its core a faith in the efficacy and ethics of violence implicit in the notion of "general strike", Gandhi's theory of protest had at its core an undying faith in the principle of non-violence which formed a part of the broader notion of "purity of ends and means". Sorel had no faith in compromises or conciliations as means to resolve conflicts because of his belief that these always served to promote the vested interest of the stronger party involved in the conflict. However, Gandhi's theory of protest accorded a due place to these means. His faith in non-violence and unlimited capacity of human beings to progress spiritually influenced him to contend that it was simultaneously possible to enter into compromises or conciliation while vindicating the essential principles or values lying at the core of the conflict. Through such an emphasis Gandhi sought to not only avoid the consequences of violent revolutions but also effectively bring about the resolution of the conflict and, thereby, the redress of the grievances of the oppressed subjects.

As senior and more experienced contemporaries, Gandhi did not fail to recognize the creative aspects of Gokhale's and Tilak's protest to realize *swaraj*. Thus, *satyagraha* is characterized by a few indices of continuum of the spirit, temper and values which Gokhale and Tilak emphasized in their protest against the British Government.

Like Gokhale, Gandhi too believed in the "spiritualization of politics" and recognized the responsibility of political governance as a moral duty, which in turn implied that a government should not only function for the fulfilment of the cherished aspirations of its subject citizens but also conform to certain principles while discharging its appointed functions. While recognizing the need for the citizens to protest a government that flouted these principles, Gokhale was emphatic about the purity and "moderation" or "constitutionalism" of the means that were adopted. Gandhi's theory of protest adopted Gokhale's advocacy as an indispensable part of the initial phase of protest against any unjust authority. However, to transcend any impasse that might persist despite the exhaustion of all available constitutional means of protest on account of the regime's reluctance to renounce its diabolic goals, Gandhi advocated the recourse to self-suffering, self-education and such forms of *satyagraha* like non-cooperation and civil disobedience to realize the envisaged goals.

The voluntary self-suffering, non-violent and ethical aspect of such forms of *satyagraha* on which Gandhi was very emphatic, distinguished Gandhi's protest from that of Tilak's advocacy of an inevitable extra-constitutional protest in the colonial setting of the British rule. Gandhi, like Tilak, admired and preferred violence to cowardice, and dearly cherished the goal of *swaraj* for the Indians; but his recognition of the need to adopt non-violence as a faith in preference to its adoption as a policy or cowardice influenced him to desist from the commendation, like Tilak, of the revolutionaries' recourse to violence and also to denounce the justification of an unethical means to realize a noble end. The means being recognized by Gandhi as the end in the process of making, he claimed that pure means alone could ensure the purity of ends. He also recognized violence to be contradictory to truth and the concomitant values and, therefore, a recourse to it as being incapable of ensuring the purity of the ends. It being so

Gandhi did not support or acquiesce in the recourse to violence while protesting an unjust or evil state.

Thus, Gandhi's heuristic theory of protest has a level of abstraction at par with the best of other theories of protest in political theory. Although evolutionary and eclectic in nature, it stands distinctly apart on account of its predominantly moral, altruistic and non-violent emphases – some quintessential values about the inevitability and inviolability of which Gandhi was thoroughly convinced due to his phenomenological enterprise and historical juxtaposition. Consequently, it defies categorization to comply with the rigours of any particular advocacy of protest. While it has the twin aspects of metaphysical foundation and practical utility, the theoretical possibilities which it throws open is enormous. For political theorists there is much to learn from Gandhi not only about the grounds of justification of defiance of the state's dictates but also the appropriate manner in which the defiance should be carried out.

Notes

1. V.R. Mehta, *Foundations of Indian Political Thought*, Manohar Publication, New Delhi, 1992, p. 211.
2. Naresh Dadhich, *Gandhi and Existentialism*, Rawat Publication, Jaipur, 1993, p. 29.
3. Judith Brown, *Gandhi: A Prisoner of Hope*, Oxford University Press, Delhi, 1992, p. 30.

Bibliography

1. Books by Gandhi and compilations of his writings

Gandhi, M.K., All Religions are True, A.T. Hingorani (ed.) Bharatiya Vidya Bhavan, Bombay, 1962.

— *An Autobiography or the Study of My Experiments With Truth*, Trans. Mahadev Desai, Navajivan Publishing House, Ahmedabad, 1966.

— *Collected Works of Mahatma Gandhi*, The Publications Division, Ministry of Information & Broadcasting, Government of India, New Delhi, 1958-93.

— *Constructive Programme: Its Meaning and Place*, Navajivan Publishing House, Ahmedabad, 1989.

— *Hind Swaraj or Indian Home Rule*, Navajivan Publishing House, Ahmedabad, 1990.

— *Non-violence in Peace and War*, Bharatan Kumrappa (ed.) Navajivan Publishing House, Ahmedabad, 1960.

— *Political and National Life and Affairs*, V.B. Kher (ed.), 2 Vols., Navajivan Publishing House, Ahmedabad, 1954.

— *Sarvodaya*, Bharatan Kumarappa (ed.), Navajivan Publishing House, Ahmedabad, 1984.

— *Satyagraha in South Africa*, V.G. Desai, Trans. Navajivan Publishing House, Ahmedabad, 1972.

— *Satyagraha*, Bharatan Kumarappa (ed.), Navajivan Publishing House, Ahmedabad, 1958.

— *Truth is God*, R.K. Prabhu (comp.), Navajivan Publishing House, Ahmedabad, 1987.

2. Books on Gandhi

Andrews, C.F., *Mahatma Gandhi's Ideas,* Allen and Unwin Ltd., London, 1949.

Bandyopadhaya, J., *Social and Political Thought of Gandhi*, Allied Publishers, Bombay, 1969.

Bari, S.A., *Gandhi's Doctrine of Civil Resistance*, Kalamkar Prakashan, Delhi, 1971.

Bhattacharya, Babhani, *Mahatma Gandhi*, Arnold Publishers (I) Pvt. Ltd., Delhi, 1977.

— Buddhdev, *Evolution of the Political Philosophy of Gandhi*, Calcutta Book House, Calcutta, 1969.

Bondurant, J.V., *Conquest of Violence: The Gandhian Philosophy of Conflict*. Princeton University Press, New Jersey, 1958.

Bose, N.K., *Selections From Gandhi*, Navajivan Publishing House, Ahmedabad, 1972.

Brown, J.M., *Gandhi and Civil Disobedience: The Mahatma in Indian Politics 1928-34*, Cambridge University Press, Cambridge, 1972.

— *Gandhi: A Prisoner of Hope*, Oxford University Press, New Delhi, 1993.

— *Gandhi's Rise to Power: Indian Politics 1915-1922*, Cambridge University Press, Cambridge, 1977.

Chaitanya, Krishna, *Gandhi's Quest of Being in Becoming*. Gandhi Peace Foundation, New Delhi, 1977.

Chandra, Bipin, (ed.) *India's Struggle for Freedom 1857-1947*, Penguin Books India (Pvt.) Ltd., New Delhi, 1991.

Chatterjee, Margaret, *Gandhi and the Challenge of Religious Diversity: Religious Pluralism Revisited*, Promilla & Co. Publishers, New Delhi, 2005.

Copley, A., *Gandhi: Raising Against the Tide*, Oxford University Press, Calcutta, 1993.

Dadhich, Naresh, *Gandhi and Existentialism*, Rawat Publications, Jaipur, 1993.

Dandavate, Madhu, *Marx and Gandhi*, Popular Prakashan, Bombay, 1967.

Datta, D.M., *The Philosophy of Mahatma Gandhi*, Gandhi Peace Foundation, New Delhi, 1990.

Dhawan, G.N., *The Political Philosophy of Mahatma Gandhi*, Gandhi Peace Foundation, New Delhi, 1990.

Diwarkar, R.R., *Gandhi: The Spiritual Seeker*, Bharatiya Vidya Bhavan, Bombay, 1964.

— *Sage of Satyagraha*, Gandhi Peace Foundation, New Delhi, 1969.

— *Satyagraha in Action*, Signet Press, Calcutta, 1949.

— *Satyagraha: Its Technique and History*, Hind Kitabs, Bombay, 1946.

Doke, J.J., *M.K. Gandhi: An Indian Patriot in South Africa*, Natesan & Co. Madras, 1909.

Erikson, E.H., *Gandhi's Truth: The Origins of Militant Non-Violence*, New York, W.W. Norton & Co., 1969.

Fischer, Louis, *The Life of Mahatma Gandhi*, Granada Publishing Ltd., London, 1982.

Ganguli, B.N., *Gandhi's Social Philosophy: Perspectives and Relevance*, Vikas Publishing House, New Delhi, 1973.

Gaur, V.V., *Mahatma Gandhi: A Study of His Message of Non-violence*, Sterling Publishers, New Delhi, 1977.

Geetha V. (ed.) *Soul Force: Gandhi's Writings on Peace*, Tara Publishing Co. Chennai, 2004.

Gregg, Richard, *The Power of Non-violence*, Navajivan Publishing House, Ahmedabad, 1960.

Hingorani, A.T., *Towards Lasting Peace*, Bhartiya Vidya Bhawan, Bombay, 1956.

Holmes, J.H., *My Gandhi*, Harper and Brothers Publishers, New York, 1953.

Horsburg, H.J.N., *Non-violence and Agression: A Study of Gandhi's Moral Equivalent of War*, Oxford University Press, London, 1971.

Iyer, Raghavan, *The Essential Writings of Mahatma Gandhi*, Oxford University Press, New Delhi, 1993.

— *The Moral and Political Thought of Mahatma Gandhi*, Oxford University Press, New Delhi, 1973.

Kapur, Sudarshan, *Raising up a Prophet, The African American Encounter with Gandhi*, Oxford University Press, Delhi, 1993.

Kriplani, J.B., *Gandhi: His Life and Thought*, The Publications Division, Ministry of Information & Broadcasting, Government of India, New Delhi, 1970.

Kumar, R. (ed.) *Essays on Gandhian Politics: The Rowlatt Satyagraha of 1919*, Oxford University Press, London, 1971.

Mahadevan, T.K., *The Year of the Phoenix*, Arnold Heineman, New Delhi, 1982.

Markovits, Claude, *The Un-Gandhian Gandhi: The Life and Afterlife of the Mahatma*, Permanent Black, Delhi, 2004.

Mathur, D.B., *Gandhi and the Liberal Bequest*, Aalekh Publishers, Jaipur, 1988.

— *Gandhi's Prolegomena of Political Ethics (The South African Phase)*, Gandhi Bhawan, University of Rajasthan, Jaipur, 1971.

— *Prefacing Gandhi*, R.B.S.A. Publishers, Jaipur, 1988.

Mazumdar, B.B., *Gandhian Concept of State*, M.C. Sarkar and Sons Pvt. Ltd., Calcutta, 1957.

Mehta J.K., *Gandhian Thought: An Analytical Study*, Ashish Publishing House, New Delhi, 1985.

Mehta, V.R., *Foundations of Indian Political Thought*, Manohar Publications, New Delhi, 1992.

— *Ideology, Modernization and Politics in India*, Manohar Publications, New Delhi, 1983.

Mishra, R.P., *Hind Swaraj: Gandhi's Challenge to Modern Civilization*, Concept Publishing Company, New Delhi, 2007.

Mukherjee, Hiren, *Gandhiji: A Study*, People's Publishing House, New Delhi, 1960.

Namboodiripad, E.M.S., *The Mahatma and the Ism*, People's Publishing House, Delhi, 1958.

Nanda, B.R., *Gandhi and His Critics*, Oxford University Press, Delhi, 1985.

— *Mahatma Gandhi: A Biography*, Oxford University Press, Delhi, 1989.

Panter-Brick, *Gandhi Against Machiavellism: Non-violence in Politics*, Trans. by P. Leon, Asia Publishing House, Bombay, 1966.

Parekh, Bhikhu and Pantham, Thomas (ed.) *Political Discourse*, Sage Publications, New Delhi, 1987.

— *Colonialism Tradition and Reform*, Sage Publications, New Delhi, 1989.

— *Gandhi: A Very Short Introduction*, Oxford University Press, New York, 2001.

Parel, Anthony J. (ed), *Hind Swaraj and Other Writings*, Foundation Books Pvt. Ltd. (India) for Cambridge University Press, New Delhi, 2005.

Patil, V.T. (ed.) *Studies on Gandhi*, Sterling Publishers, New Delhi, 1983.

— *New Dimensions and Perspectives in Gandhism*, Inter-India Publications, New Delhi, 1989.

Polak H.S.L. et.al., *Mahatma Gandhi*, Jaico Publishing House, Delhi, 1962.

Power, Paul F. (ed.) *Meanings of Gandhi*, The University of Hawaii, Hawaii, 1971.

Pyarelal, *A Pilgrimage For Peace*, Navajivan Publishing House, Ahmedabad, 1959.

— *Mahatma Gandhi: The Early Phase*, Navajivan Publishing House, Ahmedabad, 1965.

— *Mahatma Gandhi: The Last Phase*, 2 Vols. Navajivan Publishing House, Ahmedabad, 1956-58.

— *Towards New Horizons*, Navajivan Publishing House, Ahmedabad, 1959.

Radhakrishnan, N., *Gandhi: The Quest for Toleration and Survival*, Gandhi Darshan and Smriti Samiti and Gandhi Media Centre, New Delhi, 1995.

Radhakrishnan, S. (ed.) *Mahatma Gandhi: 100 Years, Gandhi Peace Foundation*, New Delhi, 1968.

Ramachandran, G. and Mahadevan, T.K. (ed.) *Quest for Gandhi*, Gandhi Peace Foundation, New Delhi, 1970.

Raman Murthy, V.V., *Non Violence in Politics: A Study of Gandhian Techniques and Thinking*, Frank Bros. & Co., New Delhi, 1958.

Rao Seshagiri, K.L., *Mahatma Gandhi and Comparative Religion*, Motilal Banarsidas, New Delhi, 1990.

Rao, M.B., *The Mahatma: A Marxist Symposium*, People's Publishing House, Bombay, 1969.

Rattan Ram, *Gandhi's Concept of Political Obligation*, The Minerva Associates, Calcutta, 1972.

Rothermund, Indira, *The Philosophy of Restraint*, Popular Prakashan, Bombay, 1963.

Roy, B.G., *Gandhian Ethics*, Navajivan Publishing House, Ahmedabad, 1950.

Roy, Ramashray, (ed.): *Contemporary Crises and Gandhi*, Discovery Publishing House, New Delhi, 1986.

— *Gandhi: Sounding in Political Philosophy*, Chankya Publications, New Delhi, 1984.

— *Self and Society: A Study in Gandhian Thought*, Sage Publications, New Delhi, 1984.

Rudolph, L.I. & Rudolph S.H. *The Modernity of Tradition*, Chicago University Press, Chicago, 1967.

Rudolph, L.I., *Gandhi: The Traditional Roots of Charisma*, Chicago University Press, Chicago, 1983.

Rudolph, L.I., *Postmodern Gandhi and Other Essays: Gandhi in the World and at Home*, Oxford University Press, New Delhi, 2006.

Sankhdheer, M.M., *Gandhi, Gandhism and the Partition of India*, Deep & Deep Publications, New Delhi, 1982.

Sethi, J.D., *Gandhi Today*, Vikas Publishing House, New Delhi, 1978.

Sharma, B.S., *Gandhi as a Political Thinker*, Indian Press Publications Pvt. Ltd. Allahabad, 1956.

Sharp, Gene. *Gandhi Wields the Weapon of Moral Power*, Navajivan Publishing House, Ahmedabad, 1960.

Sheean, *Mahatma Gandhi: A Great Life in Brief*, Publications Division, Ministry of Information & Broadcasting, Government of India, New Delhi, 1968.

Sheean, Vincent, *Lead Kindly Light*, Random House, New York, 1949.

Singh, S.N., *Gandhi and Marx: An Ethico-Philosophical Study*, Associated Book Agency, Patna, 1979.

Spratt, Phillip, *Gandhism: An Analysis*, The Huxley Press, Madras, 1939.

Swan, Maureen, *Gandhi: The South African Experience*, Ravan Press, Johannesburg, 1985.

Swarup, Ram, *Gandhi and Communism: Principles and Techniques*, Jyoti Prakashan, New Delhi, 1955.

Tendulkar, D.G., *Mahatama: Life of Mohandas Karamchand Gandhi*, 8 Vols. K. Jhaveri and D.G. Tendulkar, Bombay, 1951-54.

Tiwari, K.N., *World Religions and Gandhi*, Classical Publications, New Delhi, 1988.

Unnithan, T.K.N., *Change Without Violence: Gandhian Theory of Social Change*, Gujarat Vidhyapeeth, Ahmedabad, 1987.

Unnithan, T.K.N., *Gandhi and Social Change*, Rawat Publication, Jaipur, 1979.

Verma, M.M., *Gandhi's Technique of Mass Mobilization*, R.K. Gupta & Co., New Delhi, 1990.

Verma, S.N., *The Metaphysical Foundations of Gandhi's Thought*, Orient Longman, New Delhi, 1970.

Verma, V.P., *The Political Philosophy of Mahatma Gandhi and Sarvodaya*, Laxmi Narain Agarwal, Agra, 1965.

3. Miscellaneous

Bose, Atindranath, *A History of Anarchism*, The World Press Pvt. Ltd., Calcutta, 1967.

Camus, Albert, *The Rebel*, Trans. by A. Bower, Knopt Publications, New York, 1960.

— *The Fall*, Trans. by Justin O' Brien, Penguin Publication, New York, 1975.

— *The Plague*, Trans. by Stuart Gilber, Penguin Publication, New York, 1960.

Chandra S., *Camus and India*, National Publishing House, New Delhi, 1991.

Chopra, P.N., (ed.) *The Gazetteer of India (History & Culture)*, Vol. 2, Publications Division, Ministry of Information & Broadcasting, Government. of India, New Delhi, 1988.

Coker, F.W., *Democracy Liberty and Property: Readings in the American Political Tradition*, The Macmillan Co., New York, 1965.

Connery, R.H., (ed.) *Urban Riots: Violence and Social Change*, Academy of Political Science, New York, 1968.

Cruikschank, J., *Albert Camus and the Literature of Revolt*, Oxford University Press, London, 1959.

Denton, David, *The Philosophy of Albert Camus: A Critical Analysis*, Prime Publishers, Boston, 1967.

Deogirkar, T.R., *Builders of Modern India: Gopal Krishna Gokhale*, Publications Division, Ministry of Information & Broadcasting, Govt. of India, New Delhi, 1992.

Dolbeare, K.M., *Directions in American Political Thought*, John Wiley & Sons Inc., New York, 1969.

Downtown Jr., J.V. and Hart D.K. (ed.), *Perspectives on Political Philosophy*, The Dryden Press Inc. Hinsdale, Illinois, 1973.

Friedrich, C.J., *Man and His Government: An Empirical Theory of Politics*, McGraw Hill Book Company Inc., New York, 1963.

Godwin, William, *An Enquiry Concerning Political Justice*, I. Krammic (ed), Penguin Publication, Harmondsworth, 1996.

Grimes, A.P., *American Political Thought*, Halt Rinehart and Winston Inc. New York, 1960.

Grover, V. (ed.) *Gopal Krishna Gokhale (Political Thinkers of Modern India-2)*, Deep & Deep Publications, New Delhi, 1991.

Gusfield, J.R., (ed.) *Protest Reform and Result: A Reader in Social Movements*, John Wiley & Sons Inc., New York, 1977.

Held, Virjinia (ed.) *Philosophy and Political Action*, Oxford University Press, New Delhi, 1972.

Ippolito, D.S. et al., *Public Opinion and Responsible Democracy*, Prentice Hall Inc. Englewood Cliffs, New Jersey, 1976.

Jog, N.G., *Builders of Modern India: Lokmanya Bal Gangadhar Tilak*, Publications Division, Ministry of Information & Broadcasting, Govt. of India, New Delhi, 1990.

Joll, James, *The Anarchists*, Methuen & Co. Ltd., London, 1979.

Karve, D.G. and Ambekar, D.V. (ed.) *Speeches and Writings of Gopal Krishna Gokhale*, 3 Vols. 1966-67.

Kumar, Ravindra (ed.) *Selected Documents of Lokmanya Bal Gangadhar Tilak*, 4 Vols. Anmol Publication, New Delhi, 1992.

Majumdar, R.C. (ed.) *The History and Culture of the Indian People*, Vols. 9-11, Bhartiya Vidya Bhawan, Bombay, 1963-69.

Malick, S.C. (ed.) *Dissent Protest and Reform in Indian Civilization*, Indian Institute of Advanced Study, Simla, 1977.

Mason, G.R. (ed.) *Great American Liberals*, Starr King Press, Bosten, 1956.

Mathur, D.B., *Gokhale: A Political Biography, A Study of His Services and Political Ideas*, P.G. Manaktala and Sons Pvt. Ltd., Bombay, 1966.

Miller, David *Anarchism*, J.M. Dent & Sons Ltd., London, 1964.

Miller, W.R., *Nonviolence: A Christian Interpretation*, George Allen Unwin Ltd., London, 1964.

Parvate T.V., *Bal Gangadhar Tilak: A Narrative and Interpretative Review of His Life, Career and Contemporary Events*, Navajivan Publishing House, Ahmedabad, 1958.

Schaar J.H., *Loyalty in America*, University of California Press, Los Angeles 1957.

Sitaramayya, P., *The History of Indian National Congress*, Padma Publication, Bombay, Vol. 1, 1946.

Sorel, Georges, *Reflections on Violence*, Trans. T.E. Hulme and J. Roth, The Free Press, Glencoe, Illinois, 1950.

Thody, Philp. *Albert Cumus: A Study of His Work*, Grove Press, New York, 1959.

Tilak, B.G., *Srimad Bhagavadgita Rahasya*, Lokmanya Tilak Mandir, Pune, 1955.

— *The Arctic Home in the Vedas*, Kesari Office, Pune, 1903.

— *The Orion*, Ms. R.A. Sagoon, Bombay, 1893.

Verma, V.P., *The Life and Philosophy of Lokmanya Tilak*, Laxmi Narayan Agrawal Educational Publishers, Agra, 1979.

Wolman, B.B., (ed.) *The International Encyclopaedia of Psychiatry Psychology Psycho-analysis and Nurology*, Vol. 9, Aesculapius Publishers, New York, 1977.

Wolpert S.A., *Tilak and Gokhale: Revolution and Reform in the Making of Modern India*, Oxford University Press, New Delhi, 1991.

4. Articles

Ali, Tariq. "The Legacy of Gandhi", in *The Illustrated Weekly of India*, October 2, 1983.

Bayley, D.H., "Pedagogy of Democracy: Coercive Public Protest in India", in *American Political Science Review*, Vol. 56, September, 1962.

Bose, Anima, "The Rowlatt Act and Gandhian Satyagraha", in *Gandhi Marg*, July, 1976.

Chakravarty, Amiya, "Gandhi and the Modern World – The New Image", in *Gandhi Marg*, January, 1964.

Cox, R.H., "Ideology, History and Political Philosophy: Camus L'Homme Revolte", in *Social Research*, No. 32, Spring 1965.

Cranston, Maurice, "Albert Camus", in *Encounter*, No. 28 February, 1967.

Dadhich, Naresh and Kumar, Arun B. "Gandhi's Critique of Modern Civilization", in *Indian Journal of Politics*, Vol. 25, No. 4, 1991.

Dadhich, Naresh and Kumar, Arun B., "Thoreau's Protest: A Means to Maintain the Ontological Essence of Man", in *Gandhi Marg*, Vol. 15, No. 3, October-December, 1993.

Dagger, R.K., "What is Political Obligation", in *American Political Science Review*, Vol. 71 March 1977.

Diwakar, R.R., "Sarvodaya: A Comprehensive Concept", in *Gandhi Marg*, June, 1986.

— "The Relevance of Gandhi", in *Gandhi Marg*, June, 1966.

Eisinger, P.K., "The Condition of Protest Behaviours in American Cities", *American Political Science Review*, Vol. 67, March 1973.

— "Forms of Emerging Indices of Satyagraha in South Africa: A Study of Gandhi's Heuristic Enterprise", in *Political Science Annual* (1996), Deep and Deep Publications, New Delhi, 1996.

— "Gandhian Protest: A Conceptual Analysis" in *Gandhi Marg*, Vol. 17, No. 1, April-June, 1995.

— Satyagraha: "The Gandhian Theory of Protest", in *Political Science Annual* (1994-95) Deep and Deep Publication, New Delhi, 1995.

— Satyagraha: "The Gandhian View", *Indian Journal of Politics Vols.* 28, No. 3.4, 1994.

Ganapati, T.N., "The Individual and Society in Gandhian Ethics", in *Gandhi Marg*, November, 1981.

Gangaiah, G., "The Bases of Satyagraha in Gandhi's Philosophy", in *Gandhi Marg*, September, 1987.

Gargan, E.T., "Revolution and Morals in the Formative Thought of Albert Camus", in *Review of Politics*, No. 25, October, 1963.

Gershman, H.H., "The Structure of Revolt in Marlaux, Camus and Sartre", in *Symposium*, No. 25, September, 1970.

Gordon, J., "Nagel or Camus on the Absurd"? in *Philosophy and Phenomenological Research*, Vols. 4, No. 1, September, 1984.

Haksar, Vinit, Rawls and Gandhi on Civil Disobedience, *in Enquiry*, No. 19, 1976.

Hendrick, George. "Influence of Thoreau and Emerson on Gandhi's Satyagraha", in *Gandhi Marg*, July 1959.

Hordern, W.E., "Protestantism", in *The Encyclopedia Americana*, International Edition, Grolier Inc., Danbury Connecticut, Vol. 22, 1991.

Jesudasan, I., "Gandhi's Idea of Liberation", in *Gandhi Marg*, August, 1985.

Jones Morris, W.H., "Mahatma Gandhi: Political Philosopher"? in *Indian Journal of Political Science*, Vols. 21, No. 3, July-September, 1960.

Kalelkar, S.D., "Thoreau and Mahatma Gandhi", in *Gandhi Marg*, January, 1964.

Kalghati, T.G., "Satyagraha: A Study", in *Gandhi Marg*, May 1986.

Lewis, R.W.B., "Caligula: Or the Realm of the Impossible", in *Yale French Studies*, No. 25, 1960.

Lipsky, Michael, "Protest as a Political Resource", in *American Political Science*, Review, Vol. 32, December, 1968.

Merton, Thomas, "The Meaning of Satyagraha", in *Gandhi Marg*, April, 1966.

Morkhandikar, R.S., "The Theory of Resistance in Ancient India", in *Gandhi Marg*, January, 1972.

Mukherjee, Dhurjati, "Gandhi and Mao: Philosopher Revolutionaries of the Century", in *Gandhi Marg*, November, 1981.

Mukherjee, Subrata. "We Need Critical Assessment", in *Sunday Review*, The Times of India, October 4, 1981.

Murthy Raman, V.V., "Bubber's Dialogue and Gandhi's Satyagraha", in *Journal of History of ideas*, October, 1968.

Nandi, Ashis, "From Outside the Imperium: Gandhi's Cultural Critique of the West", in *Alternatives*, Vol. 7, No. 2, June 1981.

Narain Jai, "Power Politics: Gandhian Alternative", in *Gandhi Marg*, September, 1986.

Natesan, B., "Gandhi and Thoreau", in *Gandhi Marg*, July, 1958.

O'Brien, Edward "Camus and Christianity", in *The Personalist*, April 1963.

Palkhivala, N.A., "Relevance of Gandhi Today", in *Gandhi Marg*, April 1984.

Pantham, Thomas, "Thinking with Mahatma Gandhi: Beyond Liberal Democracy", in *Political Theory*, Vols. 2, No. 2, May 1983.

Parekh, Bhikhu, "Gandhi and His Translators", in *Gandhi Marg*, June, 1986.

Pawlowski, Ija Laz, "The Moral Philosophy of Gandhi", in *Gandhi Marg*, April, 1966.

Raychowdhary, T., "Indian Nationalism or Animal Politics", in *Historical Journal*, Vol. 22, 1979.

Saran, A.K., "Gandhi and The Concept of Politics: Towards Normal Civilization", in *Gandhi Marg*, February, 1980.

Sharp, Gene., "Gandhi's Political Significance Today", in *Gandhi Marg*, January, 1965.

Srinivasan, G., "Gandhi: A Practical Existentialist", in *Gandhi Marg*, July 1980.

Tinker, Hugh, "Non-violence as a Political Strategy: Gandhi and Western Thinkers", in *Gandhi Marg*, August, 1980.

Turner, R.R., "The Public Perception of Protest", in *American Sociological Review*, Vols. 34, No. 6, 1969.

Index